Java™ Message Service API
Tutorial and Reference

Java™ Message Service API Tutorial and Reference

Messaging for the J2EE™ Platform

Mark Hapner
Rich Burridge
Rahul Sharma
Joseph Fialli
Kim Haase

Addison-Wesley

Boston • San Francisco • New York • Toronto • Montreal
London • Munich • Paris • Madrid
Capetown • Sydney • Tokyo • Singapore • Mexico City

Library of Congress Cataloging-in-Publication Data
Java message service API tutorial and reference : messaging in the J2EE platform /
Mark Hapner ... [et al.].
    p. cm.
    Includes bibliographical references and index.
    ISBN 0-201-78472-6 (pbk.)
    1. Java (Computer program language) 2. Telecommunication–Message processing. I. Hapner, Mark.
    QA76.73.J38 J3675 2002
    005.13'3–dc21   2002018253

The publisher offers discounts on this book when ordered in quantity for special sales. For more information, please contact:

Pearson Education Corporate Sales Division
201 W. 103rd Street
Indianapolis, IN 46290
(800) 428-5331
corpsales@pearsoned.com

Visit AW on the Web: www.aw.com/cseng/

ISBN 0-201-78472-6

Text printed on recycled paper
1 2 3 4 5 6 7 8 9 10—MA—0605040302
First printing, February 2002

Contents

Preface

THE *Java*™ *Message Service Tutorial and Reference* provides an introduction to the Java Message Service (JMS) API for new users. It has the following goals:

- To introduce the JMS API to new users, with simple JMS client program examples

- To show how to use the JMS API within the Java 2 Platform, Enterprise Edition (J2EE™ platform), with additional simple examples showing how to

  - Consume messages asynchronously with a message-driven bean

  - Produce messages from an application client

  - Produce messages from a session bean

  - Access an entity bean from a message-driven bean

  - Produce and consume messages on more than one system

- To provide a full reference to the JMS API for JMS client programmers

The audience for this book is programmers who expect to write JMS applications, especially applications for the J2EE platform ("J2EE applications") that use the JMS API. We assume that you are familiar with the Java programming language and that you have some experience with earlier versions of the J2EE platform.

In order to run the tutorial examples, we recommend that you download and install the Java 2 Software Development Kit, Enterprise Edition (J2EE SDK), version 1.3 or above, which is available at no charge and runs on the Solaris™

Operating Environment and on the Linux and Windows NT/2000 operating systems. See `http://java.sun.com/j2ee/` for more information and a link to the J2EE SDK. You should first install the required version of the Java 2 Software Development Kit, Standard Edition (J2SE™ SDK), if it is not already installed.

You can download the examples in this book, along with an HTML version of the tutorial, from the following location: `http://java.sun.com/products/jms/ tutorial/`. The downloaded examples are in a directory named `jms_tutorial/ examples` (on UNIX® systems) or `jms_tutorial\examples` (on Microsoft Windows systems).

You may adapt the examples to other implementations of the JMS API and the J2EE platform, but you will need to study your vendor's documentation to determine how to modify the parts of the examples and instructions that deal with external resources, such as JMS administered objects (connection factories and destinations) and databases. For the J2EE platform examples, you will also need to adapt the instructions to use your vendor's packaging and deployment tools.

Part Two, the reference, is based on the API documentation for JMS version 1.0.2b. The reference describes all parts of the API that apply to JMS application programmers. It does not describe the methods and interfaces that are used only for implementing a JMS provider.

This book uses a few simple documentation conventions:

- `Monospace font` is used for code, which includes what would be typed in a source code file or on the command line, URLs, file names, keywords, and names of classes, interfaces, exceptions, constructors, methods, and fields.

- *`Italic code font`* is used for variables in text, command lines, and method explanations.

- *Italic font* is used for introducing new terms, for book titles, and for emphasis.

We welcome your comments, questions, and suggestions. Please send them to the following e-mail address: `jms-book@sun.com`.

Errata for this book and information on other books in the Addison-Wesley Java series will be posted at `http://java.sun.com/Series`.

Acknowledgments

MANY people contributed to the writing of this book. Mark Hapner was the creative mind behind the invention of the Java Message Service API, and he wrote the JMS Specification and API documentation with his coauthors Rich Burridge and Rahul Sharma. After they completed versions 1.0, 1.0.1, and 1.0.2 of the Specification, Joseph Fialli became the Specification Lead. Joe supervised the publication of version 1.0.2b of the JMS Specification and API documentation and became the primary technical contributor to this book. Kim Haase, with the assistance of Joe and the rest of the JMS development team, wrote the JMS Tutorial and helped edit the API documentation.

We thank the members of the JMS team, who contributed many reviews and much technical (and nontechnical) help: Kevin Osborn, Ryan Shoemaker, Irene Caruso, Bobby Bissett, Carla Carlson, Kathy Walsh, Farrukh Najmi, Dianne Jiao, Leslie Schwenk, and the current Specification Lead, Kate Stout. Many thanks are also owed to the J2EE documentation team, especially Jim Inscore, Eric Jendrock, Maydene Fisher, Dale Green, and Stephanie Bodoff.

We are also grateful to Lisa Friendly, the series editor, and to the following people at Addison-Wesley for their assistance: Mike Hendrickson, Ross Venables, John Fuller, and Elizabeth Ryan.

About the Authors

MARK **Hapner** is a Distinguished Engineer at Sun Microsystems, where he is Lead Architect for the J2EE platform. He participated in the development of the JDBC™ API, wrote the Java Message Service API specification, and coauthored the Enterprise JavaBeans™ specification.

Rich Burridge is a Staff Engineer at Sun Microsystems, where he has worked for over fifteen years. Currently with the Accessibility group, he is the creator of the Java Shared Data Toolkit (JSDT) and a coauthor of the Java Message Service API specification. Previously he worked on the "Netscape 6 for Solaris," OpenStep™, and OpenWindows™ products.

Rahul Sharma is a Senior Staff Engineer at Sun Microsystems, where he has worked for the past five years. Currently, he is the lead architect for the Java API for XML-based RPC (JAX-RPC). He architected the J2EE Connector Architecture and led its expert group. He participated in the Java Message Service API specification.

Joseph Fialli is a Senior Staff Engineer at Sun Microsystems, where he has worked for the past four years. Currently, he is the lead architect for the Java Architecture for XML Binding (JAXB). Previously, he was the technical lead for the Java Message Service API within the J2EE Software Development Kit, version 1.3, and maintained Java serialization within the Java 2 Platform, Standard Edition, version 1.2.

Kim Haase is a technical writer at Sun Microsystems, where she documents the J2EE platform. In previous positions she created documentation for compilers, debuggers, and floating-point programming. She currently writes about the Java Message Service API, the Java API for XML Registries (JAXR), and J2EE SDK tools.

Part One

$\mathbf{P}$ART One is the Java Message Service Tutorial. It contains the following chapters:

- Chapter 1, "Overview," provides a brief conceptual overview of the JMS API and its relationship to the J2EE platform.

- Chapter 2, "Basic JMS API Concepts," introduces the basic concepts of the JMS architecture, messaging domains, and message consumption.

- Chapter 3, "The JMS API Programming Model," describes the basic building blocks of a JMS application.

- Chapter 4, "Writing Simple JMS Client Applications," shows how to create and to run simple JMS client programs.

- Chapter 5, "Creating Robust JMS Applications," explains how to use features of the JMS API to achieve the level of reliability and performance your application requires.

- Chapter 6, "Using the JMS API in a J2EE Application," describes the ways in which using the JMS API in a J2EE application differs from using it in a standalone client application.

- Chapter 7, "A Simple J2EE Application that Uses the JMS API," explains how to create a J2EE application consisting of an application client and a message-driven bean.

- Chapter 8, "A J2EE Application that Uses the JMS API with a Session Bean," explains how to create a J2EE application consisting of an application client, a session bean, and a message-driven bean.

- Chapter 9, "A J2EE Application that Uses the JMS API with an Entity Bean," explains how to create a J2EE application consisting of an application client, three message-driven beans, and an entity bean.

- Chapter 10, "An Application Example that Uses Two J2EE Servers," explains how to create a J2EE application consisting of an application client and a message-driven bean, in which the message-driven bean is deployed on two different servers.

CHAPTER 1

Overview

THIS overview of the Java Message Service Application Programming Interface (the JMS API) answers the following questions.

- What is messaging?

- What is the JMS API?

- How can you use the JMS API?

- How does the JMS API work with the J2EE platform?

1.1 What Is Messaging?

Messaging is a method of communication between software components or applications. A messaging system is a peer-to-peer facility: A messaging client can send messages to, and receive messages from, any other client. Each client connects to a messaging agent that provides facilities for creating, sending, receiving, and reading messages.

Messaging enables distributed communication that is *loosely coupled*. A component sends a message to a destination, and the recipient can retrieve the message from the destination. However, the sender and the receiver do not have to be available at the same time in order to communicate. In fact, the sender does not need to know anything about the receiver; nor does the receiver need to know anything about the sender. The sender and the receiver need to know only what message format and what destination to use. In this respect, messaging differs from tightly coupled technologies, such as Remote Method Invocation (RMI), which require an application to know a remote application's methods.

Messaging also differs from electronic mail (e-mail), which is a method of communication between people or between software applications and people. Messaging is used for communication between software applications or software components.

1.2   What Is the JMS API?

The Java Message Service is a Java API that allows applications to create, send, receive, and read messages. Designed by Sun and several partner companies, the JMS API defines a common set of interfaces and associated semantics that allow programs written in the Java programming language to communicate with other messaging implementations.

The JMS API minimizes the set of concepts a programmer must learn to use messaging products but provides enough features to support sophisticated messaging applications. It also strives to maximize the portability of JMS applications across JMS providers in the same messaging domain.

The JMS API enables communication that is not only loosely coupled but also

- **Asynchronous.** A JMS provider can deliver messages to a client as they arrive; a client does not have to request messages in order to receive them.

- **Reliable.** The JMS API can ensure that a message is delivered once and only once. Lower levels of reliability are available for applications that can afford to miss messages or to receive duplicate messages.

The JMS Specification was first published in August 1998. The latest version of the JMS Specification is Version 1.0.2b, which was released in August 2001. You can download a copy of the Specification from the JMS Web site, `http://java.sun.com/products/jms/`.

1.3   When Can You Use the JMS API?

An enterprise application provider is likely to choose a messaging API over a tightly coupled API, such as Remote Procedure Call (RPC), under the following circumstances.

- The provider wants the components not to depend on information about other components' interfaces, so that components can be easily replaced.

- The provider wants the application to run whether or not all components are up and running simultaneously.

- The application business model allows a component to send information to another and to continue to operate without receiving an immediate response.

For example, components of an enterprise application for an automobile manufacturer can use the JMS API in situations like these.

- The inventory component can send a message to the factory component when the inventory level for a product goes below a certain level, so the factory can make more cars.

- The factory component can send a message to the parts components so that the factory can assemble the parts it needs.

- The parts components in turn can send messages to their own inventory and order components to update their inventories and to order new parts from suppliers.

- Both the factory and the parts components can send messages to the accounting component to update their budget numbers.

- The business can publish updated catalog items to its sales force.

Using messaging for these tasks allows the various components to interact with one another efficiently, without tying up network or other resources. Figure 1.1 illustrates how this simple example might work.

Figure 1.1   Messaging in an Enterprise Application

Manufacturing is only one example of how an enterprise can use the JMS API. Retail applications, financial services applications, health services applications, and many others can make use of messaging.

1.4   How Does the JMS API Work with the J2EE Platform?

When the JMS API was introduced in 1998, its most important purpose was to allow Java applications to access existing messaging-oriented middleware (MOM) systems, such as MQSeries from IBM. Since that time, many vendors have adopted and implemented the JMS API, so that a JMS product can now provide a complete messaging capability for an enterprise.

At the 1.2 release of the J2EE platform, a service provider based on J2EE technology ("J2EE provider") was required to provide the JMS API interfaces but was not required to implement them. Now, at the 1.3 release of the J2EE platform ("the J2EE 1.3 platform"), the JMS API is an integral part of the platform, and application developers can use messaging with components using J2EE APIs ("J2EE components").

The JMS API in the J2EE 1.3 platform has the following features.

- Application clients, Enterprise JavaBeans (EJB™) components, and Web components can send or synchronously receive a JMS message. Application clients can in addition receive JMS messages asynchronously. (Applets, however, are not required to support the JMS API.)

- A new kind of enterprise bean, the message-driven bean, enables the asynchronous consumption of messages. A JMS provider may optionally implement concurrent processing of messages by message-driven beans.

- Message sends and receives can participate in distributed transactions.

The addition of the JMS API enhances the J2EE platform by simplifying enterprise development, allowing loosely coupled, reliable, asynchronous interactions among J2EE components and legacy systems capable of messaging. A developer can easily add new behavior to a J2EE application with existing business events by adding a new message-driven bean to operate on specific business events. The J2EE platform's EJB container architecture, moreover, enhances the JMS API by providing support for distributed transactions and allowing for the concurrent consumption of messages.

Another technology new to the J2EE 1.3 platform, the J2EE Connector Architecture, provides tight integration between J2EE applications and existing Enterprise Information (EIS) systems. The JMS API, on the other hand, allows for a very loosely coupled interaction between J2EE applications and existing EIS systems.

CHAPTER 2

Basic JMS API Concepts

THIS chapter introduces the most basic JMS API concepts, the ones you must know to get started writing simple JMS client applications:

- JMS API architecture

- Messaging domains

- Message consumption

The next chapter introduces the JMS API programming model. Later chapters cover more advanced concepts, including the ones you need to write J2EE applications that use message-driven beans.

2.1 JMS API Architecture

A JMS application is composed of the following parts.

- A *JMS provider* is a messaging system that implements the JMS interfaces and provides administrative and control features. An implementation of the J2EE platform at release 1.3 and above includes a JMS provider.

- *JMS clients* are the programs or components, written in the Java programming language, that produce and consume messages.

- *Messages* are the objects that communicate information between JMS clients.

- *Administered objects* are preconfigured JMS objects created by an administrator for the use of clients. The two kinds of administered objects are destinations and connection factories, which are described in Section 3.1 on page 16.

- *Native clients* are programs that use a messaging product's native client API instead of the JMS API. An application first created before the JMS API became available and subsequently modified is likely to include both JMS and native clients.

Figure 2.1 illustrates the way these parts interact. Administrative tools allow you to bind destinations and connection factories into a Java Naming and Directory Interface™ (JNDI) API namespace. A JMS client can then look up the administered objects in the namespace and then establish a logical connection to the same objects through the JMS provider.

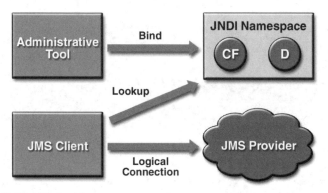

Figure 2.1   JMS API Architecture

2.2   Messaging Domains

Before the JMS API existed, most messaging products supported either the *point-to-point* or the *publish/subscribe* approach to messaging. The JMS Specification provides a separate domain for each approach and defines compliance for each domain. A standalone JMS provider may implement one or both domains. A J2EE provider must implement both domains.

In fact, most current implementations of the JMS API provide support for both the point-to-point and the publish/subscribe domains, and some JMS clients combine the use of both domains in a single application. In this way, the JMS API has extended the power and flexibility of messaging products.

2.2.1 Point-to-Point Messaging Domain

A point-to-point (PTP) product or application is built around the concept of message queues, senders, and receivers. Each message is addressed to a specific queue, and receiving clients extract messages from the queue(s) established to hold their messages. Queues retain all messages sent to them until the messages are consumed or until the messages expire.

PTP messaging has the following characteristics and is illustrated in Figure 2.2.

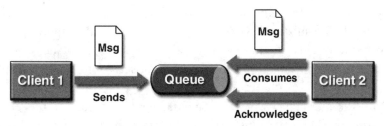

Figure 2.2   Point-to-Point Messaging

- Each message has only one consumer.

- A sender and a receiver of a message have no timing dependencies. The receiver can fetch the message whether or not it was running when the client sent the message.

- The receiver acknowledges the successful processing of a message.

Use PTP messaging when every message you send must be processed successfully by one consumer.

2.2.2 Publish/Subscribe Messaging Domain

In a publish/subscribe (pub/sub) product or application, clients address messages to a topic. Publishers and subscribers are generally anonymous and may dynamically publish or subscribe to the content hierarchy. The system takes care of distributing the messages arriving from a topic's multiple publishers to its multiple subscribers. Topics retain messages only as long as it takes to distribute them to current subscribers.

Pub/sub messaging has the following characteristics.

* Each message may have multiple consumers.

* Publishers and subscribers have a timing dependency. A client that subscribes to a topic can consume only messages published after the client has created a subscription, and the subscriber must continue to be active in order for it to consume messages.

The JMS API relaxes this timing dependency to some extent by allowing clients to create *durable subscriptions*. Durable subscriptions can receive messages sent while the subscribers are not active. Durable subscriptions provide the flexibility and reliability of queues but still allow clients to send messages to many recipients. For more information about durable subscriptions, see Section 5.2.1 on page 61.

Use pub/sub messaging when each message can be processed by zero, one, or many consumers. Figure 2.3 illustrates pub/sub messaging.

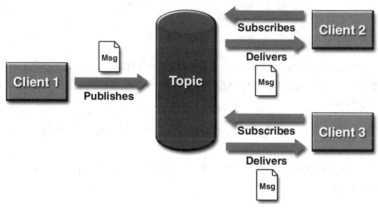

Figure 2.3   Publish/Subscribe Messaging

2.3   Message Consumption

Messaging products are inherently asynchronous in that no fundamental timing dependency exists between the production and the consumption of a message. However, the JMS Specification uses this term in a more precise sense. Messages can be consumed in either of two ways:

- **Synchronously.** A subscriber or a receiver explicitly fetches the message from the destination by calling the `receive` method. The `receive` method can block until a message arrives or can time out if a message does not arrive within a specified time limit.

- **Asynchronously.** A client can register a *message listener* with a consumer. A message listener is similar to an event listener. Whenever a message arrives at the destination, the JMS provider delivers the message by calling the listener's `onMessage` method, which acts on the contents of the message.

CHAPTER 3

The JMS API Programming Model

THE basic building blocks of a JMS application consist of

- Administered objects: connection factories and destinations
- Connections
- Sessions
- Message producers
- Message consumers
- Messages

Figure 3.1 shows how all these objects fit together in a JMS client application.

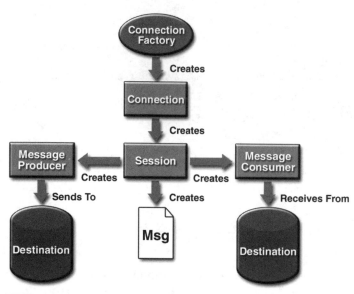

Figure 3.1   The JMS API Programming Model

This chapter describes all these objects briefly and provides sample commands and code snippets that show how to create and use the objects. The last section briefly describes JMS API exception handling.

Examples that show how to combine all these objects in applications appear in later chapters. For more details, see the JMS API documentation, which you can download from the JMS Web site, `http://java.sun.com/products/jms/`.

3.1   Administered Objects

Two parts of a JMS application—destinations and connection factories—are best maintained administratively rather than programmatically. The technology underlying these objects is likely to be very different from one implementation of the JMS API to another. Therefore, the management of these objects belongs with other administrative tasks that vary from provider to provider.

JMS clients access these objects through interfaces that are portable, so a client application can run with little or no change on more than one implementation of the JMS API. Ordinarily, an administrator configures administered objects in a Java Naming and Directory Interface (JNDI) API namespace, and JMS clients then look them up, using the JNDI API. J2EE applications always use the JNDI API.

With the J2EE Software Development Kit (SDK) version 1.3, you use a tool called `j2eeadmin` to perform administrative tasks. For help on the tool, type `j2eeadmin` with no arguments.

3.1.1   Connection Factories

A *connection factory* is the object a client uses to create a connection with a provider. A connection factory encapsulates a set of connection configuration parameters that has been defined by an administrator. A pair of connection factories come preconfigured with the J2EE SDK and are accessible as soon as you start the service. Each connection factory is an instance of either the `QueueConnectionFactory` or the `TopicConnectionFactory` interface.

With the J2EE SDK, for example, you can use the default connection factory objects, named `QueueConnectionFactory` and `TopicConnectionFactory`, to create connections. You can also create new connection factories by using the following commands:

```
j2eeadmin -addJmsFactory jndi_name queue

j2eeadmin -addJmsFactory jndi_name topic
```

At the beginning of a JMS client program, you usually perform a JNDI API lookup of the connection factory. For example, the following code fragment obtains an `InitialContext` object and uses it to look up the `QueueConnection-Factory` and the `TopicConnectionFactory` by name:

```
Context ctx = new InitialContext();

QueueConnectionFactory queueConnectionFactory =
   (QueueConnectionFactory) ctx.lookup("QueueConnectionFactory");

TopicConnectionFactory topicConnectionFactory =
   (TopicConnectionFactory) ctx.lookup("TopicConnectionFactory");
```

Calling the `InitialContext` method with no parameters results in a search of the current classpath for a vendor-specific file named `jndi.properties`. This file indicates which JNDI API implementation to use and which namespace to use.

3.1.2   Destinations

A *destination* is the object a client uses to specify the target of messages it produces and the source of messages it consumes. In the PTP messaging domain, destinations are called queues, and you use the following J2EE SDK command to create them:

```
j2eeadmin -addJmsDestination queue_name queue
```

In the pub/sub messaging domain, destinations are called topics, and you use the following J2EE SDK command to create them:

```
j2eeadmin -addJmsDestination topic_name topic
```

A JMS application may use multiple queues and/or topics.

In addition to looking up a connection factory, you usually look up a destination. For example, the following line of code performs a JNDI API lookup of the previously created topic MyTopic and assigns it to a Topic object:

```
Topic myTopic = (Topic) ctx.lookup("MyTopic");
```

The following line of code looks up a queue named MyQueue and assigns it to a Queue object:

```
Queue myQueue = (Queue) ctx.lookup("MyQueue");
```

3.2   Connections

A *connection* encapsulates a virtual connection with a JMS provider. A connection could represent an open TCP/IP socket between a client and a provider service daemon. You use a connection to create one or more sessions.

Like connection factories, connections come in two forms, implementing either the QueueConnection or the TopicConnection interface. For example, once you have a QueueConnectionFactory or a TopicConnectionFactory object, you can use it to create a connection:

```
QueueConnection queueConnection =
  queueConnectionFactory.createQueueConnection();
```

```
TopicConnection topicConnection =
    topicConnectionFactory.createTopicConnection();
```

When an application completes, you need to close any connections that you have created. Failure to close a connection can cause resources not to be released by the JMS provider. Closing a connection also closes its sessions and their message producers and message consumers.

```
queueConnection.close();
```

```
topicConnection.close();
```

Before your application can consume messages, you must call the connection's start method; for details, see Section 3.5 on page 21. If you want to stop message delivery temporarily without closing the connection, you call the stop method.

3.3   Sessions

A *session* is a single-threaded context for producing and consuming messages. You use sessions to create message producers, message consumers, and messages. Sessions serialize the execution of message listeners; for details, see Section 3.5.1 on page 22.

A session provides a transactional context with which to group a set of sends and receives into an atomic unit of work. For details, see Section 5.2.2 on page 64.

Sessions, like connections, come in two forms, implementing either the QueueSession or the TopicSession interface. For example, if you created a Topic-Connection object, you use it to create a TopicSession:

```
TopicSession topicSession =
    topicConnection.createTopicSession(false,
    Session.AUTO_ACKNOWLEDGE);
```

The first argument means that the session is not transacted; the second means that the session automatically acknowledges messages when they have been received successfully. (For more information, see Section 5.1.1 on page 56.)

Similarly, you use a `QueueConnection` object to create a `QueueSession`:

```
QueueSession queueSession =
   queueConnection.createQueueSession(true, 0);
```

Here, the first argument means that the session is transacted; the second indicates that message acknowledgment is not specified for transacted sessions.

3.4   Message Producers

A *message producer* is an object created by a session and is used for sending messages to a destination. The PTP form of a message producer implements the `Queue-Sender` interface. The pub/sub form implements the `TopicPublisher` interface.

For example, you use a `QueueSession` to create a sender for the queue `myQueue`, and you use a `TopicSession` to create a publisher for the topic `myTopic`:

```
QueueSender queueSender = queueSession.createSender(myQueue);

TopicPublisher topicPublisher =
   topicSession.createPublisher(myTopic);
```

You can create an unidentified producer by specifying `null` as the argument to `createSender` or `createPublisher`. With an unidentified producer, you can wait to specify which destination to send the message to until you send or publish a message.

Once you have created a message producer, you can use it to send messages. (You have to create the messages first; see Section 3.6 on page 23.) With a `Queue-Sender`, you use the `send` method:

```
queueSender.send(message);
```

With a `TopicPublisher`, you use the `publish` method:

```
topicPublisher.publish(message);
```

If you created an unidentified producer, use the overloaded `send` or `publish` method that specifies the destination as the first parameter.

3.5 Message Consumers

A *message consumer* is an object created by a session and is used for receiving messages sent to a destination. A message consumer allows a JMS client to register interest in a destination with a JMS provider. The JMS provider manages the delivery of messages from a destination to the registered consumers of the destination.

The PTP form of message consumer implements the QueueReceiver interface. The pub/sub form implements the TopicSubscriber interface.

For example, you use a QueueSession to create a receiver for the queue myQueue, and you use a TopicSession to create a subscriber for the topic myTopic:

```
QueueReceiver queueReceiver = queueSession.createReceiver(myQueue);

TopicSubscriber topicSubscriber =
  topicSession.createSubscriber(myTopic);
```

You use the TopicSession.createDurableSubscriber method to create a durable topic subscriber. For details, see Section 5.2.1 on page 61.

Once you have created a message consumer, it becomes active, and you can use it to receive messages. You can use the close method for a QueueReceiver or a TopicSubscriber to make the message consumer inactive. Message delivery does not begin until you start the connection you created by calling the start method (see Section 3.2 on page 18).

With either a QueueReceiver or a TopicSubscriber, you use the receive method to consume a message synchronously. You can use this method at any time after you call the start method:

```
queueConnection.start();
Message m = queueReceiver.receive();

topicConnection.start();
Message m = topicSubscriber.receive(1000); // time out after a second
```

To consume a message asynchronously, you use a message listener, described in Section 3.5.1 on page 22.

3.5.1   Message Listeners

A *message listener* is an object that acts as an asynchronous event handler for messages. This object implements the MessageListener interface, which contains one method, onMessage. In the onMessage method, you define the actions to be taken when a message arrives.

You register the message listener with a specific QueueReceiver or TopicSubscriber by using the setMessageListener method. For example, if you define a class named TopicListener that implements the MessageListener interface, you can register the message listener as follows:

```
TopicListener topicListener = new TopicListener();
topicSubscriber.setMessageListener(topicListener);
```

After you register the message listener, you call the start method on the QueueConnection or the TopicConnection to begin message delivery. (If you call start before you register the message listener, you are likely to miss messages.)

Once message delivery begins, the message consumer automatically calls the message listener's onMessage method whenever a message is delivered. The onMessage method takes one argument of type Message, which the method can cast to any of the other message types (see Section 3.6.3 on page 25).

A message listener is not specific to a particular destination type. The same listener can obtain messages from either a queue or a topic, depending on whether the listener is set by a QueueReceiver or a TopicSubscriber object. A message listener does, however, usually expect a specific message type and format. Moreover, if it needs to reply to messages, a message listener must either assume a particular destination type or obtain the destination type of the message and create a producer for that destination type.

Your onMessage method should handle all exceptions. It must not throw checked exceptions, and throwing a RuntimeException, though possible, is considered a programming error.

The session used to create the message consumer serializes the execution of all message listeners registered with the session. At any time, only one of the session's message listeners is running.

In the J2EE 1.3 platform, a message-driven bean is a special kind of message listener. For details, see Section 6.2 on page 69.

3.5.2   Message Selectors

If your messaging application needs to filter the messages it receives, you can use a JMS API message selector, which allows a message consumer to specify the messages it is interested in. Message selectors assign the work of filtering messages to the JMS provider rather than to the application. For an example of the use of a message selector, see Chapter 8.

A message selector is a String that contains an expression. The syntax of the expression is based on a subset of the SQL92 conditional expression syntax. The createReceiver, createSubscriber, and createDurableSubscriber methods each have a form that allows you to specify a message selector as an argument when you create a message consumer.

The message consumer then receives only messages whose headers and properties match the selector. (See Section 3.6.1 on page 23 and Section 3.6.2 on page 24.) A message selector cannot select messages on the basis of the content of the message body.

3.6   Messages

The ultimate purpose of a JMS application is to produce and to consume messages that can then be used by other software applications. JMS messages have a basic format that is simple but highly flexible, allowing you to create messages that match formats used by non-JMS applications on heterogeneous platforms.

A JMS message has three parts:

- A header

- Properties (optional)

- A body (optional)

For complete documentation of message headers, properties, and bodies, see the documentation of the Message interface in Chapter 25.

3.6.1   Message Headers

A JMS message header contains a number of predefined fields that contain values that both clients and providers use to identify and to route messages. (Table 3.1 lists the JMS message header fields and indicates how their values are set.) For example, every message has a unique identifier, represented in the header field JMSMessageID. The value of another header field, JMSDestination, represents the queue or the topic to which the message is sent. Other fields include a timestamp and a priority level.

Each header field has associated setter and getter methods, which are documented in the description of the Message interface. Some header fields are intended to be set by a client, but many are set automatically by the send or the publish method, which overrides any client-set values.

Table 3.1: How JMS Message Header Field Values Are Set

Header Field	Set By
JMSDestination	send or publish method
JMSDeliveryMode	send or publish method
JMSExpiration	send or publish method
JMSPriority	send or publish method
JMSMessageID	send or publish method
JMSTimestamp	send or publish method
JMSCorrelationID	Client
JMSReplyTo	Client
JMSType	Client
JMSRedelivered	JMS provider

3.6.2   Message Properties

You can create and set properties for messages if you need values in addition to those provided by the header fields. You can use properties to provide compatibility with other messaging systems, or you can use them to create message selectors (see Section 3.5.2 on page 23). For an example of setting a property to be used as a message selector, see Section 8.1.2.3 on page 102.

The JMS API provides some predefined property names that a provider may support. The use of either predefined properties or user-defined properties is optional.

3.6.3   Message Bodies

The JMS API defines five message body formats, also called message types, which allow you to send and to receive data in many different forms and provide compatibility with existing messaging formats. Table 3.2 describes these message types.

Table 3.2: JMS Message Types

Message Type	Body Contains
TextMessage	A java.lang.String object (for example, the contents of an Extensible Markup Language file).
MapMessage	A set of name/value pairs, with names as String objects and values as primitive types in the Java programming language. The entries can be accessed sequentially by enumerator or randomly by name. The order of the entries is undefined.
BytesMessage	A stream of uninterpreted bytes. This message type is for literally encoding a body to match an existing message format.
StreamMessage	A stream of primitive values in the Java programming language, filled and read sequentially.
ObjectMessage	A Serializable object in the Java programming language.
Message	Nothing. Composed of header fields and properties only. This message type is useful when a message body is not required.

The JMS API provides methods for creating messages of each type and for filling in their contents. For example, to create and send a TextMessage to a queue, you might use the following statements:

```
TextMessage message = queueSession.createTextMessage();
message.setText(msg_text);      // msg_text is a String
queueSender.send(message);
```

At the consuming end, a message arrives as a generic Message object and must be cast to the appropriate message type. You can use one or more getter methods to extract the message contents. The following code fragment uses the getText method:

```
Message m = queueReceiver.receive();
if (m instanceof TextMessage) {
    TextMessage message = (TextMessage) m;
    System.out.println("Reading message: " + message.getText());
} else {
    // Handle error
}
```

3.7   Exception Handling

The root class for exceptions thrown by JMS API methods is JMSException. Catching JMSException provides a generic way of handling all exceptions related to the JMS API. The JMSException class includes the following subclasses:

- IllegalStateException
- InvalidClientIDException
- InvalidDestinationException
- InvalidSelectorException
- JMSSecurityException
- MessageEOFException
- MessageFormatException
- MessageNotReadableException
- MessageNotWriteableException
- ResourceAllocationException
- TransactionInProgressException
- TransactionRolledBackException

All the examples in this book catch and handle JMSException when it is appropriate to do so.

CHAPTER 4

Writing Simple JMS Client Applications

THIS chapter shows how to create and to run simple JMS client programs. A J2EE application client commonly accesses J2EE components installed in a server based on J2EE technology ("J2EE server"). The clients in this chapter, however, are simple standalone programs that run outside the server as class files. The clients demonstrate the basic tasks that a JMS application must perform:

- Creating a connection and a session

- Creating message producers and consumers

- Sending and receiving messages

In a J2EE application, some of these tasks are performed, in whole or in part, by the EJB container. If you learn about these tasks, you will have a good basis for understanding how a JMS application works on the J2EE platform.

The chapter covers the following topics:

- Setting your environment to run J2EE clients and applications

- A point-to-point example that uses synchronous receives

- A publish/subscribe example that uses a message listener

- Running JMS client programs on multiple systems

Each example consists of two programs: one that sends messages and one that receives them. You can run the programs in two terminal windows.

When you write a JMS application to run in a J2EE component, you use many of the same methods in much the same sequence as you do for a JMS client program. However, there are some significant differences. Chapter 6 describes these differences, and the following chapters provide examples that illustrate them.

4.1   Setting Your Environment for Running Applications

Before you can run the examples, you need to make sure that your environment is set appropriately. Table 4.1 shows how to set the environment variables needed to run J2EE applications on Microsoft Windows and UNIX platforms.

**Table 4.1: Environment Settings for Compiling and Running
J2EE Applications**

Platform	Variable Name	Values
Microsoft Windows	%JAVA_HOME%	Directory in which the Java 2 SDK, Standard Edition, version 1.3.1, is installed
	%J2EE_HOME%	Directory in which the J2EE SDK 1.3 is installed, usually `C:\j2sdkee1.3`

	%CLASSPATH%	Include the following:
		`.;%J2EE_HOME%\lib\j2ee.jar;`
		`%J2EE_HOME%\lib\locale`

	%PATH%	Include `%J2EE_HOME%\bin`
UNIX	$JAVA_HOME	Directory in which the Java 2 SDK, Standard Edition, version 1.3.1, is installed
	$J2EE_HOME	Directory in which the J2EE SDK 1.3 is installed, usually `$HOME/j2sdkee1.3`

	$CLASSPATH	Include the following:
		`.:$J2EE_HOME/lib/j2ee.jar:`
		`$J2EE_HOME/lib/locale`

	$PATH	Include `$J2EE_HOME/bin`

The appendix provides more examples of client programs that demonstrate additional features of the JMS API. You can download still more examples of JMS client programs from the JMS API Web site, `http://java.sun.com/products/jms/`. If you downloaded the tutorial examples as described in the preface, you will find the examples for this chapter in the directory `jms_tutorial/examples/simple` (on UNIX systems) or `jms_tutorial\examples\simple` (on Microsoft Windows systems).

4.2   A Simple Point-to-Point Example

This section describes the sending and receiving programs in a PTP example that uses the `receive` method to consume messages synchronously. This section then explains how to compile and run the programs, using the J2EE SDK 1.3.

4.2.1   Writing the PTP Client Programs

The sending program, `SimpleQueueSender.java`, performs the following steps:

1. Performs a Java Naming and Directory Interface (JNDI) API lookup of the `QueueConnectionFactory` and queue

2. Creates a connection and a session

3. Creates a `QueueSender`

4. Creates a `TextMessage`

5. Sends one or more messages to the queue

6. Sends a control message to indicate the end of the message stream

7. Closes the connection in a `finally` block, automatically closing the session and `QueueSender`

The receiving program, `SimpleQueueReceiver.java`, performs the following steps:

1. Performs a JNDI API lookup of the `QueueConnectionFactory` and queue

2. Creates a connection and a session

3. Creates a `QueueReceiver`

4. Starts the connection, causing message delivery to begin

5. Receives the messages sent to the queue until the end-of-message-stream control message is received

6. Closes the connection in a `finally` block, automatically closing the session and `QueueReceiver`

The `receive` method can be used in several ways to perform a synchronous receive. If you specify no arguments or an argument of `0`, the method blocks indefinitely until a message arrives:

```
Message m = queueReceiver.receive();
```

```
Message m = queueReceiver.receive(0);
```

For a simple client program, this may not matter. But if you do not want your program to consume system resources unnecessarily, use a timed synchronous receive. Do one of the following:

- Call the `receive` method with a timeout argument greater than `0`:

```
Message m = queueReceiver.receive(1); // 1 millisecond
```

- Call the `receiveNoWait` method, which receives a message only if one is available:

```
Message m = queueReceiver.receiveNoWait();
```

The `SimpleQueueReceiver` program uses an indefinite `while` loop to receive messages, calling `receive` with a timeout argument. Calling `receiveNoWait` would have the same effect.

The following subsections show the two programs:

- `SimpleQueueSender.java`
- `SimpleQueueReceiver.java`

4.2.1.1   Sending Messages to a Queue: `SimpleQueueSender.java`

The sending program is `SimpleQueueSender.java`.

```java
/**
 * The SimpleQueueSender class consists only of a main method,
 * which sends several messages to a queue.
 *
 * Run this program in conjunction with SimpleQueueReceiver.
 * Specify a queue name on the command line when you run the
 * program.  By default, the program sends one message.  Specify
 * a number after the queue name to send that number of messages.
 */
import javax.jms.*;
import javax.naming.*;

public class SimpleQueueSender {

    /**
     * Main method.
     *
     * @param args      the queue used by the example and,
     *                  optionally, the number of messages to send
     */
    public static void main(String[] args) {
        String                 queueName = null;
        Context                jndiContext = null;
        QueueConnectionFactory queueConnectionFactory = null;
        QueueConnection        queueConnection = null;
        QueueSession           queueSession = null;
        Queue                  queue = null;
        QueueSender            queueSender = null;
        TextMessage            message = null;
        final int              NUM_MSGS;
```

```java
if ( (args.length < 1) || (args.length > 2) ) {
    System.out.println("Usage: java SimpleQueueSender " +
        "<queue-name> [<number-of-messages>]");
    System.exit(1);
}

queueName = new String(args[0]);
System.out.println("Queue name is " + queueName);
if (args.length == 2){
    NUM_MSGS = (new Integer(args[1])).intValue();
} else {
    NUM_MSGS = 1;
}

/*
 * Create a JNDI API InitialContext object if none exists
 * yet.
 */
try {
    jndiContext = new InitialContext();
} catch (NamingException e) {
    System.out.println("Could not create JNDI API " +
        "context: " + e.toString());
    System.exit(1);
}

/*
 * Look up connection factory and queue.  If either does
 * not exist, exit.
 */
try {
    queueConnectionFactory = (QueueConnectionFactory)
        jndiContext.lookup("QueueConnectionFactory");
    queue = (Queue) jndiContext.lookup(queueName);
} catch (NamingException e) {
    System.out.println("JNDI API lookup failed: " +
        e.toString());
    System.exit(1);
```

```java
        }

        /*
         * Create connection.
         * Create session from connection; false means session is
         * not transacted.
         * Create sender and text message.
         * Send messages, varying text slightly.
         * Send end-of-messages message.
         * Finally, close connection.
         */
        try {
            queueConnection =
                queueConnectionFactory.createQueueConnection();
            queueSession =
                queueConnection.createQueueSession(false,
                    Session.AUTO_ACKNOWLEDGE);
            queueSender = queueSession.createSender(queue);
            message = queueSession.createTextMessage();
            for (int i = 0; i < NUM_MSGS; i++) {
                message.setText("This is message " + (i + 1));
                System.out.println("Sending message: " +
                    message.getText());
                queueSender.send(message);
            }

            /*
             * Send a non-text control message indicating end of
             * messages.
             */
            queueSender.send(queueSession.createMessage());
        } catch (JMSException e) {
            System.out.println("Exception occurred: " +
                e.toString());
        } finally {
            if (queueConnection != null) {
                try {
                    queueConnection.close();
                } catch (JMSException e) {}
```

```
        }
      }
    }
  }
```

Code Example 4.1   SimpleQueueSender.java

4.2.1.2   Receiving Messages from a Queue: SimpleQueueReceiver.java

The receiving program is SimpleQueueReceiver.java.

```
/**
 * The SimpleQueueReceiver class consists only of a main method,
 * which fetches one or more messages from a queue using
 * synchronous message delivery.  Run this program in conjunction
 * with SimpleQueueSender.  Specify a queue name on the command
 * line when you run the program.
 */
import javax.jms.*;
import javax.naming.*;

public class SimpleQueueReceiver {

    /**
     * Main method.
     *
     * @param args     the queue used by the example
     */
    public static void main(String[] args) {
        String                  queueName = null;
        Context                 jndiContext = null;
        QueueConnectionFactory  queueConnectionFactory = null;
        QueueConnection         queueConnection = null;
        QueueSession            queueSession = null;
        Queue                   queue = null;
```

```
QueueReceiver          queueReceiver = null;
TextMessage            message = null;

/*
 * Read queue name from command line and display it.
 */
if (args.length != 1) {
    System.out.println("Usage: java " +
        "SimpleQueueReceiver <queue-name>");
    System.exit(1);
}
queueName = new String(args[0]);
System.out.println("Queue name is " + queueName);

/*
 * Create a JNDI API InitialContext object if none exists
 * yet.
 */
try {
    jndiContext = new InitialContext();
} catch (NamingException e) {
    System.out.println("Could not create JNDI API " +
        "context: " + e.toString());
    System.exit(1);
}

/*
 * Look up connection factory and queue.  If either does
 * not exist, exit.
 */
try {
    queueConnectionFactory = (QueueConnectionFactory)
        jndiContext.lookup("QueueConnectionFactory");
    queue = (Queue) jndiContext.lookup(queueName);
} catch (NamingException e) {
    System.out.println("JNDI API lookup failed: " +
        e.toString());
    System.exit(1);
}
```

```java
/*
 * Create connection.
 * Create session from connection; false means session is
 * not transacted.
 * Create receiver, then start message delivery.
 * Receive all text messages from queue until
 * a non-text message is received indicating end of
 * message stream.
 * Close connection.
 */
try {
    queueConnection =
        queueConnectionFactory.createQueueConnection();
    queueSession =
        queueConnection.createQueueSession(false,
            Session.AUTO_ACKNOWLEDGE);
    queueReceiver = queueSession.createReceiver(queue);
    queueConnection.start();
    while (true) {
        Message m = queueReceiver.receive(1);
        if (m != null) {
            if (m instanceof TextMessage) {
                message = (TextMessage) m;
                System.out.println("Reading message: " +
                    message.getText());
            } else {
                break;
            }
        }
    }
} catch (JMSException e) {
    System.out.println("Exception occurred: " +
        e.toString());
} finally {
    if (queueConnection != null) {
        try {
            queueConnection.close();
        } catch (JMSException e) {}
    }
```

```
            }
        }
    }
```

Code Example 4.2 `SimpleQueueReceiver.java`

4.2.2   Compiling the PTP Clients

To compile the PTP example, do the following.

1. Make sure that you have set the environment variables shown in Table 4.1 on page 28.

2. At a command line prompt, compile the two source files:

```
javac SimpleQueueSender.java
javac SimpleQueueReceiver.java
```

4.2.3   Starting the JMS Provider

When you use the J2EE SDK 1.3, your JMS provider is the SDK. At another command line prompt, start the J2EE server as follows:

```
j2ee -verbose
```

Wait until the server displays the message "J2EE server startup complete."

4.2.4   Creating the JMS Administered Objects

In the window in which you compiled the clients, use the `j2eeadmin` command to create a queue named `MyQueue`. The last argument tells the command what kind of destination to create.

```
j2eeadmin -addJmsDestination MyQueue queue
```

To make sure that the queue has been created, use the following command:

```
j2eeadmin -listJmsDestination
```

This example uses the default `QueueConnectionFactory` object supplied with the J2EE SDK 1.3. With a different J2EE product, you might need to create a connection factory yourself.

4.2.5   Running the PTP Clients

Run the clients as follows.

1. Run the `SimpleQueueSender` program, sending three messages. You need to define a value for `jms.properties`.

   - On a Microsoft Windows system, type the following command on a single line:

   ```
   java -Djms.properties=%J2EE_HOME%\config\jms_client.properties
   SimpleQueueSender MyQueue 3
   ```

   - On a UNIX system, type the following command on a single line:

   ```
   java -Djms.properties=$J2EE_HOME/config/jms_client.properties
   SimpleQueueSender MyQueue 3
   ```

   The output of the program looks like this:

   ```
   Queue name is MyQueue
   Sending message: This is message 1
   Sending message: This is message 2
   Sending message: This is message 3
   ```

2. In the same window, run the `SimpleQueueReceiver` program, specifying the queue name. The `java` commands look like this:

   - Microsoft Windows systems:

   ```
   java -Djms.properties=%J2EE_HOME%\config\jms_client.properties
   SimpleQueueReceiver MyQueue
   ```

   - UNIX systems:

   ```
   java -Djms.properties=$J2EE_HOME/config/jms_client.properties
   SimpleQueueReceiver MyQueue
   ```

The output of the program looks like this:

```
Queue name is MyQueue
Reading message: This is message 1
Reading message: This is message 2
Reading message: This is message 3
```

3. Now try running the programs in the opposite order. Start the SimpleQueue-Receiver program. It displays the queue name and then appears to hang, waiting for messages.

4. In a different terminal window, run the SimpleQueueSender program. When the messages have been sent, the SimpleQueueReceiver program receives them and exits.

4.2.6   Deleting the Queue

You can delete the queue you created as follows:

```
j2eeadmin -removeJmsDestination MyQueue
```

You will use it again in Section 4.4.1 on page 51, however.

4.3   A Simple Publish/Subscribe Example

This section describes the publishing and subscribing programs in a pub/sub example that uses a message listener to consume messages asynchronously. This section then explains how to compile and run the programs, using the J2EE SDK 1.3.

4.3.1   Writing the Pub/Sub Client Programs

The publishing program, SimpleTopicPublisher.java, performs the following steps:

1. Performs a JNDI API lookup of the TopicConnectionFactory and topic

2. Creates a connection and a session

3. Creates a TopicPublisher

4. Creates a `TextMessage`

5. Publishes one or more messages to the topic

6. Closes the connection, which automatically closes the session and `Topic-Publisher`

The receiving program, `SimpleTopicSubscriber.java`, performs the following steps:

1. Performs a JNDI API lookup of the `TopicConnectionFactory` and topic

2. Creates a connection and a session

3. Creates a `TopicSubscriber`

4. Creates an instance of the `TextListener` class and registers it as the message listener for the `TopicSubscriber`

5. Starts the connection, causing message delivery to begin

6. Listens for the messages published to the topic, stopping when the user enters the character q or Q

7. Closes the connection, which automatically closes the session and `TopicSubscriber`

The message listener, `TextListener.java`, follows these steps:

1. When a message arrives, the `onMessage` method is called automatically.

2. The `onMessage` method converts the incoming message to a `TextMessage` and displays its content.

The following subsections show the three source files:

- `SimpleTopicPublisher.java`

- `SimpleTopicSubscriber.java`

- `TextListener.java`

4.3.1.1 Publishing Messages to a Topic: `SimpleTopicPublisher.java`

The publisher program is `SimpleTopicPublisher.java`.

```java
/**
 * The SimpleTopicPublisher class consists only of a main method,
 * which publishes several messages to a topic.
 *
 * Run this program in conjunction with SimpleTopicSubscriber.
 * Specify a topic name on the command line when you run the
 * program.  By default, the program sends one message.
 * Specify a number after the topic name to send that number
 * of messages.
 */
import javax.jms.*;
import javax.naming.*;

public class SimpleTopicPublisher {

    /**
     * Main method.
     *
     * @param args      the topic used by the example and,
     *                  optionally, the number of messages to send
     */
    public static void main(String[] args) {
        String                  topicName = null;
        Context                 jndiContext = null;
        TopicConnectionFactory  topicConnectionFactory = null;
        TopicConnection         topicConnection = null;
        TopicSession            topicSession = null;
        Topic                   topic = null;
        TopicPublisher          topicPublisher = null;
        TextMessage             message = null;
        final int               NUM_MSGS;

        if ( (args.length < 1) || (args.length > 2) ) {
            System.out.println("Usage: java " +
```

```java
                "SimpleTopicPublisher <topic-name> " +
            "[<number-of-messages>]");
        System.exit(1);
    }
    topicName = new String(args[0]);
    System.out.println("Topic name is " + topicName);
    if (args.length == 2){
        NUM_MSGS = (new Integer(args[1])).intValue();
    } else {
        NUM_MSGS = 1;
    }

    /*
     * Create a JNDI API InitialContext object if none exists
     * yet.
     */
    try {
        jndiContext = new InitialContext();
    } catch (NamingException e) {
        System.out.println("Could not create JNDI API " +
            "context: " + e.toString());
        e.printStackTrace();
        System.exit(1);
    }

    /*
     * Look up connection factory and topic.  If either does
     * not exist, exit.
     */
    try {
        topicConnectionFactory = (TopicConnectionFactory)
            jndiContext.lookup("TopicConnectionFactory");
        topic = (Topic) jndiContext.lookup(topicName);
    } catch (NamingException e) {
        System.out.println("JNDI API lookup failed: " +
            e.toString());
        e.printStackTrace();
        System.exit(1);
    }
```

```java
    /*
     * Create connection.
     * Create session from connection; false means session is
     * not transacted.
     * Create publisher and text message.
     * Send messages, varying text slightly.
     * Finally, close connection.
     */
    try {
        topicConnection =
            topicConnectionFactory.createTopicConnection();
        topicSession =
            topicConnection.createTopicSession(false,
                Session.AUTO_ACKNOWLEDGE);
        topicPublisher = topicSession.createPublisher(topic);
        message = topicSession.createTextMessage();
        for (int i = 0; i < NUM_MSGS; i++) {
            message.setText("This is message " + (i + 1));
            System.out.println("Publishing message: " +
                message.getText());
            topicPublisher.publish(message);
        }
    } catch (JMSException e) {
        System.out.println("Exception occurred: " +
            e.toString());
    } finally {
        if (topicConnection != null) {
            try {
                topicConnection.close();
            } catch (JMSException e) {}
        }
    }
    }
}
```

Code Example 4.3 SimpleTopicPublisher.java

4.3.1.2 Receiving Messages Asynchronously: `SimpleTopicSubscriber.java`

The subscriber program is `SimpleTopicSubscriber.java`.

```java
/**
 * The SimpleTopicSubscriber class consists only of a main
 * method, which receives one or more messages from a topic using
 * asynchronous message delivery.  It uses the message listener
 * TextListener.  Run this program in conjunction with
 * SimpleTopicPublisher.
 *
 * Specify a topic name on the command line when you run the
 * program. To end the program, enter Q or q on the command line.
 */
import javax.jms.*;
import javax.naming.*;
import java.io.*;

public class SimpleTopicSubscriber {

    /**
     * Main method.
     *
     * @param args     the topic used by the example
     */
    public static void main(String[] args) {
        String                  topicName = null;
        Context                 jndiContext = null;
        TopicConnectionFactory  topicConnectionFactory = null;
        TopicConnection         topicConnection = null;
        TopicSession            topicSession = null;
        Topic                   topic = null;
        TopicSubscriber         topicSubscriber = null;
        TextListener            topicListener = null;
        TextMessage             message = null;
        InputStreamReader       inputStreamReader = null;
        char                    answer = '\0';
```

```java
/*
 * Read topic name from command line and display it.
 */
if (args.length != 1) {
    System.out.println("Usage: java " +
        "SimpleTopicSubscriber <topic-name>");
    System.exit(1);
}
topicName = new String(args[0]);
System.out.println("Topic name is " + topicName);

/*
 * Create a JNDI API InitialContext object if none exists
 * yet.
 */
try {
    jndiContext = new InitialContext();
} catch (NamingException e) {
    System.out.println("Could not create JNDI API " +
        "context: " + e.toString());
    e.printStackTrace();
    System.exit(1);
}

/*
 * Look up connection factory and topic.  If either does
 * not exist, exit.
 */
try {
    topicConnectionFactory = (TopicConnectionFactory)
        jndiContext.lookup("TopicConnectionFactory");
    topic = (Topic) jndiContext.lookup(topicName);
} catch (NamingException e) {
    System.out.println("JNDI API lookup failed: " +
        e.toString());
    e.printStackTrace();
    System.exit(1);
}
```

```java
/*
 * Create connection.
 * Create session from connection; false means session is
 * not transacted.
 * Create subscriber.
 * Register message listener (TextListener).
 * Receive text messages from topic.
 * When all messages have been received, enter Q to quit.
 * Close connection.
 */
try {
    topicConnection =
        topicConnectionFactory.createTopicConnection();
    topicSession =
        topicConnection.createTopicSession(false,
            Session.AUTO_ACKNOWLEDGE);
    topicSubscriber =
        topicSession.createSubscriber(topic);
    topicListener = new TextListener();
    topicSubscriber.setMessageListener(topicListener);
    topicConnection.start();
    System.out.println("To end program, enter Q or q, " +
        "then <return>");
    inputStreamReader = new InputStreamReader(System.in);
    while (!((answer == 'q') || (answer == 'Q'))) {
        try {
            answer = (char) inputStreamReader.read();
        } catch (IOException e) {
            System.out.println("I/O exception: "
                + e.toString());
        }
    }
} catch (JMSException e) {
    System.out.println("Exception occurred: " +
        e.toString());
} finally {
    if (topicConnection != null) {
        try {
            topicConnection.close();
```

```
            } catch (JMSException e) {}
        }
    }
}
}
```

Code Example 4.4 `SimpleTopicSubscriber.java`

4.3.1.3 The Message Listener: `TextListener.java`

The message listener is `TextListener.java`.

```java
/**
 * The TextListener class implements the MessageListener
 * interface by defining an onMessage method that displays
 * the contents of a TextMessage.
 *
 * This class acts as the listener for the SimpleTopicSubscriber
 * class.
 */
import javax.jms.*;

public class TextListener implements MessageListener {

    /**
     * Casts the message to a TextMessage and displays its text.
     *
     * @param message      the incoming message
     */

    public void onMessage(Message message) {
        TextMessage msg = null;

        try {
            if (message instanceof TextMessage) {
                msg = (TextMessage) message;
```

```
                    System.out.println("Reading message: " +
                        msg.getText());
                } else {
                    System.out.println("Message of wrong type: " +
                        message.getClass().getName());
                }
            } catch (JMSException e) {
                System.out.println("JMSException in onMessage(): " +
                    e.toString());
            } catch (Throwable t) {
                System.out.println("Exception in onMessage():" +
                    t.getMessage());
            }
        }
    }
}
```

Code Example 4.5 `TextListener.java`

4.3.2   Compiling the Pub/Sub Clients

To compile the pub/sub example, do the following.

1. Make sure that you have set the environment variables shown in Table 4.1 on page 28.

2. Compile the programs and the message listener class:

```
javac SimpleTopicPublisher.java
javac SimpleTopicSubscriber.java
javac TextListener.java
```

4.3.3   Starting the JMS Provider

If you did not do so before, start the J2EE server in another terminal window:

```
j2ee -verbose
```

Wait until the server displays the message "J2EE server startup complete."

4.3.4   Creating the JMS Administered Objects

In the window in which you compiled the clients, use the `j2eeadmin` command to create a topic named `MyTopic`. The last argument tells the command what kind of destination to create.

```
j2eeadmin -addJmsDestination MyTopic topic
```

To verify that the queue has been created, use the following command:

```
j2eeadmin -listJmsDestination
```

This example uses the default `TopicConnectionFactory` object supplied with the J2EE SDK 1.3. With a different J2EE product, you might need to create a connection factory.

4.3.5   Running the Pub/Sub Clients

Run the clients as follows.

1. Run the `SimpleTopicSubscriber` program, specifying the topic name. You need to define a value for `jms.properties`.

   - On a Microsoft Windows system, type the following command on a single line:

   ```
   java -Djms.properties=%J2EE_HOME%\config\jms_client.properties
   SimpleTopicSubscriber MyTopic
   ```

   - On a UNIX system, type the following command on a single line:

   ```
   java -Djms.properties=$J2EE_HOME/config/jms_client.properties
   SimpleTopicSubscriber MyTopic
   ```

   The program displays the following lines and appears to hang:

   ```
   Topic name is MyTopic
   To end program, enter Q or q, then <return>
   ```

2. In another terminal window, run the `SimpleTopicPublisher` program, publishing three messages. The `java` commands look like this:

- Microsoft Windows systems:

```
java -Djms.properties=%J2EE_HOME%\config\jms_client.properties
SimpleTopicPublisher MyTopic 3
```

- UNIX systems:

```
java -Djms.properties=$J2EE_HOME/config/jms_client.properties
SimpleTopicPublisher MyTopic 3
```

The output of the program looks like this:

```
Topic name is MyTopic
Publishing message: This is message 1
Publishing message: This is message 2
Publishing message: This is message 3
```

In the other window, the program displays the following:

```
Reading message: This is message 1
Reading message: This is message 2
Reading message: This is message 3
```

Enter Q or q to stop the program.

4.3.6   Deleting the Topic and Stopping the Server

1. You can delete the topic you created as follows:

```
j2eeadmin -removeJmsDestination MyTopic
```

You will use it again in Section 4.4.2 on page 52, however.

2. If you wish, you can stop the J2EE server as well:

```
j2ee -stop
```

4.4 Running JMS Client Programs on Multiple Systems

JMS client programs can communicate with each other when they are running on different systems in a network. The systems must be visible to each other by name—the UNIX host name or the Microsoft Windows computer name—and must both be running the J2EE server.

This section explains how to produce and to consume messages in two different situations:

- When a J2EE server is running on both systems
- When a J2EE server is running on only one system

4.4.1 Communicating Between Two J2EE Servers

Suppose that you want to run the `SimpleQueueSender` program on one system, `mars`, and the `SimpleQueueReceiver` program on another system, `earth`. To do so, follow these steps.

1. Start the J2EE server on both systems. Enter the following command in a terminal window on each system:

   ```
   j2ee -verbose
   ```

2. On `earth`, create a `QueueConnectionFactory` object, using a command like the following:

   ```
   j2eeadmin -addJmsFactory jms/EarthQCF queue
   ```

3. On `mars`, create a connection factory with the same name that points to the server on `earth`. Enter, on one line, a command like the following:

   ```
   j2eeadmin -addJmsFactory jms/EarthQCF queue -props
   url=corbaname:iiop:earth:1050#earth
   ```

4. In each source program, change the line that looks up the connection factory so that it refers to the new connection factory:

   ```
   queueConnectionFactory =
       (QueueConnectionFactory) jndiContext.lookup("jms/EarthQCF");
   ```

5. Recompile the programs; then run them by using the instructions in Section 4.2.5 on page 38. Because both connection factories have the same name, you can run either the sender or the receiver on either system. (Note: A bug in the JMS provider in the J2EE SDK may cause a runtime failure to create a connection to systems that use the Dynamic Host Configuration Protocol [DHCP] to obtain an IP address.)

You can run the pub/sub example in the same way by creating a `Topic-ConnectionFactory` object on both systems. For an example showing how to deploy J2EE applications on two different systems, see Chapter 10.

4.4.2   Communicating Between a J2EE Server and a System Not Running a J2EE Server

In order for two standalone client programs to communicate, both must have the J2EE SDK installed locally. However, the J2EE server does not have to be running on both systems. Suppose that you want to run the `SimpleTopicPublisher` and the `SimpleTopicSubscriber` programs on two systems called `earth` and `mars`, as in Section 4.4.1, but that the J2EE server will be running only on `earth`. To specify the system running the server, you can either

- Use the command line, which allows you to access different applications on different servers for maximum flexibility

- Set a configurable property, which allows applications to run only on the system specified in the property

When the server is running only on the remote system, you do *not* have to create a connection factory on the local system that refers to the remote system.

The procedure for using the command line is as follows:

1. Start the J2EE server on `earth`:

    j2ee -verbose

2. Set the `J2EE_HOME` environment variable and the classpath on `mars` so that they point to the J2EE SDK 1.3 installation on `mars` (see Table 4.1 on page 28).

3. To access a client program on a system running the server from a client program on a system not running the server, use the following option, where *hostname* is the name of the system running the J2EE server:

```
-Dorg.omg.CORBA.ORBInitialHost=hostname
```

This option allows you to access the naming service on the remote system. For example, if the server is running on earth, use a command like the following to run the SimpleTopicSubscriber program on mars. Make sure that the destination you specify exists on the server running on earth.

- On a Microsoft Windows system, type the following command on a single line:

```
java -Djms.properties=%J2EE_HOME%\config\jms_client.properties
-Dorg.omg.CORBA.ORBInitialHost=earth SimpleTopicSubscriber MyTopic
```

- On a UNIX system, type the following command on a single line:

```
java -Djms.properties=$J2EE_HOME/config/jms_client.properties
-Dorg.omg.CORBA.ORBInitialHost=earth SimpleTopicSubscriber MyTopic
```

If all the remote programs you need to access are on the same system, you can edit the file %J2EE_HOME%\config\orb.properties (on Microsoft Windows systems) or $J2EE_HOME/config/orb.properties (on UNIX systems) on the local system. The second line of this file looks like this:

```
host=localhost
```

Change localhost to the name of the system on which the J2EE server is running—for example, earth:

```
host=earth
```

You can now run the client program as before, but you do not need to specify the option -Dorg.omg.CORBA.ORBInitialHost.

CHAPTER 5

Creating Robust JMS Applications

THIS chapter explains how to use features of the JMS API to achieve the level of reliability and performance your application requires. Many JMS applications cannot tolerate dropped or duplicate messages and require that every message be received once and only once.

The most reliable way to produce a message is to send a PERSISTENT message within a transaction. JMS messages are PERSISTENT by default. A *transaction* is a unit of work into which you can group a series of operations, such as message sends and receives, so that the operations either all succeed or all fail. For details, see Section 5.1.2 on page 58 and Section 5.2.2 on page 64.

The most reliable way to consume a message is to do so within a transaction, either from a nontemporary queue—in the PTP messaging domain—or from a durable subscription—in the pub/sub messaging domain. For details, see Section 5.1.5 on page 60, Section 5.2.1 on page 61, and Section 5.2.2 on page 64.

For other applications, a lower level of reliability can reduce overhead and improve performance. You can send messages with varying priority levels—see Section 5.1.3 on page 59—and you can set them to expire after a certain length of time (see Section 5.1.4 on page 59).

The JMS API provides several ways to achieve various kinds and degrees of reliability. This chapter divides them into two categories:

- Basic reliability mechanisms
- Advanced reliability mechanisms

The following sections describe these features as they apply to JMS clients. Some of the features work differently in J2EE applications; in these cases, the differences are noted here and are explained in detail in Chapter 6.

5.1   Using Basic Reliability Mechanisms

The basic mechanisms for achieving or affecting reliable message delivery are as follows:

- **Controlling message acknowledgment.** You can specify various levels of control over message acknowledgment.

- **Specifying message persistence.** You can specify that messages are persistent, meaning that they must not be lost in the event of a provider failure.

- **Setting message priority levels.** You can set various priority levels for messages, which can affect the order in which the messages are delivered.

- **Allowing messages to expire.** You can specify an expiration time for messages, so that they will not be delivered if they are obsolete.

- **Creating temporary destinations.** You can create temporary destinations that last only for the duration of the connection in which they are created.

5.1.1   Controlling Message Acknowledgment

Until a JMS message has been acknowledged, it is not considered to be successfully consumed. The successful consumption of a message ordinarily takes place in three stages.

1. The client receives the message.

2. The client processes the message.

3. The message is acknowledged. Acknowledgment is initiated either by the JMS provider or by the client, depending on the session acknowledgment mode.

In transacted sessions (see Section 5.2.2 on page 64), acknowledgment happens automatically when a transaction is committed. If a transaction is rolled back, all consumed messages are redelivered.

In nontransacted sessions, when and how a message is acknowledged depends on the value specified as the second argument of the `createQueueSession` or `createTopicSession` method. The three possible argument values are:

- `Session.AUTO_ACKNOWLEDGE`. The session automatically acknowledges a client's receipt of a message either when the client has successfully returned from a call to `receive` or when the `MessageListener` it has called to process the message returns successfully. A synchronous receive in an `AUTO_ACKNOWLEDGE` session is the one exception to the rule that message consumption is a three-stage process. In this case, the receipt and acknowledgment take place in one step, followed by the processing of the message.

- `Session.CLIENT_ACKNOWLEDGE`. A client acknowledges a message by calling the message's `acknowledge` method. In this mode, acknowledgment takes place on the session level: Acknowledging a consumed message automatically acknowledges the receipt of all messages that have been consumed by its session. For example, if a message consumer consumes ten messages and then acknowledges the fifth message delivered, all ten messages are acknowledged.

- `Session.DUPS_OK_ACKNOWLEDGE`. This option instructs the session to lazily acknowledge the delivery of messages. This is likely to result in the delivery of some duplicate messages if the JMS provider fails, so it should be used only by consumers that can tolerate duplicate messages. (If it redelivers a message, the JMS provider must set the value of the `JMSRedelivered` message header to `true`.) This option can reduce session overhead by minimizing the work the session does to prevent duplicates.

If messages have been received but not acknowledged when a `QueueSession` terminates, the JMS provider retains them and redelivers them when a consumer next accesses the queue. The provider also retains unacknowledged messages for a terminated `TopicSession` with a durable `TopicSubscriber`. (See Section 5.2.1 on page 61.) Unacknowledged messages for a nondurable `TopicSubscriber` are dropped when the session is closed.

If you use a queue or a durable subscription, you can use the `Session.recover` method to stop a nontransacted session and restart it with its first unacknowledged message. In effect, the session's series of delivered messages is reset to the point after its last acknowledged message. The messages it now delivers may be different from those that were originally delivered, if messages have expired or higher-priority messages have arrived. For a nondurable TopicSubscriber, the provider may drop unacknowledged messages when its session is recovered.

The sample program in Section A.3 on page 464 demonstrates two ways to ensure that a message will not be acknowledged until processing of the message is complete.

5.1.2 Specifying Message Persistence

The JMS API supports two delivery modes for messages to specify whether messages are lost if the JMS provider fails. These delivery modes are fields of the DeliveryMode interface.

- The PERSISTENT delivery mode, which is the default, instructs the JMS provider to take extra care to ensure that a message is not lost in transit in case of a JMS provider failure. A message sent with this delivery mode is logged to stable storage when it is sent.

- The NON_PERSISTENT delivery mode does not require the JMS provider to store the message or otherwise guarantee that it is not lost if the provider fails.

You can specify the delivery mode in either of two ways.

- You can use the setDeliveryMode method of the MessageProducer interface—the parent of the QueueSender and the TopicPublisher interfaces—to set the delivery mode for all messages sent by that producer.

- You can use the long form of the send or the publish method to set the delivery mode for a specific message. The second argument sets the delivery mode. For example, the following publish call sets the delivery mode for message to NON_PERSISTENT:

```
topicPublisher.publish(message, DeliveryMode.NON_PERSISTENT, 3,
    10000);
```

The third and fourth arguments set the priority level and expiration time, which are described in the next two subsections.

If you do not specify a delivery mode, the default is PERSISTENT. Using the NON_PERSISTENT delivery mode may improve performance and reduce storage overhead, but you should use it only if your application can afford to miss messages.

5.1.3   Setting Message Priority Levels

You can use message priority levels to instruct the JMS provider to deliver urgent messages first. You can set the priority level in either of two ways.

- You can use the `setPriority` method of the `MessageProducer` interface to set the priority level for all messages sent by that producer.

- You can use the long form of the `send` or the `publish` method to set the priority level for a specific message. The third argument sets the priority level. For example, the following `publish` call sets the priority level for `message` to 3:

```
topicPublisher.publish(message, DeliveryMode.NON_PERSISTENT, 3,
    10000);
```

The ten levels of priority range from 0 (lowest) to 9 (highest). If you do not specify a priority level, the default level is 4. A JMS provider tries to deliver higher-priority messages before lower-priority ones but does not have to deliver messages in exact order of priority.

5.1.4   Allowing Messages to Expire

By default, a message never expires. If a message will become obsolete after a certain period, however, you may want to set an expiration time. You can do this in either of two ways.

- You can use the `setTimeToLive` method of the `MessageProducer` interface to set a default expiration time for all messages sent by that producer.

- You can use the long form of the `send` or the `publish` method to set an expiration time for a specific message. The fourth argument sets the expiration time in milliseconds. For example, the following `publish` call sets a time to live of 10 seconds:

```
topicPublisher.publish(message, DeliveryMode.NON_PERSISTENT, 3,
    10000);
```

If the specified *timeToLive* value is 0, the message never expires.

When the message is published, the specified *timeToLive* is added to the current time to give the expiration time. Any message not delivered before the specified expiration time is destroyed. The destruction of obsolete messages conserves storage and computing resources.

5.1.5   Creating Temporary Destinations

Normally, you create JMS destinations—queues and topics—administratively rather than programmatically. Your JMS or J2EE provider includes a tool that you use to create and to remove destinations, and it is common for destinations to be long lasting.

The JMS API also enables you to create destinations—TemporaryQueue and TemporaryTopic objects—that last only for the duration of the connection in which they are created. You create these destinations dynamically, using the QueueSession.createTemporaryQueue and the TopicSession.createTemporary-Topic methods.

The only message consumers that can consume from a temporary destination are those created by the same connection that created the destination. Any message producer can send to the temporary destination. If you close the connection that a temporary destination belongs to, the destination is closed and its contents lost.

You can use temporary destinations to implement a simple request/reply mechanism. If you create a temporary destination and specify it as the value of the JMSReplyTo message header field when you send a message, the consumer of the message can use the value of the JMSReplyTo field as the destination to which it sends a reply and can also reference the original request by setting the JMSCorrelationID header field of the reply message to the value of the JMSMessageID header field of the request. For examples, see Chapters 9 and 10.

5.2   Using Advanced Reliability Mechanisms

The more advanced mechanisms for achieving reliable message delivery are the following:

- **Creating durable subscriptions.** You can create durable topic subscriptions, which receive messages published while the subscriber is not active. Durable subscriptions offer the reliability of queues to the publish/subscribe message domain.

- **Using local transactions.** You can use local transactions, which allow you to group a series of sends and receives into an atomic unit of work. Transactions are rolled back if they fail at any time.

5.2.1   Creating Durable Subscriptions

To make sure that a pub/sub application receives all published messages, use PERSISTENT delivery mode for the publishers. In addition, use durable subscriptions for the subscribers.

The `TopicSession.createSubscriber` method creates a nondurable subscriber. A nondurable subscriber can receive only messages that are published while it is active.

At the cost of higher overhead, you can use the `TopicSession.create-DurableSubscriber` method to create a durable subscriber. A durable subscription can have only one active subscriber at a time.

A durable subscriber registers a durable subscription with a unique identity that is retained by the JMS provider. Subsequent subscriber objects with the same identity resume the subscription in the state in which it was left by the previous subscriber. If a durable subscription has no active subscriber, the JMS provider retains the subscription's messages until they are received by the subscription or until they expire.

You establish the unique identity of a durable subscriber by setting the following:

- A client ID for the connection

- A topic and a subscription name for the subscriber

You set the client ID administratively for a client-specific connection factory using the `j2eeadmin` command. For example:

```
j2eeadmin -addJmsFactory MY_CON_FAC topic -props clientID=MyID
```

After using this connection factory to create the connection and the session, you call the createDurableSubscriber method with two arguments—the topic and a string that specifies the name of the subscription:

```
String subName = "MySub";
TopicSubscriber topicSubscriber =
   topicSession.createDurableSubscriber(myTopic, subName);
```

The subscriber becomes active after you start the TopicConnection. Later on, you might close the TopicSubscriber:

```
topicSubscriber.close();
```

The JMS provider stores the messages published to the topic, as it would store messages sent to a queue. If the program or another application calls create-DurableSubscriber with the same connection factory and its client ID, the same topic, and the same subscription name, the subscription is reactivated, and the JMS provider delivers the messages that were published while the subscriber was inactive.

To delete a durable subscription, first close the subscriber, and then use the unsubscribe method, with the subscription name as the argument:

```
topicSubscriber.close();
topicSession.unsubscribe("MySub");
```

The unsubscribe method deletes the state that the provider maintains for the subscriber.

Figures 5.1 and 5.2 show the difference between a nondurable and a durable subscriber. With an ordinary, nondurable, subscriber, the subscriber and the subscription are coterminous and, in effect, identical. When a subscriber is closed, the subscription ends as well. Here, create stands for a call to TopicSession.create-Subscriber, and close stands for a call to TopicSubscriber.close. Any messages published to the topic between the time of the first close and the time of the second create are not consumed by the subscriber. In Figure 5.1, the subscriber consumes messages M1, M2, M5, and M6, but messages M3 and M4 are lost.

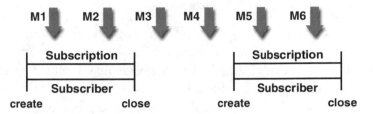

Figure 5.1 Nondurable Subscribers and Subscriptions

With a durable subscriber, the subscriber can be closed and recreated, but the subscription continues to exist and to hold messages until the application calls the unsubscribe method. In Figure 5.2, `create` stands for a call to `TopicSession.createDurableSubscriber`, `close` stands for a call to `TopicSubscriber.close`, and `unsubscribe` stands for a call to `TopicSession.unsubscribe`. Messages published while the subscriber is closed are received when the subscriber is created again. So even though messages M2, M4, and M5 arrive while the subscriber is closed, they are not lost.

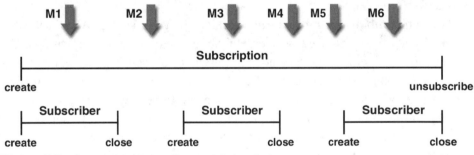

Figure 5.2 A Durable Subscriber and Subscription

See Chapter 8 for an example of a J2EE application that uses durable subscriptions. See Section A.1 on page 429 for an example of a client application that uses durable subscriptions.

5.2.2   Using JMS API Local Transactions

You can group a series of operations together into an atomic unit of work called a transaction. If any one of the operations fails, the transaction can be rolled back, and the operations can be attempted again from the beginning. If all the operations succeed, the transaction can be committed.

In a JMS client, you can use local transactions to group message sends and receives. The JMS API `Session` interface provides `commit` and `rollback` methods that you can use in a JMS client. A transaction commit means that all produced messages are sent and all consumed messages are acknowledged. A transaction rollback means that all produced messages are destroyed and all consumed messages are recovered and redelivered unless they have expired (see Section 5.1.4 on page 59).

A transacted session is always involved in a transaction. As soon as the `commit` or the `rollback` method is called, one transaction ends and another transaction begins. Closing a transacted session rolls back its transaction in progress, including any pending sends and receives.

In an Enterprise JavaBeans component, you cannot use the `Session.commit` and `Session.rollback` methods. Instead, you use distributed transactions, which are described in Chapter 6.

You can combine several sends and receives in a single JMS API local transaction. If you do so, you need to be careful about the order of the operations. You will have no problems if the transaction consists of all sends or all receives or if the receives come before the sends. But if you try to use a request-reply mechanism, whereby you send a message and then try to receive a reply to the sent message in the same transaction, the program will hang, because the send cannot take place until the transaction is committed. Because a message sent during a transaction is not actually sent until the transaction is committed, the transaction cannot contain any receives that depend on that message's having been sent.

It is also important to note that the production and the consumption of a message cannot both be part of the same transaction. The reason is that the transactions take place between the clients and the JMS provider, which intervenes between the production and the consumption of the message. Figure 5.3 illustrates this interaction.

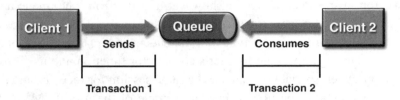

Figure 5.3   Using JMS API Local Transactions

The sending of one or more messages to a queue by Client 1 can form a single transaction, because it forms a single set of interactions with the JMS provider. Similarly, the receiving of one or more messages from the queue by Client 2 also forms a single transaction. But because the two clients have no direct interaction, no transactions take place between them. Another way of putting this is that the act of producing and/or consuming messages in a session can be transactional, but the act of producing and consuming a specific message across different sessions cannot be transactional.

This is the fundamental difference between messaging and synchronized processing. Instead of tightly coupling the sending and receiving of data, message producers and consumers use an alternative approach to reliability, one that is built on a JMS provider's ability to supply a once-and-only-once message delivery guarantee.

When you create a session, you specify whether it is transacted. The first argument to the `createQueueSession` and the `createTopicSession` methods is a `boolean` value. A value of `true` means that the session is transacted; a value of `false` means that it is not transacted. The second argument to these methods is the acknowledgment mode, which is relevant only to nontransacted sessions (see Section 5.1.1 on page 56). If the session is transacted, the second argument is ignored, so it is a good idea to specify `0` to make the meaning of your code clear. For example:

```
topicSession = topicConnection.createTopicSession(true, 0);
```

Because the `commit` and the `rollback` methods for local transactions are associated with the session, you cannot combine queue and topic operations in a single transaction. For example, you cannot receive a message from a queue and then publish a related message to a topic in the same transaction, because the `Queue-Receiver` and the `TopicPublisher` are associated with a `QueueSession` and a

TopicSession, respectively. You can, however, receive from one queue and send to another queue in the same transaction, assuming that you use the same Queue-Session to create the QueueReceiver and the QueueSender. You can pass a client program's session to a message listener's constructor function and use it to create a message producer, so that you can use the same session for receives and sends in asynchronous message consumers. For an example of the use of JMS API local transactions, see Section A.2 on page 439.

CHAPTER 6

Using the JMS API in a J2EE Application

THIS chapter describes the ways in which using the JMS API in a J2EE application differs from using it in a standalone client application:

- Using enterprise beans to produce and to synchronously receive messages

- Using message-driven beans to receive messages asynchronously

- Managing distributed transactions

- Using application clients and Web components

This chapter assumes that you have some knowledge of the J2EE platform and J2EE components. If you have not already done so, you may wish to read the J2EE Tutorial (`http://java.sun.com/j2ee/tutorial/`) or the Java 2 Platform, Enterprise Edition Specification, v1.3 (available from `http://java.sun.com/j2ee/download.html`).

6.1 Using Enterprise Beans to Produce and to Synchronously Receive Messages

A J2EE application that produces messages or synchronously receives them may use any kind of enterprise bean to perform these operations. The example in Chapter 8 uses a stateless session bean to publish messages to a topic.

Because a blocking synchronous receive ties up server resources, it is not a good programming practice to use such a `receive` call in an enterprise bean.

Instead, use a timed synchronous receive, or use a message-driven bean to receive messages asynchronously. For details about blocking and timed synchronous receives, see Section 4.2.1 on page 29.

Using the JMS API in a J2EE application is in many ways similar to using it in a standalone client. The main differences are in administered objects, resource management, and transactions.

6.1.1   Administered Objects

The Platform Specification recommends that you use `java:comp/env/jms` as the environment subcontext for Java Naming and Directory Interface (JNDI) API lookups of connection factories and destinations. With the J2EE SDK 1.3, you use the Application Deployment Tool, commonly known as the deploytool, to specify JNDI API names that correspond to those in your source code.

Instead of looking up a JMS API connection factory or destination each time it is used in a method, it is recommended that you look up these instances once in the enterprise bean's `ejbCreate` method and cache them for the lifetime of the enterprise bean.

6.1.2   Resource Management

A JMS API resource is a JMS API connection or a JMS API session. In general, it is important to release JMS resources when they are no longer being used. Here are some useful practices to follow.

- If you wish to maintain a JMS API resource only for the life span of a business method, it is a good idea to close the resource in a `finally` block within the method.

- If you would like to maintain a JMS API resource for the life span of an enterprise bean instance, it is a good idea to use the component's `ejbCreate` method to create the resource and to use the component's `ejbRemove` method to close the resource. If you use a stateful session bean or an entity bean and you wish to maintain the JMS API resource in a cached state, you must close the resource in the `ejbPassivate` method and set its value to `null`, and you must create it again in the `ejbActivate` method.

6.1.3 Transactions

Instead of using local transactions, you use the deploytool to specify container-managed transactions for bean methods that perform sends and receives, allowing the EJB container to handle transaction demarcation. (You can use bean-managed transactions and the `javax.transaction.UserTransaction` interface's transaction demarcation methods, but you should do so only if your application has special requirements and you are an expert in using transactions. Usually, container-managed transactions produce the most efficient and correct behavior.)

6.2 Using Message-Driven Beans

As we noted in Section 1.4 on page 6, the J2EE platform supports a new kind of enterprise bean, the message-driven bean, which allows J2EE applications to process JMS messages asynchronously. Session beans and entity beans allow you to send messages and to receive them synchronously but not asynchronously.

A message-driven bean is a message listener that can reliably consume messages from a queue or a durable subscription. The messages may be sent by any J2EE component—from an application client, another enterprise bean, or a Web component—or from an application or a system that does not use J2EE technology.

Like a message listener in a standalone JMS client, a message-driven bean contains an `onMessage` method that is called automatically when a message arrives. Like a message listener, a message-driven bean class may implement helper methods invoked by the `onMessage` method to aid in message processing.

A message-driven bean differs from a standalone client's message listener in five ways, however.

- The EJB container automatically performs several setup tasks that a standalone client has to do:

  - Creating a message consumer (a `QueueReceiver` or a `TopicSubscriber`) to receive the messages. You associate the message-driven bean with a destination and a connection factory at deployment time. If you want to specify a durable subscription or use a message selector, you do this at deployment time also.

  - Registering the message listener. (You must not call `setMessageListener`.)

- Specifying a message acknowledgment mode. (For details, see Section 6.3 on page 71.)

• Your bean class must implement the javax.ejb.MessageDrivenBean and the javax.jms.MessageListener interfaces.

• Your bean class must implement the ejbCreate method in addition to the onMessage method. The method has the following signature:

```
public void ejbCreate() {}
```

If your message-driven bean produces messages or does synchronous receives from another destination, you use its ejbCreate method to look up JMS API connection factories and destinations and to create the JMS API connection.

• Your bean class must implement an ejbRemove method. The method has the following signature:

```
public void ejbRemove() {}
```

If you used the message-driven bean's ejbCreate method to create the JMS API connection, you ordinarily use the ejbRemove method to close the connection.

• Your bean class must implement the setMessageDrivenContext method. A MessageDrivenContext object provides some additional methods that you can use for transaction management. The method has the following signature:

```
public void setMessageDrivenContext(MessageDrivenContext mdc) {}
```

See Section 7.1.2 on page 79 for a simple example of a message-driven bean.

The main difference between a message-driven bean and other enterprise beans is that a message-driven bean has no home or remote interface. Rather, it has only a bean class.

A message-driven bean is similar in some ways to a stateless session bean: its instances are relatively short-lived and retain no state for a specific client. The instance variables of the message-driven bean instance can contain some state across the handling of client messages: for example, a JMS API connection, an open database connection, or an object reference to an enterprise bean object.

Like a stateless session bean, a message-driven bean can have many inter-changeable instances running at the same time. The container can pool these instances to allow streams of messages to be processed concurrently. Concurrency can affect the order in which messages are delivered, so you should write your application to handle messages that arrive out of sequence.

To create a new instance of a message-driven bean, the container instantiates the bean and then

1. Calls the `setMessageDrivenContext` method to pass the context object to the instance

2. Calls the instance's `ejbCreate` method

Figure 6.1 shows the life cycle of a message-driven bean.

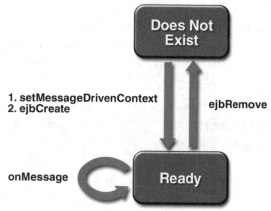

Figure 6.1   Life Cycle of a Message-Driven Bean

6.3   Managing Distributed Transactions

JMS client applications use JMS API local transactions, described in Section 5.2.2 on page 64, which allow the grouping of sends and receives within a specific JMS session. J2EE applications commonly use distributed transactions in order to ensure the integrity of accesses to external resources. For example, distributed transactions allow multiple applications to perform atomic updates on the same database, and they allow a single application to perform atomic updates on multiple databases.

In a J2EE application that uses the JMS API, you can use transactions to combine message sends or receives with database updates and other resource manager operations. You can access resources from multiple application components within a single transaction. For example, a servlet may start a transaction, access multiple databases, invoke an enterprise bean that sends a JMS message, invoke another enterprise bean that modifies an EIS system using the Connector architecture, and finally commit the transaction. Your application cannot, however, both send a JMS message and receive a reply to it within the same transaction; the restriction described in Section 5.2.2 on page 64 still applies.

Distributed transactions can be either of two kinds:

- **Container-managed transactions.** The EJB container controls the integrity of your transactions without your having to call `commit` or `rollback`. Container-managed transactions are recommended for J2EE applications that use the JMS API. You can specify appropriate transaction attributes for your enterprise bean methods.

  Use the `Required` transaction attribute to ensure that a method is always part of a transaction. If a transaction is in progress when the method is called, the method will be part of that transaction; if not, a new transaction will be started before the method is called and will be committed when the method returns.

- **Bean-managed transactions.** You can use these in conjunction with the `javax.transaction.UserTransaction` interface, which provides its own `commit` and `rollback` methods that you can use to delimit transaction boundaries.

You can use either container-managed transactions or bean-managed transactions with message-driven beans.

To ensure that all messages are received and handled within the context of a transaction, use container-managed transactions and specify the `Required` transaction attribute for the `onMessage` method. This means that a new transaction will be started before the method is called and will be committed when the method returns. An `onMessage` call is always a separate transaction, because there is never a transaction in progress when the method is called.

When you use container-managed transactions, you can call the following `MessageDrivenContext` methods:

- `setRollbackOnly`. Use this method for error handling. If an exception occurs, `setRollbackOnly` marks the current transaction so that the only possible outcome of the transaction is a rollback.

- `getRollbackOnly`. Use this method to test whether the current transaction has been marked for rollback.

If you use bean-managed transactions, the delivery of a message to the `onMessage` method takes place outside of the distributed transaction context. The transaction begins when you call the `UserTransaction.begin` method within the `onMessage` method and ends when you call `UserTransaction.commit`. If you call `UserTransaction.rollback`, the message is not redelivered, whereas calling `setRollbackOnly` for container-managed transactions does cause a message to be redelivered.

Neither the JMS API Specification nor the Enterprise JavaBeans Specification (available from `http://java.sun.com/products/ejb/`) specifies how to handle calls to JMS API methods outside transaction boundaries. The Enterprise JavaBeans Specification does state that the EJB container is responsible for acknowledging a message that is successfully processed by the `onMessage` method of a message-driven bean that uses bean-managed transactions. Using bean-managed transactions allows you to process the message by using more than one transaction or to have some parts of the message processing take place outside a transaction context. In most cases, however, container-managed transactions provide greater reliability and are therefore preferable.

When you create a session in an enterprise bean, the container ignores the arguments you specify, because it manages all transactional properties for enterprise beans. It is still a good idea to specify arguments of `true` and `0` to the `createQueueSession` or the `createTopicSession` method to make this situation clear:

```
queueSession = queueConnection.createQueueSession(true, 0);
```

When you use container-managed transactions, you usually specify the `Required` transaction attribute for your enterprise bean's business methods.

You do not specify a message acknowledgment mode when you create a message-driven bean that uses container-managed transactions. The container acknowledges the message automatically when it commits the transaction.

If a message-driven bean uses bean-managed transactions, the message receipt cannot be part of the bean-managed transaction, so the container acknowledges the message outside of the transaction. When you package a message-driven bean using the deploytool, the Message-Driven Bean Settings dialog box allows you to specify the acknowledgment mode, which can be either AUTO_ACKNOWLEDGE (the default) or DUPS_OK_ACKNOWLEDGE.

If the onMessage method throws a RuntimeException, the container does not acknowledge processing the message. In that case, the JMS provider will redeliver the unacknowledged message in the future.

6.4   Using the JMS API with Application Clients and Web Components

An application client can use the JMS API in much the same way a standalone client program does. It can produce messages, and it can consume messages by using either synchronous receives or message listeners. See Chapter 7 for an example of an application client that produces messages; see Chapters 9 and 10 for examples of using application clients to produce and to consume messages.

The J2EE Platform Specification does not define how Web components implement a JMS provider. In the J2EE SDK 1.3, a Web component—one that uses either the Java Servlet API or JavaServerPages™ (JSP™) technology—may send messages and consume them synchronously but may not consume them asynchronously.

Because a blocking synchronous receive ties up server resources, it is not a good programming practice to use such a receive call in a Web component. Instead, use a timed synchronous receive. For details about blocking and timed synchronous receives, see Section 4.2.1 on page 29.

CHAPTER 7

A Simple J2EE Application that Uses the JMS API

THIS chapter explains how to write, compile, package, deploy, and run a simple J2EE application that uses the JMS API. The application in this chapter uses the following components:

- An application client that sends several messages to a queue

- A message-driven bean that asynchronously receives and processes the messages

The chapter covers the following topics:

- Writing and compiling the application components

- Creating and packaging the application

- Deploying and running the application

If you downloaded the tutorial examples as described in the preface, you will find the source code files for this chapter in `jms_tutorial/examples/client_mdb` (on UNIX systems) or `jms_tutorial\examples\client_mdb` (on Microsoft Windows systems). The directory `ear_files` in the `examples` directory contains a built application called `SampleMDBApp.ear`. If you run into difficulty at any time, you can open this file in the deploytool and compare that file to your own version.

7.1   Writing and Compiling the Application Components

The first and simplest application contains the following components:

- An application client that sends several messages to a queue

- A message-driven bean that asynchronously receives and processes the messages

Figure 7.1 illustrates the structure of this application.

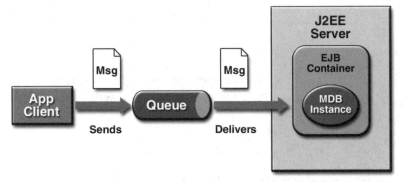

Figure 7.1   A Simple J2EE Application: Client to Message-Driven Bean

The application client sends messages to the queue, which is created administratively, using the `j2eeadmin` command. The JMS provider—in this case, the J2EE server—delivers the messages to the message-driven bean instances, which then process the messages.

Writing and compiling the components of this application involve

- Coding the application client

- Coding the message-driven bean

- Compiling the source files

7.1.1   Coding the Application Client: `SimpleClient.java`

The application client class, `SimpleClient.java`, is almost identical to `Simple-QueueSender.java` in Section 4.2.1.1 on page 31. The only significant differences are as follows.

- You do not specify the queue name on the command line. Instead, the client obtains the queue name through a Java Naming and Directory Interface (JNDI) API lookup.

- You do not specify the number of messages on the command line; the number of messages is set at 3 for simplicity, and no end-of-messages message is sent.

- The JNDI API lookup uses the `java:/comp/env/jms` naming context.

```java
import javax.jms.*;
import javax.naming.*;

/**
 * The SimpleClient class sends several messages to a queue.
 */
public class SimpleClient {

    /**
     * Main method.
     */
    public static void main(String[] args) {
        Context                 jndiContext = null;
        QueueConnectionFactory  queueConnectionFactory = null;
        QueueConnection         queueConnection = null;
        QueueSession            queueSession = null;
        Queue                   queue = null;
        QueueSender             queueSender = null;
        TextMessage             message = null;
        final int               NUM_MSGS = 3;

        /*
         * Create a JNDI API InitialContext object.
         */
```

```java
        try {
            jndiContext = new InitialContext();
        } catch (NamingException e) {
            System.out.println("Could not create JNDI API " +
                "context: " + e.toString());
            System.exit(1);
        }

        /*
         * Look up connection factory and queue.  If either does
         * not exist, exit.
         */
        try {
            queueConnectionFactory = (QueueConnectionFactory)
    jndiContext.lookup("java:comp/env/jms/MyQueueConnectionFactory");
            queue = (Queue)
                jndiContext.lookup("java:comp/env/jms/QueueName");
        } catch (NamingException e) {
            System.out.println("JNDI API lookup failed: " +
                e.toString());
            System.exit(1);
        }

        /*
         * Create connection.
         * Create session from connection; false means session is
         * not transacted.
         * Create sender and text message.
         * Send messages, varying text slightly.
         * Finally, close connection.
         */
        try {
            queueConnection =
                queueConnectionFactory.createQueueConnection();
            queueSession =
                queueConnection.createQueueSession(false,
                    Session.AUTO_ACKNOWLEDGE);
            queueSender = queueSession.createSender(queue);
            message = queueSession.createTextMessage();
```

```
            for (int i = 0; i < NUM_MSGS; i++) {
                message.setText("This is message " + (i + 1));
                System.out.println("Sending message: " +
                    message.getText());
                queueSender.send(message);
            }
        } catch (JMSException e) {
            System.out.println("Exception occurred: " +
                e.toString());
        } finally {
            if (queueConnection != null) {
                try {
                    queueConnection.close();
                } catch (JMSException e) {}
            }
            System.exit(0);
        }
    }
}
```

Code Example 7.1 `SimpleClient.java`

7.1.2   Coding the Message-Driven Bean: `MessageBean.java`

The message-driven bean class, `MessageBean.java`, implements the methods `set-MessageDrivenContext`, `ejbCreate`, `onMessage`, and `ejbRemove`. The `onMessage` method, almost identical to that of `TextListener.java` in Section 4.3.1.3 on page 47, casts the incoming message to a `TextMessage` and displays the text. The only significant difference is that it calls the `MessageDrivenContext.setRollback-Only` method in case of an exception. This method rolls back the transaction so that the message will be redelivered.

```
import javax.ejb.*;
import javax.naming.*;
import javax.jms.*;
```

```java
/**
 * The MessageBean class is a message-driven bean.  It implements
 * the javax.ejb.MessageDrivenBean and javax.jms.MessageListener
 * interfaces. It is defined as public (but not final or
 * abstract).  It defines a constructor and the methods
 * setMessageDrivenContext, ejbCreate, onMessage, and
 * ejbRemove.
 */
public class MessageBean implements MessageDrivenBean,
        MessageListener {

    private transient MessageDrivenContext mdc = null;
    private Context context;

    /**
     * Constructor, which is public and takes no arguments.
     */
    public MessageBean() {
        System.out.println("In MessageBean.MessageBean()");
    }

    /**
     * setMessageDrivenContext method, declared as public (but
     * not final or static), with a return type of void, and
     * with one argument of type javax.ejb.MessageDrivenContext.
     *
     * @param mdc     the context to set
     */
    public void setMessageDrivenContext(MessageDrivenContext mdc)
    {
        System.out.println("In " +
            "MessageBean.setMessageDrivenContext()");
        this.mdc = mdc;
    }

    /**
     * ejbCreate method, declared as public (but not final or
     * static), with a return type of void, and with no
     * arguments.
```

```java
 */
public void ejbCreate() {
    System.out.println("In MessageBean.ejbCreate()");
}


/**
 * onMessage method, declared as public (but not final or
 * static), with a return type of void, and with one argument
 * of type javax.jms.Message.
 *
 * Casts the incoming Message to a TextMessage and displays
 * the text.
 *
 * @param inMessage    the incoming message
 */
public void onMessage(Message inMessage) {
    TextMessage msg = null;

    try {
        if (inMessage instanceof TextMessage) {
            msg = (TextMessage) inMessage;
            System.out.println("MESSAGE BEAN: Message " +
                "received: " + msg.getText());
        } else {
            System.out.println("Message of wrong type: " +
                inMessage.getClass().getName());
        }
    } catch (JMSException e) {
        System.err.println("MessageBean.onMessage: " +
            "JMSException: " + e.toString());
        mdc.setRollbackOnly();
    } catch (Throwable te) {
        System.err.println("MessageBean.onMessage: " +
            "Exception: " + te.toString());
    }
}
```

```
/**
 * ejbRemove method, declared as public (but not final or
 * static), with a return type of void, and with no
 * arguments.
 */
public void ejbRemove() {
    System.out.println("In MessageBean.remove()");
}
}
```

Code Example 7.2 `MessageBean.java`

7.1.3   Compiling the Source Files

To compile the files in the application, go to the `client_mdb` directory and do the following.

1. Make sure that you have set the environment variables shown in Table 4.1 on page 28: `JAVA_HOME`, `J2EE_HOME`, `CLASSPATH`, and `PATH`.

2. At a command line prompt, compile the source files:

   ```
   javac *.java
   ```

7.2   Creating and Packaging the Application

Creating and packaging this application involve several steps:

1. Starting the J2EE server and the Application Deployment Tool

2. Creating a queue

3. Creating the J2EE application

4. Packaging the application client

5. Packaging the message-driven bean

6. Checking the JNDI API names ("JNDI names")

7.2.1   Starting the J2EE Server and the Deploytool

Before you can create and package the application, you must start the J2EE server and the deploytool. Follow these steps.

1. At the command line prompt, start the J2EE server:

   ```
   j2ee -verbose
   ```

   Wait until the server displays the message "J2EE server startup complete."

   (To stop the server, type `j2ee -stop`.)

2. At another command line prompt, start the deploytool:

   ```
   deploytool
   ```

   (To access the tool's context-sensitive help, press F1.)

7.2.2   Creating a Queue

In Section 4.2.4 on page 37, you used the `j2eeadmin` command to create a queue. This time, you will create it by using the deploytool, as follows.

1. In the deploytool, select the Tools menu.

2. From the Tools menu, choose Server Configuration.

3. Under the JMS folder, select Destinations.

4. In the JMS Queue Destinations area, click Add.

5. In the text field, enter `jms/MyQueue`. (We will observe the J2EE convention of placing the queue in the `jms` namespace.)

6. Click OK.

7. Verify that the queue was created:

   ```
   j2eeadmin -listJmsDestination
   ```

7.2.3   Creating the J2EE Application

Create a new J2EE application called MDBApp and store it in the file named MDBApp.ear. Follow these steps.

1. In the deploytool, select the File menu.

2. From the File menu, choose New → Application.

3. Click Browse next to the Application File Name field and use the file chooser to locate the directory client_mdb.

4. In the File Name field, enter MDBApp.

5. Click New Application.

6. Click OK.

A diamond icon labeled MDBApp appears in the tree view on the left side of the deploytool window. The full path name of MDBApp.ear appears in the General tabbed pane on the right side.

7.2.4   Packaging the Application Client

In this section, you will run the New Application Client Wizard of the deploytool to package the application client. The New Application Client Wizard does the following:

- Identifies the application toward which the client is targeted

- Identifies the main class for the application client

- Identifies the queue and the connection factory referenced by the application client

To start the New Application Client Wizard, follow these steps.

1. In the tree view, select MDBApp.

2. From the File menu, choose New → Application Client. The wizard displays a series of dialog boxes.

7.2.4.1   Introduction Dialog Box

1. Read this explanatory text for an overview of the wizard's features.

2. Click Next.

7.2.4.2   JAR File Contents Dialog Box

1. In the combo box labeled Create Archive Within Application, select MDBApp.

2. Click the Edit button next to the Contents text area.

3. In the dialog box Edit Contents of <Application Client>, choose the client_mdb directory. If the directory is not already in the Starting Directory field, type it in the field, or locate it by browsing through the Available Files tree.

4. Select SimpleClient.class from the Available Files tree area and click Add.

5. Click OK.

6. Click Next.

7.2.4.3   General Dialog Box

1. Verify that the Main Class and the Display Name are both SimpleClient.

2. In the Callback Handler Class combo box, verify that container-managed authentication is selected.

3. Click Next.

7.2.4.4   Environment Entries Dialog Box

Click Next.

7.2.4.5   Enterprise Bean References Dialog Box

Click Next.

7.2.4.6 Resource References Dialog Box

In this dialog box, you associate the JNDI API context name for the connection factory in the `SimpleClient.java` source file with the name of the `QueueConnectionFactory`. You also specify container authentication for the connection factory resource, defining the user name and the password that the user must enter in order to be able to create a connection. Follow these steps.

1. Click Add.

2. In the Coded Name field, enter `jms/MyQueueConnectionFactory`—the logical name referenced by `SimpleClient`.

3. In the Type field, select `javax.jms.QueueConnectionFactory`.

4. In the Authentication field, select Container.

5. In the Sharable field, make sure that the checkbox is checked. This allows the container to optimize connections.

6. In the JNDI Name field, enter `jms/QueueConnectionFactory`.

7. In the User Name field, enter `j2ee`.

8. In the Password field, enter `j2ee`.

9. Click Next.

7.2.4.7 JMS Destination References Dialog Box

In this dialog box, you associate the JNDI API context name for the queue in the `SimpleClient.java` source file with the name of the queue you created using `j2eeadmin`. Follow these steps.

1. Click Add.

2. In the Coded Name field, enter `jms/QueueName`—the logical name referenced by `SimpleClient`.

3. In the Type field, select `javax.jms.Queue`.

4. In the JNDI Name field, enter `jms/MyQueue`.

5. Click Next.

7.2.4.8 Review Settings Dialog Box

1. Check the settings for the deployment descriptor.

2. Click Finish.

7.2.5 Packaging the Message-Driven Bean

In this section, you will run the New Enterprise Bean Wizard of the deploytool to perform these tasks:

- Create the bean's deployment descriptor

- Package the deployment descriptor and the bean class in an enterprise bean JAR file

- Insert the enterprise bean JAR file into the application's MDBApp.ear file

    To start the New Enterprise Bean Wizard, follow these steps.

1. In the tree view, select MDBApp.

2. From the File menu, choose New → Enterprise Bean. The wizard displays a series of dialog boxes.

7.2.5.1 Introduction Dialog Box

Click Next.

7.2.5.2 EJB JAR Dialog Box

1. In the combo box labeled JAR File Location, verify that Create New JAR File in Application and MDBApp are selected.

2. In the JAR Display Name field, verify that the name is Ejb1, the default display name. Representing the enterprise bean JAR file that contains the bean, this name will be displayed in the tree view.

3. Click the Edit button next to the Contents text area.

4. In the dialog box Edit Contents of Ejb1, choose the client_mdb directory. If the directory is not already in the Starting Directory field, type it in the field, or locate it by browsing through the Available Files tree.

5. Select the `MessageBean.class` file from the Available Files tree area and click Add.

6. Click OK.

7. Click Next.

7.2.5.3   General Dialog Box

1. In the Bean Type combo box, select the Message-Driven radio button.

2. Under Enterprise Bean Class, select `MessageBean`. The combo boxes for the local and remote interfaces are grayed out.

3. In the Enterprise Bean Name field, enter `MessageBean`. This name will represent the message-driven bean in the tree view. The display name does not have to be different from the bean class name.

4. Click Next.

7.2.5.4   Transaction Management Dialog Box

In this dialog box, you specify how transactions for the `onMessage` method should be handled. Although an ordinary enterprise bean has six possible transaction attributes, a message-driven bean has only two. (The others are meaningful only if there might be a preexisting transaction context, which doesn't exist for a message-driven bean.) Follow these steps.

1. Select the Container-Managed radio button.

2. In the Transaction Attribute field opposite the `onMessage` method, verify that Required is selected.

3. Click Next.

7.2.5.5   Message-Driven Bean Settings Dialog Box

In this dialog box, you specify the deployment properties for the bean. Because you are using container-managed transactions, the Acknowledgment field is grayed out. Follow these steps.

1. In the Destination Type combo box, select Queue.

2. In the Destination field, select `jms/MyQueue`.

3. In the Connection Factory field, select `jms/QueueConnectionFactory`.

4. Click Next.

7.2.5.6 Environment Entries Dialog Box

Click Next.

7.2.5.7 Enterprise Bean References Dialog Box

Click Next.

7.2.5.8 Resource References Dialog Box

Click Next. (You do not need to specify the connection factory for the message-driven bean, because it is not referred to in the message-driven bean code. You specified the connection factory in the Message-Driven Bean Settings dialog box.)

7.2.5.9 Resource Environment References Dialog Box

Click Next. (You do not need to specify the queue name here, because it is not referred to in the message-driven bean code. You specified it in the Message-Driven Bean Settings dialog box.)

7.2.5.10 Security Dialog Box

Use the default Security Identity setting for a message-driven bean, Run As Specified Role. Click Next.

7.2.5.11 Review Settings Dialog Box

1. Check the settings for the deployment descriptor.

2. Click Finish.

7.2.6   Checking the JNDI Names

Verify that the JNDI names for the application components are correct.

- You give the JNDI name of the destination—in this case, the queue—to the message-driven bean component.

- You check to make sure that the context names for the connection factory and the destination are correctly matched to their JNDI names.

1. In the tree view, select the MDBApp application.

2. Select the JNDI Names tabbed pane.

3. Verify that the JNDI names appear as shown in Tables 7.1 and 7.2.

Table 7.1: Application Pane

Component Type	Component	JNDI Name
EJB	MessageBean	jms/MyQueue

Table 7.2: References Pane

Ref. Type	Referenced By	Reference Name	JNDI Name
Resource	SimpleClient	jms/MyQueue-ConnectionFactory	jms/Queue-ConnectionFactory
Env Resource	SimpleClient	jms/QueueName	jms/MyQueue

7.3   Deploying and Running the Application

Deploying and running this application involve several steps:

1. Looking at the deployment descriptor

2. Adding the server, if necessary

3. Deploying the application

4. Running the client

5. Undeploying the application

6. Removing the application and stopping the server

7.3.1   Looking at the Deployment Descriptor

As you package an application, the deploytool creates a deployment descriptor in accordance with the packaging choices you make. To see some of the JMS API-related elements of the enterprise bean deployment descriptor, follow these steps.

1. Select Ejb1 in the tree view.

2. Choose Descriptor Viewer from the Tools menu.

3. Select SimpleClient in the tree view and repeat step 2.

In the Deployment Descriptor Viewer window, click Save As if you want to save the contents as an XML file for future reference. Table 7.3 describes the elements that are related to the JMS API.

Table 7.3: JMS API-Related Deployment Descriptor Elements

Element Name	Description
`<message-driven>`	Declares a message-driven bean.
`<message-selector>`	Specifies the JMS API message selector to be used in determining which messages a message-driven bean is to receive.
`<message-driven-destination>`	Tells the Deployer whether a message-driven bean is intended for a queue or a topic, and if it is intended for a topic, whether the subscription is durable. Contains the element `<destination-type>` and optionally, for topics, `<subscription-durability>`.
`<destination-type>`	Specifies the type of the JMS API destination (either `javax.jms.Queue` or `javax.jms.Topic`). In this case, the value is `javax.jms.Queue`.

(continued)

Table 7.3: JMS API-Related Deployment Descriptor Elements (Cont.)

Element Name	Description
`<subscription-durability>`	Optionally specifies whether a topic subscription is intended to be durable or nondurable.
`<resource-env-ref>`	Declares an enterprise bean's reference to an administered object associated with a resource in the enterprise bean's environment—in this case, a JMS API destination. Contains the elements `<resource-env-ref-name>` and `<resource-env-ref-type>`.
`<resource-env-ref-name>`	Specifies the name of a resource environment reference; its value is the environment entry name used in the enterprise bean code—in this case, jms/QueueName.
`<resource-env-ref-type>`	Specifies the type of a resource environment reference—in this case, javax.jms.Queue.
`<resource-ref>`	Contains a declaration of the enterprise bean's reference to an external resource—in this case, a JMS API connection factory. Contains the elements `<res-ref-name>`, `<res-type>`, and `<res-auth>`.
`<res-ref-name>`	Specifies the name of a resource manager connection factory reference—in this case, jms/MyQueueConnectionFactory.
`<res-type>`	Specifies the type of the data source—in this case, javax.jms.QueueConnectionFactory.
`<res-auth>`	Specifies whether the enterprise bean code signs on programmatically to the resource manager (Application) or whether the Container will sign on to the resource manager on behalf of the bean. In the latter case, the Container uses information that is supplied by the Deployer.
`<res-sharing-scope>`	Specifies whether connections obtained through the given resource manager connection factory reference can be shared. In this case, the value is Shareable.

7.3.2   Adding the Server

Before you can deploy the application, you must make available to the deploytool the J2EE server you started in Section 7.2.1 on page 83. Because you started the J2EE server before you started the deploytool, the server, named `localhost`, probably appears in the tree under `Servers`. If it does not, do the following.

1. From the File menu, choose Add Server.

2. In the Add Server dialog box, enter `localhost` in the Server Name field.

3. Click OK. A `localhost` node appears under `Servers` in the tree view.

7.3.3   Deploying the Application

You have now created an application that consists of an application client and a message-driven bean. To deploy the application, perform the following steps.

1. From the File menu, choose Save to save the application.

2. From the Tools menu, choose Deploy.

3. In the Introduction dialog box, verify that the Object to Deploy selection is `MDBApp` and that the Target Server selection is `localhost`.

4. Click Next.

5. In the JNDI Names dialog box, verify that the JNDI names are correct.

6. Click Next.

7. Click Finish.

8. In the Deployment Progress dialog box, click OK when the "Deployment of MDBApp is complete" message appears.

9. In the tree view, expand `Servers` and select `localhost`. Verify that `MDBApp` is deployed.

7.3.4   Running the Client

To run the client, you use the MDBApp.ear file that you created in Section 7.2.3 on page 84. Make sure that you are in the directory client_mdb. Then perform the following steps.

1. At the command line prompt, enter the following:

```
runclient -client MDBApp.ear -name SimpleClient
```

2. When the Login for user: dialog box appears, enter j2ee for the user name and j2ee for the password.

3. Click OK.

The client program runs in the command window, generating output that looks like this:

```
Binding name:'java:comp/env/jms/QueueName'
Binding name:'java:comp/env/jms/MyQueueConnectionFactory'
Java(TM) Message Service 1.0.2 Reference Implementation (build b14)
Sending message: This is message 1
Sending message: This is message 2
Sending message: This is message 3
Unbinding name:'java:comp/env/jms/QueueName'
Unbinding name:'java:comp/env/jms/MyQueueConnectionFactory'
```

Output from the application appears in the window in which you started the J2EE server. By default, the server creates three instances of the MessageBean to receive messages.

```
In MessageBean.MessageBean()
In MessageBean.setMessageDrivenContext()
In MessageBean.ejbCreate()
MESSAGE BEAN: Message received: This is message 1
In MessageBean.MessageBean()
In MessageBean.setMessageDrivenContext()
In MessageBean.ejbCreate()
In MessageBean.MessageBean()
In MessageBean.setMessageDrivenContext()
```

```
In MessageBean.ejbCreate()
MESSAGE BEAN: Message received: This is message 2
MESSAGE BEAN: Message received: This is message 3
```

7.3.5   Undeploying the Application

To undeploy the J2EE application, follow these steps.

1. In the tree view, select localhost.

2. Select MDBApp in the Deployed Objects area.

3. Click Undeploy.

4. Answer Yes in the confirmation dialog.

7.3.6   Removing the Application and Stopping the Server

To remove the application from the deploytool, follow these steps.

1. Select MDBApp in the tree view.

2. Select Close from the File menu.

To delete the queue you created, enter the following at the command line prompt:

```
j2eeadmin -removeJmsDestination jms/MyQueue
```

To stop the J2EE server, use the following command:

```
j2ee -stop
```

To exit the deploytool, choose Exit from the File menu.

CHAPTER 8

A J2EE Application that Uses the JMS API with a Session Bean

THIS chapter explains how to write, compile, package, deploy, and run a J2EE application that uses the JMS API in conjunction with a session bean. The application contains the following components:

- An application client that calls an enterprise bean
- A session bean that publishes several messages to a topic
- A message-driven bean that receives and processes the messages, using a durable topic subscriber and a message selector

The chapter covers the following topics:

- Writing and compiling the application components
- Creating and packaging the application
- Deploying and running the application

If you downloaded the tutorial examples as described in the preface, you will find the source code files for this chapter in `jms_tutorial/examples/client_ses_mdb` (on UNIX systems) or `jms_tutorial\examples\client_ses_mdb` (on Microsoft Windows systems). The directory `ear_files` in the `examples` directory contains a built application called `SamplePubSubApp.ear`. If you run into difficulty at any time, you can open this file in the deploytool and compare that file to your own version.

8.1   Writing and Compiling the Application Components

This application demonstrates how to send messages from an enterprise bean—in this case, a session bean—rather than from an application client, as in the example in Chapter 7. Figure 8.1 illustrates the structure of this application.

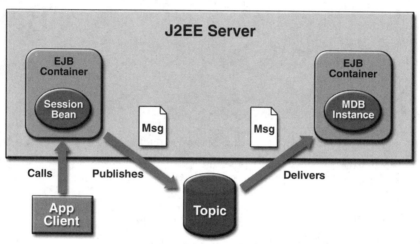

Figure 8.1   A J2EE Application: Client to Session Bean to Message-Driven Bean

The Publisher enterprise bean in this example is the enterprise-application equivalent of a wire-service news feed that categorizes news events into six news categories. The message-driven bean could represent a newsroom, where the Sports desk, for example, would set up a subscription for all news events pertaining to sports news.

The application client in the example obtains a handle to the Publisher enterprise bean's home interface and calls the enterprise bean's business method. The enterprise bean creates 18 text messages. For each message, it sets a `String` property randomly to one of six values representing the news categories and then publishes the message to a topic. The message-driven bean uses a message selector for the property to limit which of the published messages it receives.

Writing and compiling the components of the application involve

- Coding the application client
- Coding the Publisher session bean
- Coding the message-driven bean
- Compiling the source files

8.1.1   Coding the Application Client: `MyAppClient.java`

The application client program, `MyAppClient.java`, performs no JMS API operations and so is simpler than the client program in Chapter 7. The program obtains a handle to the Publisher enterprise bean's home interface, using the Java Naming and Directory Interface (JNDI) API naming context `java:comp/env`. The program then creates an instance of the bean and calls the bean's business method twice.

```java
import javax.ejb.EJBHome;
import javax.naming.*;
import javax.rmi.PortableRemoteObject;
import javax.jms.*;

/**
 * The MyAppClient class is the client program for this J2EE
 * application.  It obtains a reference to the home interface
 * of the Publisher enterprise bean and creates an instance of
 * the bean.  After calling the publisher's publishNews method
 * twice, it removes the bean.
 */
public class MyAppClient {

    public static void main (String[] args) {
        MyAppClient client = new MyAppClient();
        client.doTest();
        System.exit(0);
    }

    public void doTest() {
```

```
try {

    Context ic = new InitialContext();

    System.out.println("Looking up EJB reference");
    java.lang.Object objref =
        ic.lookup("java:comp/env/ejb/MyEjbReference");
    System.err.println("Looked up home");

    PublisherHome pubHome = (PublisherHome)
        PortableRemoteObject.narrow(objref,
            PublisherHome.class);
    System.err.println("Narrowed home");

    /*
     * Create bean instance, invoke business method
     * twice, and remove bean instance.
     */
    Publisher phr = pubHome.create();
    System.err.println("Got the EJB");
    phr.publishNews();
    phr.publishNews();
    phr.remove();
} catch (Exception ex) {
    ex.printStackTrace();
}
    }
}
```

Code Example 8.1 `MyAppClient.java`

8.1.2   Coding the Publisher Session Bean

The Publisher bean is a stateless session bean with one `create` method and one business method. The Publisher bean uses remote interfaces rather than local interfaces because it is accessed from outside the EJB container.

8.1.2.1 The Remote Home Interface: `PublisherHome.java`

The remote home interface source file is `PublisherHome.java`.

```java
import java.rmi.RemoteException;
import javax.ejb.EJBHome;
import javax.ejb.CreateException;

/**
 * Home interface for Publisher enterprise bean.
 */
public interface PublisherHome extends EJBHome {
    Publisher create() throws RemoteException, CreateException;
}
```

Code Example 8.2   `PublisherHome.java`

8.1.2.2 The Remote Interface: `Publisher.java`

The remote interface, `Publisher.java`, declares a single business method, `publishNews`.

```java
import javax.ejb.*;
import java.rmi.RemoteException;

/**
 * Remote interface for Publisher enterprise bean. Declares one
 * business method.
 */
public interface Publisher extends EJBObject {
    void publishNews() throws RemoteException;
```

```
        }
```

Code Example 8.3 `Publisher.java`

8.1.2.3   The Bean Class: `PublisherBean.java`

The bean class, `PublisherBean.java`, implements the `publishNews` method and its helper method `chooseType`. The bean class also implements the required methods `ejbCreate`, `setSessionContext`, `ejbRemove`, `ejbActivate`, and `ejbPassivate`.

The `ejbCreate` method of the bean class allocates resources—in this case, by looking up the `TopicConnectionFactory` and the topic and creating the `Topic-Connection`. The business method `publishNews` creates a `TopicSession` and a `TopicPublisher` and publishes the messages.

The `ejbRemove` method must deallocate the resources that were allocated by the `ejbCreate` method. In this case, the `ejbRemove` method closes the `Topic-Connection`.

```java
import java.rmi.RemoteException;
import java.util.*;
import javax.ejb.*;
import javax.naming.*;
import javax.jms.*;

/**
 * Bean class for Publisher enterprise bean. Defines publishNews
 * business method as well as required methods for a stateless
 * session bean.
 */
public class PublisherBean implements SessionBean {
    SessionContext      sc = null;
    TopicConnection     topicConnection = null;
    Topic               topic = null;
    final static String messageTypes[] = {"Nation/World",
        "Metro/Region", "Business", "Sports", "Living/Arts",
        "Opinion"};
```

```java
public PublisherBean() {
    System.out.println("In PublisherBean() (constructor)");
}

/**
 * Sets the associated session context. The container calls
 * this method after the instance creation.
 */
public void setSessionContext(SessionContext sc) {
    this.sc = sc;
}

/**
 * Instantiates the enterprise bean.  Creates the
 * TopicConnection and looks up the topic.
 */
public void ejbCreate() {
    Context context = null;
    TopicConnectionFactory topicConnectionFactory = null;

    System.out.println("In PublisherBean.ejbCreate()");
    try {
        context = new InitialContext();
        topic = (Topic)
            context.lookup("java:comp/env/jms/TopicName");

        // Create a TopicConnection
        topicConnectionFactory = (TopicConnectionFactory)
context.lookup("java:comp/env/jms/MyTopicConnectionFactory");
        topicConnection =
            topicConnectionFactory.createTopicConnection();
    } catch (Throwable t) {
        // JMSException or NamingException could be thrown
        System.err.println("PublisherBean.ejbCreate:" +
            "Exception: " + t.toString());
    }
}

/**
```

```java
 * Chooses a message type by using the random number
 * generator found in java.util.  Called by publishNews().
 *
 * @return    the String representing the message type
 */
private String chooseType() {
    int     whichMsg;
    Random rgen = new Random();

    whichMsg = rgen.nextInt(messageTypes.length);
    return messageTypes[whichMsg];
}


/**
 * Creates TopicSession, publisher, and message.  Publishes
 * messages after setting their NewsType property and using
 * the property value as the message text. Messages are
 * received by MessageBean, a message-driven bean that uses a
 * message selector to retrieve messages whose NewsType
 * property has certain values.
 */
public void publishNews() throws EJBException {
    TopicSession    topicSession = null;
    TopicPublisher topicPublisher = null;
    TextMessage     message = null;
    int             numMsgs = messageTypes.length * 3;
    String          messageType = null;

    try {
        topicSession =
            topicConnection.createTopicSession(true, 0);
        topicPublisher = topicSession.createPublisher(topic);
        message = topicSession.createTextMessage();
        for (int i = 0; i < numMsgs; i++) {
            messageType = chooseType();
            message.setStringProperty("NewsType",
                messageType);
            message.setText("Item " + i + ": " +
                messageType);
```

```java
                    System.out.println("PUBLISHER: Setting " +
                        "message text to: " + message.getText());
                    topicPublisher.publish(message);
                }
            } catch (Throwable t) {
                // JMSException could be thrown
                System.err.println("PublisherBean.publishNews: " +
                    "Exception: " + t.toString());
                sc.setRollbackOnly();
            } finally {
                if (topicSession != null) {
                    try {
                        topicSession.close();
                    } catch (JMSException e) {}
                }
            }
        }


        /**
         * Closes the TopicConnection.
         */
        public void ejbRemove() throws RemoteException {
            System.out.println("In PublisherBean.ejbRemove()");
            if (topicConnection != null) {
                try {
                    topicConnection.close();
                } catch (Exception e) {
                    e.printStackTrace();
                }
            }
        }


        public void ejbActivate() {}
        public void ejbPassivate() {}
    }
```

Code Example 8.4 `PublisherBean.java`

8.1.3   Coding the Message-Driven Bean: `MessageBean.java`

The message-driven bean class, `MessageBean.java`, is identical to the one in Section 7.1.2 on page 79.

```java
import javax.ejb.*;
import javax.naming.*;
import javax.jms.*;

/**
 * The MessageBean class is a message-driven bean.  It implements
 * the javax.ejb.MessageDrivenBean and javax.jms.MessageListener
 * interfaces. It is defined as public (but not final or
 * abstract).  It defines a constructor and the methods
 * setMessageDrivenContext, ejbCreate, onMessage, and
 * ejbRemove.
 */
public class MessageBean implements MessageDrivenBean,
    MessageListener {

    private transient MessageDrivenContext mdc = null;
    private Context context;

    /**
     * Constructor, which is public and takes no arguments.
     */
    public MessageBean() {
        System.out.println("In MessageBean.MessageBean()");
    }

    /**
     * setMessageDrivenContext method, declared as public (but
     * not final or static), with a return type of void, and
     * with one argument of type javax.ejb.MessageDrivenContext.
     *
     * @param mdc     the context to set
     */
```

```java
public void setMessageDrivenContext(MessageDrivenContext mdc)
{
    System.out.println("In " +
        "MessageBean.setMessageDrivenContext()");
    this.mdc = mdc;
}


/**
 * ejbCreate method, declared as public (but not final or
 * static), with a return type of void, and with no
 * arguments.
 */
public void ejbCreate() {
    System.out.println("In MessageBean.ejbCreate()");
}




/**
 * onMessage method, declared as public (but not final or
 * static), with a return type of void, and with one argument
 * of type javax.jms.Message.
 *
 * Casts the incoming Message to a TextMessage and displays
 * the text.
 *
 * @param inMessage     the incoming message
 */
public void onMessage(Message inMessage) {
    TextMessage msg = null;

    try {
        if (inMessage instanceof TextMessage) {
            msg = (TextMessage) inMessage;
            System.out.println("MESSAGE BEAN: Message " +
                "received: " + msg.getText());
        } else {
            System.out.println("Message of wrong type: " +
                inMessage.getClass().getName());
```

```
            }
        } catch (JMSException e) {
            System.err.println("MessageBean.onMessage: " +
                "JMSException: " + e.toString());
            mdc.setRollbackOnly();
        } catch (Throwable te) {
            System.err.println("MessageBean.onMessage: " +
                "Exception: " + te.toString());
        }
    }


    /**
     * ejbRemove method, declared as public (but not final or
     * static), with a return type of void, and with no
     * arguments.
     */
    public void ejbRemove() {
        System.out.println("In MessageBean.remove()");
    }
}
```

Code Example 8.5 `MessageBean.java`

8.1.4   Compiling the Source Files

To compile all the files in the application, go to the directory `client_ses_mdb` and do the following.

1. Make sure that you have set the environment variables shown in Table 4.1 on page 28: `JAVA_HOME`, `J2EE_HOME`, `CLASSPATH`, and `PATH`.

2. At a command line prompt, compile the source files:

   `javac *.java`

8.2 Creating and Packaging the Application

Creating and packaging this application involve several steps:

1. Starting the J2EE server and the deploytool*
2. Creating a topic
3. Creating a connection factory
4. Creating the J2EE application
5. Packaging the application client
6. Packaging the session bean
7. Packaging the message-driven bean
8. Specifying the JNDI names

Step 1, marked with an asterisk (*), is not needed if the server and deploytool are still running.

8.2.1 Starting the J2EE Server and the Deploytool

Before you can create and package the application, you must start the J2EE server and the deploytool. Follow these steps.

1. At the command line prompt, start the J2EE server:

   ```
   j2ee -verbose
   ```

   Wait until the server displays the message "J2EE server startup complete."

   (To stop the server, type `j2ee -stop`.)

2. At another command line prompt, start the deploytool:

   ```
   deploytool
   ```

   (To access the tool's context-sensitive help, press F1.)

8.2.2   Creating a Topic

In Section 4.3.4 on page 49, you used the j2eeadmin command to create a topic. This time, you will create the topic by using the deploytool. Follow these steps.

1. In the deploytool, select the Tools menu.

2. From the Tools menu, choose Server Configuration.

3. Under the JMS folder, select Destinations.

4. In the JMS Topic Destinations area, click Add.

5. In the text field, enter jms/MyTopic. (We will observe the J2EE convention of placing the topic in the jms namespace.)

6. Click OK.

7. If you wish, you can verify that the topic was created:

   ```
   j2eeadmin -listJmsDestination
   ```

8.2.3   Creating a Connection Factory

For this application, you create a new connection factory. This application will use a durable subscriber, so you need a connection factory that has a client ID. (For more information, see Section 5.2.1 on page 61.) Follow these steps.

1. At the command line prompt, enter the following command (all on one line):

   ```
   j2eeadmin -addJmsFactory jms/DurableTopicCF topic -props
   clientID=MyID
   ```

2. Verify that the connection factory was created:

   ```
   j2eeadmin -listJmsFactory
   ```

You can also create connection factories by using the deploytool's Server Configuration dialog.

8.2.4   Creating the J2EE Application

Create a new J2EE application called PubSubApp and store it in the file named PubSubApp.ear. Follow these steps.

1. In the deploytool, select the File menu.

2. From the File menu, choose New → Application.

3. Click Browse next to the Application File Name field and use the file chooser to locate the directory client_ses_mdb.

4. In the File Name field, enter PubSubApp.

5. Click New Application.

6. Click OK.

A diamond icon labeled PubSubApp appears in the tree view on the left side of the deploytool window. The full path name of PubSubApp.ear appears in the General tabbed pane on the right side.

8.2.5   Packaging the Application Client

In this section, you will run the New Application Client Wizard of the deploytool to package the application client. To start the New Application Client Wizard, follow these steps.

1. In the tree view, select PubSubApp.

2. From the File menu, choose New → Application Client. The wizard displays a series of dialog boxes.

8.2.5.1   Introduction Dialog Box

Click Next.

8.2.5.2   JAR File Contents Dialog Box

1. In the combo box labeled Create Archive Within Application, select PubSubApp.

2. Click the Edit button next to the Contents text area.

3. In the dialog box Edit Contents of <Application Client>, choose the client_ses_mdb directory. If the directory is not already in the Starting Directory field, type it in the field, or locate it by browsing through the Available Files tree.

4. Select the MyAppClient.class file from the Available Files tree area and click Add.

5. Click OK.

6. Click Next.

8.2.5.3   General Dialog Box

1. In the Application Client combo box, select MyAppClient in the Main Class field, and enter MyAppClient in the Display Name field.

2. In the Callback Handler Class combo box, verify that container-managed authentication is selected.

3. Click Next.

8.2.5.4   Environment Entries Dialog Box

Click Next.

8.2.5.5   Enterprise Bean References Dialog Box

In this dialog box, you associate the JNDI API context name for the EJB reference in the MyAppClient.java source file with the home and remote interfaces of the Publisher enterprise bean. Follow these steps.

1. Click Add.

2. In the Coded Name column, enter ejb/MyEjbReference.

3. In the Type column, select Session.

4. In the Interfaces column, select Remote.

5. In the Home Interface column, enter PublisherHome.

6. In the Local/Remote Interface column, enter Publisher.

7. In the Deployment Settings combo box, select JNDI Name. In the JNDI Name field, enter `MyPublisher`.

8. Click Finish. You do not need to enter anything in the other dialog boxes.

8.2.6 Packaging the Session Bean

In this section, you will run the New Enterprise Bean Wizard of the deploytool to package the session bean. Follow these steps.

1. In the tree view, select `PubSubApp`.

2. From the File menu, choose New → Enterprise Bean. The wizard displays a series of dialog boxes.

8.2.6.1 Introduction Dialog Box

Click Next.

8.2.6.2 EJB JAR Dialog Box

1. In the combo box labeled JAR File Location, verify that Create New JAR File in Application and `PubSubApp` are selected.

2. In the JAR Display Name field, verify that the name is `Ejb1`, the default display name. Representing the enterprise bean JAR file that contains the bean, this name will be displayed in the tree view.

3. Click the Edit button next to the Contents text area.

4. In the dialog box Edit Contents of Ejb1, choose the `client_ses_mdb` directory. If the directory is not already in the Starting Directory field, type it in the field, or locate it by browsing through the Available Files tree.

5. Select the files `Publisher.class`, `PublisherBean.class`, and `PublisherHome.class` from the Available Files tree area and click Add.

6. Click OK.

7. Click Next.

8.2.6.3   General Dialog Box

1. In the Bean Type combo box, select the Session radio button.

2. Select the Stateless radio button.

3. In the Enterprise Bean Class combo box, select `PublisherBean`.

4. In the Enterprise Bean Name field, enter `PublisherEJB`.

5. In the Remote Interfaces combo box, select `PublisherHome` for Remote Home Interface and `Publisher` for Remote Interface. Ignore the Local Interfaces combo box.

6. Click Next.

8.2.6.4   Transaction Management Dialog Box

1. Select the Container-Managed radio button.

2. In the Transaction Attribute field opposite the `publishNews` method, verify that Required is selected.

3. Click Next.

8.2.6.5   Environment Entries Dialog Box

Click Next.

8.2.6.6   Enterprise Bean References Dialog Box

Click Next.

8.2.6.7   Resource References Dialog Box

1. Click Add.

2. In the Coded Name field, enter `jms/MyTopicConnectionFactory`.

3. In the Type field, select `javax.jms.TopicConnectionFactory`.

4. In the Authentication field, select Container.

5. In the JNDI Name field, enter `jms/DurableTopicCF`.

6. In the User Name field, enter `j2ee`.

7. In the Password field, enter j2ee.

8. Click Next.

8.2.6.8   Resource Environment References Dialog Box

1. Click Add.

2. In the Coded Name field, enter jms/TopicName—the logical name referenced by the PublisherBean.

3. In the Type field, select javax.jms.Topic.

4. In the JNDI Name field, enter jms/MyTopic.

5. Click Next.

8.2.6.9   Security Dialog Box

Use the default Security Identity setting for a session or an entity bean, Use Caller ID. Click Next.

8.2.6.10 Review Settings Dialog Box

1. Check the settings for the deployment descriptor.

2. Click Finish.

8.2.7   Packaging the Message-Driven Bean

In this section, you will run the New Enterprise Bean Wizard of the deploytool to package the message-driven bean. To start the New Enterprise Bean Wizard, follow these steps.

1. In the tree view, select PubSubApp.

2. From the File menu, choose New → Enterprise Bean. The wizard displays a series of dialog boxes.

8.2.7.1   Introduction Dialog Box

Click Next.

8.2.7.2   EJB JAR Dialog Box

1. In the combo box labeled JAR File Location, verify that Create New JAR File in Application and PubSubApp are selected.

2. In the JAR Display Name field, verify that the name is Ejb2, the default display name.

3. Click the Edit button next to the Contents text area.

4. In the dialog box Edit Contents of Ejb2, choose the client_ses_mdb directory. If the directory is not already in the Starting Directory field, type it in the field, or locate it by browsing through the Available Files tree.

5. Select the MessageBean.class file from the Available Files tree area and click Add.

6. Click OK.

7. Click Next.

8.2.7.3   General Dialog Box

1. In the Bean Type combo box, select the Message-Driven radio button.

2. In the Enterprise Bean Class combo box, select MessageBean.

3. In the Enterprise Bean Name field, enter MessageBean.

4. Click Next.

8.2.7.4   Transaction Management Dialog Box

1. Select the Container-Managed radio button.

2. In the Transaction Type field opposite the onMessage method, verify that Required is selected.

3. Click Next.

8.2.7.5   Message-Driven Bean Settings Dialog Box

1. In the Destination Type combo box, select Topic.

2. Check the Durable Subscriber checkbox.

3. In the Subscription Name field, enter `MySub`.

4. In the Destination field, select `jms/MyTopic`.

5. In the Connection Factory field, select `jms/DurableTopicCF`.

6. In the JMS Message Selector field, enter the following exactly as shown:

```
NewsType = 'Opinion' OR NewsType = 'Sports'
```

This will cause the message-driven bean to receive only messages whose `NewsType` property is set to one of these values.

7. Click Finish. You do not need to enter anything in the other dialog boxes.

8.2.8 Specifying the JNDI Names

Verify that the JNDI names are correct, and add one for the `PublisherEJB` component. Follow these steps.

1. In the tree view, select the `PubSubApp` application.

2. Select the JNDI Names tabbed pane.

3. Make sure that the JNDI names appear as shown in Tables 8.1 and 8.2. You will need to enter `MyPublisher` as the JNDI name for the `PublisherEJB` component.

Table 8.1: Application Pane

Component Type	Component	JNDI Name
EJB	MessageBean	jms/MyTopic
EJB	PublisherEJB	MyPublisher

Table 8.2: References Pane

Ref. Type	Referenced By	Reference Name	JNDI Name
Resource	PublisherEJB	jms/MyTopic-ConnectionFactory	jms/DurableTopicCF
Env Resource	PublisherEJB	jms/TopicName	jms/MyTopic
EJB Ref	MyAppClient	ejb/MyEjbReference	MyPublisher

8.3   Deploying and Running the Application

Deploying and running this application involve several steps:

1. Adding the server, if necessary

2. Deploying the application

3. Running the client

4. Undeploying the application

5. Removing the application and stopping the server

8.3.1   Adding the Server

Before you can deploy the application, you must make available to the deploytool the J2EE server you started in Section 8.2.1 on page 109. Because you started the J2EE server before you started the deploytool, the server, named localhost, probably appears in the tree under Servers. If it does not, do the following.

1. From the File menu, choose Add Server.

2. In the Add Server dialog box, enter localhost in the Server Name field.

3. Click OK. A localhost node appears under Servers in the tree view.

8.3.2   Deploying the Application

To deploy the application, perform the following steps.

1. From the File menu, choose Save to save the application.

2. From the Tools menu, choose Deploy.

3. In the Introduction dialog box, verify that the Object to Deploy selection is PubSubApp and that the Target Server selection is localhost.

4. Click Next.

5. In the JNDI Names dialog box, verify that the JNDI names are correct.

6. Click Next.

7. Click Finish.

8. In the Deployment Progress dialog box, click OK when the "Deployment of PubSubApp is complete" message appears.

9. In the tree view, expand Servers and select localhost. Verify that PubSubApp is deployed.

8.3.3   Running the Client

To run the client, perform the following steps.

1. At the command line prompt, enter the following:

```
runclient -client PubSubApp.ear -name MyAppClient -textauth
```

2. At the login prompts, enter j2ee as the user name and j2ee as the password.

3. Click OK.

The client program runs in the command window and has output that looks like this:

```
Binding name:'java:comp/env/ejb/MyEjbReference'
Looking up EJB reference
Looked up home
Narrowed home
```

```
Got the EJB
Unbinding name: 'java:comp/env/ejb/MyEjbReference'
```

Output from the application appears in the window in which you started the J2EE server. Suppose that the last few messages from the Publisher session bean look like this:

```
PUBLISHER: Setting message text to: Item 13: Opinion
PUBLISHER: Setting message text to: Item 14: Sports
PUBLISHER: Setting message text to: Item 15: Nation/World
PUBLISHER: Setting message text to: Item 16: Living/Arts
PUBLISHER: Setting message text to: Item 17: Opinion
```

Because of the message selector, the last few messages received by the message-driven bean will look like this:

```
MESSAGE BEAN: Message received: Item 13: Opinion
MESSAGE BEAN: Message received: Item 14: Sports
MESSAGE BEAN: Message received: Item 17: Opinion
```

8.3.4   Undeploying the Application

To undeploy the J2EE application, follow these steps.

1. In the tree view, select localhost.

2. Select PubSubApp in the Deployed Objects area.

3. Click Undeploy.

4. Answer Yes in the confirmation dialog.

8.3.5   Removing the Application and Stopping the Server

To remove the application from the deploytool, follow these steps.

1. Select PubSubApp in the tree view.

2. Select Close from the File menu.

To delete the topic you created, enter the following at the command line prompt:

```
j2eeadmin -removeJmsDestination jms/MyTopic
```

To delete the connection factory you created, enter the following:

```
j2eeadmin -removeJmsFactory jms/DurableTopicCF
```

To stop the J2EE server, use the following command:

```
j2ee -stop
```

CHAPTER 9

A J2EE Application that Uses the JMS API with an Entity Bean

THIS chapter explains how to write, compile, package, deploy, and run a J2EE application that uses the JMS API with an entity bean. The application uses the following components:

- An application client that both sends and receives messages

- Three message-driven beans

- An entity bean that uses container-managed persistence

  The chapter covers the following topics:

- An overview of the application

- Writing and compiling the application components

- Creating and packaging the application

- Deploying and running the application

  If you downloaded the tutorial examples as described in the preface, you will find the source code files for this chapter in `jms_tutorial/examples/client_mdb_ent` (on UNIX systems) or `jms_tutorial\examples\client_mdb_ent` (on Microsoft Windows systems). The directory `ear_files` in the `examples` directory contains a built application called `SampleNewHireApp.ear`. If you run into difficulty at any time, you can open this file in the deploytool and compare that file to your own version.

9.1   Overview of the Human Resources Application

This application simulates, in a simplified way, the work flow of a company's human resources (HR) department when it processes a new hire. This application also demonstrates how to use the J2EE platform to accomplish a task that many JMS client applications perform.

A JMS client must often wait for several messages from various sources. It then uses the information in all these messages to assemble a message that it then sends to another destination. (The common term for this process is *joining messages*.) Such a task must be transactional, with all the receives and the send as a single transaction. If all the messages are not received successfully, the transaction can be rolled back. For a client example that illustrates this task, see Section A.2 on page 439.

A message-driven bean can process only one message at a time in a transaction. To provide the ability to join messages, a J2EE application can have the message-driven bean store the interim information in an entity bean. The entity bean can then determine whether all the information has been received; when it has, the entity bean can create and send the message to the other destination. Once it has completed its task, the entity bean can be removed.

The basic steps of the application are as follows.

1. The HR department's application client generates an employee ID for each new hire and then publishes a message containing the new hire's name and employee ID. The client then creates a temporary queue with a message listener that waits for a reply to the message.

2. Two message-driven beans process each message: One bean assigns the new hire's office number, and one bean assigns the new hire's equipment. The first bean to process the message creates an entity bean to store the information it has generated. The second bean locates the existing entity bean and adds its information.

3. When both the office and the equipment have been assigned, the entity bean sends to the reply queue a message describing the assignments. The application client's message listener retrieves the information. The entity bean also

sends to a Schedule queue a message that contains a reference to the entity bean.

4. The Schedule message-driven bean receives the message from the entity bean. This message serves as a notification that the entity bean has finished joining all messages. The message contains the primary key to look up the entity bean instance that aggregates the data of the joined messages. The message-driven bean accesses information from the entity bean to complete its task and then removes the entity bean instance.

Figure 9.1 illustrates the structure of this application. An actual HR application would have more components, of course; other beans could set up payroll and benefits records, schedule orientation, and so on.

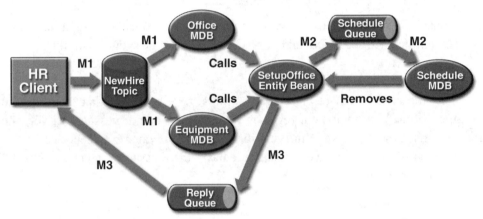

Figure 9.1   A J2EE Application: Client to Message-Driven Beans to Entity Beans

9.2   Writing and Compiling the Application Components

Writing and compiling the components of the application involve

- Coding the application client
- Coding the message-driven beans
- Coding the entity bean
- Compiling the source files

9.2.1   Coding the Application Client: `HumanResourceClient.java`

The application client program, `HumanResourceClient.java`, performs the following steps:

1. Uses the Java Naming and Directory Interface (JNDI) API naming context `java:comp/env` to look up a `TopicConnectionFactory`, a `QueueConnection-Factory`, and a topic

2. Creates a `TemporaryQueue` to receive notification of processing that occurs, based on new-hire events it has published

3. Creates a `QueueReceiver` for the `TemporaryQueue`, sets the `QueueReceiver`'s message listener, and starts the connection

4. Creates a `TopicPublisher` and a `MapMessage`

5. Creates five new employees with randomly generated names, positions, and ID numbers (in sequence) and publishes five messages containing this information

The message listener, `HRListener`, waits for messages that contain the assigned office and equipment for each employee. When a message arrives, the message listener displays the information received and checks to see whether all five messages have arrived yet. When they have, the message listener notifies the main program, which then exits.

```
import javax.jms.*;
import javax.naming.*;
import java.util.*;

/**
 * The HumanResourceClient class is the client program for this
 * J2EE application. It publishes a message describing a new
 * hire business event that other departments can act upon. It
 * also listens for a message reporting the completion of the
 * other departments' actions and displays the results.
 */
public class HumanResourceClient {
    static Object     waitUntilDone = new Object();
```

```java
static SortedSet  outstandingRequests =
    Collections.synchronizedSortedSet(new TreeSet());

public static void main (String[] args) {
    InitialContext          ic = null;
    TopicConnectionFactory  topicConnectionFactory = null;
    TopicConnection         tConnection = null;
    TopicSession            tSession = null;
    Topic                   pubTopic = null;
    TopicPublisher          tPublisher = null;
    MapMessage              message = null;
    QueueConnectionFactory  queueConnectionFactory = null;
    QueueConnection         qConnection = null;
    QueueSession            qSession = null;
    Queue                   replyQueue = null;
    QueueReceiver           qReceiver = null;

    /*
     * Create a JNDI API InitialContext object.
     */
    try {
        ic = new InitialContext();
    } catch (NamingException e) {
        System.err.println("HumanResourceClient: " +
            "Could not create JNDI API context: " +
            e.toString());
        System.exit(1);
    }


    /*
     * Look up connection factories and topic.  If any do not
     * exist, exit.
     */
    try {
        topicConnectionFactory = (TopicConnectionFactory)
        ic.lookup("java:comp/env/jms/TopicConnectionFactory");
        pubTopic =
          (Topic) ic.lookup("java:comp/env/jms/NewHireTopic");
```

```java
        queueConnectionFactory = (QueueConnectionFactory)
          ic.lookup("java:comp/env/jms/QueueConnectionFactory");
    } catch (NamingException e) {
        System.err.println("HumanResourceClient: " +
            "JNDI API lookup failed: " + e.toString());
        System.exit(1);
    }


    /*
     * Create topic and queue connections.
     * Create sessions from connections for the publisher
     *   and receiver; false means session is not
     *   transacted.
     * Create temporary queue and receiver, set message
     *   listener, and start connection.
     * Create publisher and MapMessage.
     * Publish new hire business events.
     * Wait for all messages to be processed.
     * Finally, close connection.
     */
    try {
        Random rand = new Random();
        int nextHireID = rand.nextInt(100);

        String[] positions = { "Programmer",
            "Senior Programmer", "Manager", "Director" };
        String[] firstNames = { "Fred", "Robert", "Tom",
            "Steve", "Alfred", "Joe", "Jack", "Harry",
            "Bill", "Gertrude", "Jenny", "Polly", "Ethel",
            "Mary", "Betsy", "Carol", "Edna", "Gwen" };
        String[] lastNames = { "Astaire", "Preston", "Tudor",
            "Stuart", "Drake", "Jones", "Windsor",
            "Hapsburg", "Robinson", "Lawrence", "Wren",
            "Parrott", "Waters", "Martin", "Blair",
            "Bourbon", "Merman", "Verdon" };

        tConnection =
            topicConnectionFactory.createTopicConnection();
```

```
tSession = tConnection.createTopicSession(false,
    Session.AUTO_ACKNOWLEDGE);

qConnection =
    queueConnectionFactory.createQueueConnection();
qSession = qConnection.createQueueSession(false,
    Session.AUTO_ACKNOWLEDGE);
replyQueue = qSession.createTemporaryQueue();
qReceiver = qSession.createReceiver(replyQueue);
qReceiver.setMessageListener(new HRListener());
qConnection.start();

tPublisher = tSession.createPublisher(pubTopic);

message = tSession.createMapMessage();
message.setJMSReplyTo(replyQueue);
for (int i = 0; i < 5; i++) {
    int currentHireID = nextHireID++;
        String.valueOf(currentHireID));
    message.setString("Name",
        firstNames[rand.nextInt(firstNames.length)]
        + " " +
        lastNames[rand.nextInt(lastNames.length)]);
    message.setString("Position",
        positions[rand.nextInt(positions.length)]);
    System.out.println("PUBLISHER: Setting hire " +
        "ID to " + message.getString("HireID") +
        ", name " + message.getString("Name") +
        ", position " +
        message.getString("Position"));
    tPublisher.publish(message);
 outstandingRequests.add(new Integer(currentHireID));
}

System.out.println("Waiting for " +
    outstandingRequests.size() + " message(s)");
synchronized (waitUntilDone) {
    waitUntilDone.wait();
}
```

```java
                } catch (Exception e) {
                    System.err.println("HumanResourceClient: " +
                        "Exception: " + e.toString());
                } finally {
                    if (tConnection != null) {
                        try {
                            tConnection.close();
                        } catch (Exception e) {
                            System.err.println("HumanResourceClient: " +
                                "Close exception: " + e.toString());
                        }
                    }
                    if (qConnection != null) {
                        try {
                            qConnection.close();
                        } catch (Exception e) {
                            System.out.println("HumanResourceClient: " +
                                             "Close exception: " +
                                             e.toString());
                        }
                    }
                    System.exit(0);
                }
        }


        /**
         * The HRListener class implements the MessageListener
         * interface by defining an onMessage method.
         */
        static class HRListener implements MessageListener {

            /**
             * onMessage method, which displays the contents of a
             * MapMessage describing the results of processing the
             * new employee, then removes the employee ID from the
             * list of outstanding requests.
             *
             * @param message    the incoming message
             */
```

```java
    public void onMessage(Message message) {
        MapMessage msg = (MapMessage) message;
        try {
            System.out.println("New hire event processed:");
            Integer id =
                Integer.valueOf(msg.getString("employeeId"));
            System.out.println("  Name: " +
                msg.getString("employeeName"));
            System.out.println("  Equipment: " +
                msg.getString("equipmentList"));
            System.out.println("  Office number: " +
                msg.getString("officeNumber"));
            outstandingRequests.remove(id);
        } catch (JMSException je) {
            System.out.println("HRListener.onMessage(): " +
                "Exception: " + je.toString());
        }

        if (outstandingRequests.size() == 0) {
            synchronized(waitUntilDone) {
                waitUntilDone.notify();
            }
        } else {
            System.out.println("Waiting for " +
                outstandingRequests.size() + " message(s)");
        }
    }
  }
}
```

Code Example 9.1 `HumanResourceClient.java`

9.2.2   Coding the Message-Driven Beans

This example uses three message-driven beans. Two of them, `ReserveEquipment-MsgBean.java` and `ReserveOfficeMsgBean.java`, take the following steps.

1. The `ejbCreate` method gets a handle to the home interface of the entity bean.

2. The `onMessage` method retrieves the information in the message. The `ReserveEquipmentMsgBean`'s `onMessage` method chooses equipment, based on the new hire's position; the `ReserveOfficeMsgBean`'s `onMessage` method randomly generates an office number.

3. After a slight delay to simulate real-world processing hitches, the `onMessage` method calls a helper method, `compose`.

4. The `compose` method either creates or finds, by primary key, the `SetupOffice` entity bean and uses it to store the equipment or the office information in the database.

```java
import java.io.Serializable;
import java.rmi.RemoteException;
import javax.rmi.PortableRemoteObject;
import javax.ejb.*;
import javax.naming.*;
import javax.jms.*;
import java.util.Random;
/**
 * The ReserveEquipmentMsgBean class is a message-driven bean.
 * It implements the javax.ejb.MessageDrivenBean and
 * javax.jms.MessageListener interfaces. It is defined as public
 * (but not final or abstract).  It defines a constructor and the
 * methods ejbCreate, onMessage, setMessageDrivenContext, and
 * ejbRemove.
 */
public class ReserveEquipmentMsgBean implements
        MessageDrivenBean, MessageListener {

    private transient MessageDrivenContext mdc = null;
    private SetupOfficeLocalHome soLocalHome = null;
    private Random processingTime = new Random();
```

```java
/**
 * Constructor, which is public and takes no arguments.
 */
public ReserveEquipmentMsgBean() {
    System.out.println("In " +
        "ReserveEquipmentMsgBean.ReserveEquipmentMsgBean()");
}


/**
 * setMessageDrivenContext method, declared as public (but
 * not final or static), with a return type of void, and with
 * one argument of type javax.ejb.MessageDrivenContext.
 *
 * @param mdc    the context to set
 */
public void setMessageDrivenContext(MessageDrivenContext mdc)
{
    System.out.println("In " +
        "ReserveEquipmentMsgBean.setMessageDrivenContext()");
    this.mdc = mdc;
}


/**
 * ejbCreate method, declared as public (but not final or
 * static), with a return type of void, and with no
 * arguments. It looks up the entity bean and gets a handle
 * to its home interface.
 */
public void ejbCreate() {
    System.out.println("In " +
        "ReserveEquipmentMsgBean.ejbCreate()");
    try {
        Context initial = new InitialContext();
        Object objref =
            initial.lookup("java:comp/env/ejb/MyEjbReference");
        soLocalHome = (SetupOfficeLocalHome)
            PortableRemoteObject.narrow(objref,
                SetupOfficeLocalHome.class);
    } catch (Exception ex) {
```

```
              System.err.println("ReserveEquipmentMsgBean." +
                  "ejbCreate: Exception: " + ex.toString());
        }
    }


    /**
     * onMessage method, declared as public (but not final or
     * static), with a return type of void, and with one argument
     * of type javax.jms.Message.
     *
     * Casts the incoming Message to a MapMessage, retrieves its
     * contents, and assigns equipment appropriate to the new
     * hire's position.  Calls the compose method to store the
     * information in the entity bean.
     *
     * @param inMessage     the incoming message
     */
    public void onMessage(Message inMessage) {
        MapMessage msg = null;
        String key = null;
        String name = null;
        String position = null;
        String equipmentList = null;

        try {
            if (inMessage instanceof MapMessage) {
                msg = (MapMessage) inMessage;
                System.out.println("  ReserveEquipmentMsgBean:" +
                    " Message received.");
                key = msg.getString("HireID");
                name = msg.getString("Name");
                position = msg.getString("Position");

                if (position.equals("Programmer")) {
                    equipmentList = "Desktop System";
                } else if (position.equals("Senior Programmer")){
                    equipmentList = "Laptop";
                } else if (position.equals("Manager")) {
                    equipmentList = "Pager";
```

```
            } else if (position.equals("Director")) {
                equipmentList = "Java Phone";
            } else {
                equipmentList = "Baton";
            }

            // Simulate processing time taking 1 to 10 seconds.
            Thread.sleep( processingTime.nextInt(10) * 1000);
            compose(key, name, equipmentList, msg);
        } else {
            System.err.println("Message of wrong type: " +
                inMessage.getClass().getName());
        }
    } catch (JMSException e) {
        System.err.println("ReserveEquipmentMsgBean." +
            "onMessage: JMSException: " + e.toString());
        mdc.setRollbackOnly();
    } catch (Throwable te) {
        System.err.println("ReserveEquipmentMsgBean." +
            "onMessage: Exception: " + te.toString());
    }
}

/**
 * compose method, helper to onMessage method.
 *
 * Locates the row of the database represented by the primary
 * key and adds the equipment allocated for the new hire.
 *
 * @param key          employee ID, primary key
 * @param name         employee name
 * @param equipmentList equipment allocated based on position
 * @param msg          the message received
 */
void compose (String key, String name, String equipmentList,
        Message msg) {
    int num = 0;
    SetupOffice so = null;
```

```java
        try {
            try {
                so = soLocalHome.findByPrimaryKey(key);
                System.out.println("  ReserveEquipmentMsgBean:" +
                    " Found join entity bean for employeeId " +
                    key);
            } catch (ObjectNotFoundException onfe) {
                System.err.println("  ReserveEquipmentMsgBean:" +
                    " Creating join entity bean for " +
                    " employeeId " + key);
                so = soLocalHome.createLocal(key, name);
            }
            so.doEquipmentList(equipmentList, msg);
            System.out.println("  ReserveEquipmentMsgBean: " +
                "employeeId " + key + " (" +
                so.getEmployeeName() + ") has the following " +
                "equipment: " + so.getEquipmentList());
        } catch (Exception ex) {
            System.err.println(" ReserveEquipmentMsgBean." +
                "compose: Exception: " + ex.toString());
            mdc.setRollbackOnly();
        }
    }


    /**
     * ejbRemove method, declared as public (but not final or
     * static), with a return type of void, and with no
     * arguments.
     */
    public void ejbRemove() {
        System.out.println("In " +
            "ReserveEquipmentMsgBean.ejbRemove()");
    }
}
```

Code Example 9.2 `ReserveEquipmentMsgBean.java`

```java
import java.io.Serializable;
import java.rmi.RemoteException;
import javax.rmi.PortableRemoteObject;
import javax.ejb.*;
import javax.naming.*;
import javax.jms.*;
import java.util.Random;

/**
 * The ReserveOfficeMsgBean class is a message-driven bean. It
 * implements the javax.ejb.MessageDrivenBean and
 * javax.jms.MessageListener interfaces. It is defined as public
 * (but not final or abstract).  It defines a constructor and the
 * methods ejbCreate, onMessage, setMessageDrivenContext, and
 * ejbRemove.
 */
public class ReserveOfficeMsgBean implements MessageDrivenBean,
    MessageListener {

    private transient MessageDrivenContext mdc = null;
    private SetupOfficeLocalHome soLocalHome = null;
    private Random processingTime = new Random();

    /**
     * Constructor, which is public and takes no arguments.
     */
    public ReserveOfficeMsgBean() {
        System.out.println("In " +
            "ReserveOfficeMsgBean.ReserveOfficeMsgBean()");
    }

    /**
     * setMessageDrivenContext method, declared as public (but
     * not final or static), with a return type of void, and with
     * one argument of type javax.ejb.MessageDrivenContext.
     *
     * @param mdc    the context to set
```

```java
    */
    public void setMessageDrivenContext(MessageDrivenContext mdc)
    {
        System.out.println("In " +
            "ReserveOfficeMsgBean.setMessageDrivenContext()");
        this.mdc = mdc;
    }


    /**
     * ejbCreate method, declared as public (but not final or
     * static), with a return type of void, and with no
     * arguments. It looks up the entity bean and gets a handle
     * to its home interface.
     */
    public void ejbCreate() {
        System.out.println("In " +
            "ReserveOfficeMsgBean.ejbCreate()");
        try {
            Context initial = new InitialContext();
            Object objref =
                initial.lookup("java:comp/env/ejb/MyEjbReference");
            soLocalHome = (SetupOfficeLocalHome)
                PortableRemoteObject.narrow(objref,
                    SetupOfficeLocalHome.class);
        } catch (Exception ex) {
            System.err.println("ReserveOfficeMsgBean." +
                "ejbCreate: Exception: " + ex.toString());
        }
    }


    /**
     * onMessage method, declared as public (but not final or
     * static), with a return type of void, and with one argument
     * of type javax.jms.Message.
     *
     * Casts the incoming Message to a MapMessage, retrieves its
     * contents, and assigns the new hire to an office. Calls the
     * compose method to store the information in the entity
     * bean.
```

```java
 *
 * @param inMessage     the incoming message
 */
public void onMessage(Message inMessage) {
    MapMessage msg = null;
    String key = null;
    String name = null;
    String position = null;
    int officeNumber = 0;

    try {
        if (inMessage instanceof MapMessage) {
            msg = (MapMessage) inMessage;
            System.out.println("  >>> ReserveOfficeMsgBean:" +
                " Message received.");
            key = msg.getString("HireID");
            name = msg.getString("Name");
            position = msg.getString("Position");

            officeNumber = new Random().nextInt(300) + 1;

            // Simulate processing time taking 1 to 10 seconds.
            Thread.sleep( processingTime.nextInt(10) * 1000);
            compose(key, name, officeNumber, msg);
        } else {
            System.err.println("Message of wrong type: " +
                inMessage.getClass().getName());
        }
    } catch (JMSException e) {
        System.err.println("ReserveOfficeMsgBean." +
            "onMessage: JMSException: " + e.toString());
        mdc.setRollbackOnly();
    } catch (Throwable te) {
        System.err.println("ReserveOfficeMsgBean." +
            "onMessage: Exception: " + te.toString());
    }
}
```

```java
/**
 * compose method, helper to onMessage method.
 *
 * Locates the row of the database represented by the primary
 * key and adds the office number allocated for the new hire.
 *
 * @param key          employee ID, primary key
 * @param name         employee name
 * @param officeNumber office number
 * @param msg          the message received
 */
void compose (String key, String name, int officeNumber,
        Message msg) {
    int num = 0;
    SetupOffice so = null;

    try {
        try {
            so = soLocalHome.findByPrimaryKey(key);
            System.out.println("  ReserveOfficeMsgBean: " +
                "Found join entity bean for employeeId " +
                key);
        } catch (ObjectNotFoundException onfe) {
            System.out.println("  ReserveOfficeMsgBean: " +
                "Creating join entity bean for " +
                "employeeId " + key);
            so = soLocalHome.createLocal(key, name);
        }
        so.doOfficeNumber(officeNumber, msg);
        System.out.println("  ReserveOfficeMsgBean: " +
            "employeeId " + key + " (" +
            so.getEmployeeName() + ") has the following " +
            "office: " + so.getOfficeNumber());
    } catch (Exception ex) {
        System.err.println(" ReserveOfficeMsgBean." +
            "compose: Exception: " + ex.toString());
        mdc.setRollbackOnly();
    }
}
```

```
/**
 * ejbRemove method, declared as public (but not final or
 * static), with a return type of void, and with no
 * arguments.
 */
public void ejbRemove() {
    System.out.println("In " +
        "ReserveOfficeMsgBean.ejbRemove()");
}
}
```

Code Example 9.3 `ReserveOfficeMsgBean.java`

The third message-driven bean, `ScheduleMsgBean.java`, is notified when the `SetupOfficeBean` entity bean instance has aggregated data from all messages needed to set up an office. The message contains the primary key to look up the correct composite entity bean instance. The `ScheduleMsgBean`'s `onMessage` method then schedules the office setup, based on the information aggregated in the entity bean instance. Finally, the `ScheduleMsgBean`'s `onMessage` method removes the entity bean instance.

```
import java.rmi.RemoteException;
import javax.rmi.PortableRemoteObject;
import javax.ejb.*;
import javax.naming.*;
import javax.jms.*;
import java.util.Random;

/**
 * The ScheduleMsgBean class is a message-driven bean.
 * It implements the javax.ejb.MessageDrivenBean and
 * javax.jms.MessageListener interfaces. It is defined as public
 * (but not final or abstract).  It defines a constructor and the
 * methods ejbCreate, onMessage, setMessageDrivenContext, and
 * ejbRemove.
```

```java
    */
public class ScheduleMsgBean implements MessageDrivenBean,
    MessageListener {

    private transient MessageDrivenContext mdc = null;

    private SetupOfficeLocalHome soLocalHome = null;

    /**
     * Constructor, which is public and takes no arguments.
     */
    public ScheduleMsgBean() {
        System.out.println("In " +
            "ScheduleMsgBean.ScheduleMsgBean()");
    }


    /**
     * setMessageDrivenContext method, declared as public (but
     * not final or static), with a return type of void, and with
     * one argument of type javax.ejb.MessageDrivenContext.
     *
     * @param mdc      the context to set
     */
    public void setMessageDrivenContext(MessageDrivenContext mdc)
    {
        System.out.println("In " +
            "ScheduleMsgBean.setMessageDrivenContext()");
        this.mdc = mdc;
    }


    /**
     * ejbCreate method, declared as public (but not final or
     * static), with a return type of void, and with no arguments.
     * It looks up the entity bean and gets a handle to its home
     * interface.
     */

    public void ejbCreate() {
        System.out.println("In ScheduleMsgBean.ejbCreate()");
```

```java
    try {
        Context initial = new InitialContext();
        Object objref =
    initial.lookup("java:comp/env/ejb/CompositeEjbReference");
        soLocalHome = (SetupOfficeLocalHome)
            PortableRemoteObject.narrow(objref,
                SetupOfficeLocalHome.class);
    } catch (Exception ex) {
        System.err.println("ScheduleMsgBean.ejbCreate: " +
            "Exception: " + ex.toString());
    }
}


/**
 * onMessage method, declared as public (but not final or
 * static), with a return type of void, and with one argument
 * of type javax.jms.Message.
 *
 * Casts the incoming Message to a TextMessage, retrieves its
 * handle to the SetupOffice entity bean, and schedules
 * office setup based on information joined in the entity
 * bean. When finished with data, deletes the entity bean.
 *
 * @param inMessage     the incoming message
 */
public void onMessage(Message inMessage) {
    String key = null;
    SetupOffice setupOffice = null;

    try {
        if (inMessage instanceof TextMessage) {
            System.out.println("  ScheduleMsgBean:" +
                " Message received.");
            key = ((TextMessage)inMessage).getText();
            System.out.println("  ScheduleMsgBean: " +
                "Looking up SetupOffice bean by primary " +
                "key=" + key);
            setupOffice = soLocalHome.findByPrimaryKey(key);
```

```
                    /*
                     * Schedule office setup using contents of
                     * SetupOffice entity bean.
                     */
                    System.out.println("  ScheduleMsgBean: " +
                        "SCHEDULE employeeId=" +
                        setupOffice.getEmployeeId() + ", Name=" +
                        setupOffice.getEmployeeName() +
                        " to be set up in office #" +
                        setupOffice.getOfficeNumber() + " with " +
                        setupOffice.getEquipmentList());

                    // All done. Remove SetupOffice entity bean.
                    setupOffice.remove();
                } else {
                    System.err.println("Message of wrong type: " +
                        inMessage.getClass().getName());
                }
            } catch (JMSException e) {
                System.err.println("ScheduleMsgBean.onMessage: " +
                    "JMSException: " + e.toString());
                mdc.setRollbackOnly();

            } catch (Throwable te) {
                System.err.println("ScheduleMsgBean.onMessage: " +
                    "Exception: " + te.toString());
            }
        }


    /**
     * ejbRemove method, declared as public (but not final or
     * static), with a return type of void, and with no
     * arguments.
     */
    public void ejbRemove() {
        System.out.println("In ScheduleMsgBean.ejbRemove()");
    }
```

```
    }
```

Code Example 9.4 `ScheduleMsgBean.java`

9.2.3 Coding the Entity Bean

The `SetupOffice` bean is an entity bean that uses a local interface. The local interface allows the entity bean and the message-driven beans to be packaged in the same EJB JAR file for maximum efficiency. The entity bean has these components:

- The local home interface, `SetupOfficeLocalHome.java`

- The local interface, `SetupOffice.java`

- The bean class, `SetupOfficeBean.java`

9.2.3.1 The Local Home Interface: **`SetupOfficeLocalHome.java`**

The local home interface source file is `SetupOfficeLocalHome.java`. It declares the create method, called `createLocal` for a bean that uses a local interface, and one finder method, `findByPrimaryKey`.

```java
import java.rmi.RemoteException;
import java.util.Collection;
import javax.ejb.*;

public interface SetupOfficeLocalHome extends EJBLocalHome {

    public SetupOffice createLocal(String hireID, String name)
        throws CreateException;
    public SetupOffice findByPrimaryKey(String hireID)
        throws FinderException;
}
```

Code Example 9.5 `SetupOfficeLocalHome.java`

9.2.3.2   The Local Interface: `SetupOffice.java`

The local interface, `SetupOffice.java`, declares several business methods that get and manipulate new-hire data.

```java
import javax.ejb.*;
import javax.jms.*;

public interface SetupOffice extends EJBLocalObject {

    public String getEmployeeId();
    public String getEmployeeName();
    public String getEquipmentList();
    public int    getOfficeNumber();

    public void   doEquipmentList(String list, Message msg)
        throws JMSException;
    public void   doOfficeNumber(int number, Message msg)
        throws JMSException;
}
```

Code Example 9.6   `SetupOffice.java`

9.2.3.3   The Bean Class: `SetupOfficeBean.java`

The bean class, `SetupOfficeBean.java`, implements the business methods and their helper method, `checkIfSetupComplete`. The bean class also implements the required methods `ejbCreateLocal`, `ejbPostCreateLocal`, `setEntityContext`, `unsetEntityContext`, `ejbRemove`, `ejbActivate`, `ejbPassivate`, `ejbLoad`, and `ejb-Store`. The `ejbFindByPrimaryKey` method is generated automatically.

The only methods called by the message-driven beans are the business methods declared in the local interface, the `findByPrimaryKey` method, and the `createLocal` method. The entity bean uses container-managed persistence, so all database calls are generated automatically.

```java
import java.io.*;
import java.util.*;
import javax.ejb.*;
import javax.naming.*;
import javax.jms.*;

/**
 * The SetupOfficeBean class implements the business methods of
 * the entity bean.  Because the bean uses version 2.0 of
 * container-managed persistence, the bean class and the
 * accessor methods for fields to be persisted are all declared
 * abstract.
 */
public abstract class SetupOfficeBean implements EntityBean {

    abstract public String getEmployeeId();
    abstract public void setEmployeeId(String id);

    abstract public String getEmployeeName();
    abstract public void setEmployeeName(String name);

    abstract public int getOfficeNumber();
    abstract public void setOfficeNumber(int officeNum);

    abstract public String getEquipmentList();
    abstract public void setEquipmentList(String equip);

    abstract public byte[] getSerializedReplyDestination();
    abstract public void setSerializedReplyDestination(byte[]
        byteArray);

    abstract public String getReplyCorrelationMsgId();
    abstract public void setReplyCorrelationMsgId(String msgId);
    /*
     * There should be a list of replies for each message being
     * joined.  This example is joining the work of separate
     * departments on the same original request, so it is all
```

```
 * right to have only one reply destination.  In theory, this
 * should be a set of destinations, with one reply for each
 * unique destination.
 *
 * Because a Destination is not a data type that can be
 * persisted, the persisted field is a byte array,
 * serializedReplyDestination, that is created and accessed
 * with the setReplyDestination and getReplyDestination
 * methods.
 */

transient private Destination       replyDestination;
transient private Queue             scheduleQueue;
transient private QueueConnection   queueConnection;
private EntityContext context;

/**
 * The getReplyDestination method extracts the
 * replyDestination from the serialized version that is
 * persisted, using a ByteArrayInputStream and
 * ObjectInputStream to read the object and casting it to a
 * Destination object.
 *
 * @return     the reply destination
 */
private Destination getReplyDestination() {
    ByteArrayInputStream bais = null;
    ObjectInputStream ois = null;
    byte[] srd = null;

    srd = getSerializedReplyDestination();
    if (replyDestination == null && srd != null) {
        try {
            bais = new ByteArrayInputStream(srd);
            ois = new ObjectInputStream(bais);
            replyDestination = (Destination)ois.readObject();
            ois.close();
        } catch (IOException io) {
        } catch (ClassNotFoundException cnfe) {}
```

```
        }
        return replyDestination;
    }


    /**
     * The setReplyDestination method serializes the reply
     * destination so that it can be persisted.  It uses a
     * ByteArrayOutputStream and an ObjectOutputStream.
     *
     * @param replyDestination    the reply destination
     */
    private void setReplyDestination(Destination
            replyDestination) {
        ByteArrayOutputStream baos = null;
        ObjectOutputStream oos = null;
        this.replyDestination = replyDestination;
        try {
            baos = new ByteArrayOutputStream();
            oos = new ObjectOutputStream(baos);
            oos.writeObject(replyDestination);
            oos.close();
            setSerializedReplyDestination(baos.toByteArray());
        } catch (IOException io) {
        }
    }


    /**
     * The doEquipmentList method stores the assigned equipment
     * in the database and retrieves the reply destination, then
     * determines if setup is complete.
     *
     * @param list      assigned equipment
     * @param msg       the message received
     */
    public void doEquipmentList(String list, Message msg)
            throws JMSException {
        setEquipmentList(list);
        setReplyDestination(msg.getJMSReplyTo());
        setReplyCorrelationMsgId(msg.getJMSMessageID());
```

```java
        System.out.println("  SetupOfficeBean." +
            "doEquipmentList: equipment is " +
            getEquipmentList() + " (office number " +
            getOfficeNumber() + ")");
        checkIfSetupComplete();
    }


    /**
     * The doOfficeNumber method stores the assigned office
     * number in the database and retrieves the reply
     * destination, then determines if setup is complete.
     *
     * @param officeNum assigned office
     * @param msg       the message received
     */
    public void doOfficeNumber(int officeNum, Message msg)
            throws JMSException {
        setOfficeNumber(officeNum);
        setReplyDestination(msg.getJMSReplyTo());
        setReplyCorrelationMsgId(msg.getJMSMessageID());
        System.out.println("  SetupOfficeBean." +
            "doOfficeNumber: office number is " +
            getOfficeNumber() + " (equipment " +
            getEquipmentList() + ")");
        checkIfSetupComplete();
    }


    /**
     * The checkIfSetupComplete method determines whether
     * both the office and the equipment have been assigned.  If
     * so, it sends messages to the schedule queue and the reply
     * queue with the information about the assignments.
     */

    private void checkIfSetupComplete() {
        QueueConnection qCon = null;
        QueueSession    qSession = null;
        QueueSender     qSender = null;
        TextMessage     schedMsg = null;
```

```
MapMessage        replyMsg = null;

if (getEquipmentList() != null &&
    getOfficeNumber() != -1) {
    System.out.println("  SetupOfficeBean." +
        "checkIfSetupComplete: SCHEDULE" +
        " employeeId=" + getEmployeeId() + ", Name=" +
        getEmployeeName() + " to be set up in office #" +
        getOfficeNumber() + " with " +
        getEquipmentList());

    try {
        qCon = getQueueConnection();
    } catch (Exception ex) {
        throw new EJBException("Unable to connect to " +
            "JMS provider: " + ex.toString());
    }

    try {
        /*
         * Compose and send message to schedule office
         * setup queue.
         */
        qSession = qCon.createQueueSession(true, 0);
        qSender = qSession.createSender(null);
        schedMsg =
            qSession.createTextMessage(getEmployeeId());
        qSender.send(scheduleQueue, schedMsg);

        /*
         * Send reply to messages aggregated by this
         * composite entity bean.
         */
        replyMsg = qSession.createMapMessage();
        replyMsg.setString("employeeId",
            getEmployeeId());
        replyMsg.setString("employeeName",
            getEmployeeName());
```

```
                    replyMsg.setString("equipmentList",
                        getEquipmentList());
                    replyMsg.setInt("officeNumber",
                        getOfficeNumber());
            replyMsg.setJMSCorrelationID(getReplyCorrelationMsgId());
                    qSender.send((Queue)getReplyDestination(),
                        replyMsg);
                } catch (JMSException je) {
                    System.err.println("SetupOfficeBean." +
                        "checkIfSetupComplete: " + "JMSException: " +
                        je.toString());
                }
            }
        }


    /**
     * ejbCreateLocal method, declared as public (but not final
     * or static).  Stores the available information about the
     * new hire in the database.
     *
     * @param newhireID    ID assigned to the new hire
     * @param name         name of the new hire
     *
     * @return             null (required for CMP 2.0)
     */
    public String ejbCreateLocal(String newhireID, String name)
        throws CreateException {

        setEmployeeId(newhireID);
        setEmployeeName(name);
        setEquipmentList(null);
        setOfficeNumber(-1);

        this.queueConnection = null;
        return null;
    }

    public void ejbRemove() {
        closeQueueConnection();
```

```java
            System.out.println(" SetupOfficeBean.ejbRemove: " +
                "REMOVING SetupOffice bean employeeId=" +
                getEmployeeId() + ", Name=" + getEmployeeName());
    }

    public void setEntityContext(EntityContext context) {
        this.context = context;
    }

    public void unsetEntityContext() {
        this.context = null;
    }

    public void ejbActivate() {
        setEmployeeId((String) context.getPrimaryKey());
    }

    public void ejbPassivate() {
        setEmployeeId(null);
        closeQueueConnection();
    }

    public void ejbLoad() {}

    public void ejbStore() {}

    public void ejbPostCreateLocal(String newhireID, String name) {}

    /**
     * The getQueueConnection method, called by the
     * checkIfSetupComplete method, looks up the schedule queue
     * and connection factory and creates a QueueConnection.
     *
     * @return    a QueueConnection object
     */
    private QueueConnection getQueueConnection()
            throws NamingException, JMSException {
```

```
        if (queueConnection == null) {
            InitialContext ic = new InitialContext();

            QueueConnectionFactory queueConnectionFactory =
                (QueueConnectionFactory)
          ic.lookup("java:comp/env/jms/QueueConnectionFactory");
            scheduleQueue =
            (Queue) ic.lookup("java:comp/env/jms/ScheduleQueue");
            queueConnection =
                queueConnectionFactory.createQueueConnection();
        }
        return queueConnection;
    }


    /**
     * The closeQueueConnection method, called by the ejbRemove
     * and ejbPassivate methods, closes the QueueConnection that
     * was created by the getQueueConnection method.
     */
    private void closeQueueConnection() {
        if (queueConnection != null) {
            try {
                queueConnection.close();
            } catch (JMSException je) {
                System.err.println("SetupOfficeBean." +
                    "closeQueueConnection: JMSException: " +
                    je.toString());
            }
            queueConnection = null;
        }
    }
}
```

Code Example 9.7   `SetupOfficeBean.java`

9.2.4　Compiling the Source Files

To compile all the files in the application, go to the directory `client_mdb_ent` and do the following.

1. Make sure that you have set the environment variables shown in Table 4.1 on page 28: `JAVA_HOME`, `J2EE_HOME`, `CLASSPATH`, and `PATH`.

2. At a command line prompt, compile the source files:

```
javac *.java
```

9.3　Creating and Packaging the Application

Creating and packaging this application involve several steps:

1. Starting the J2EE server and the deploytool*
2. Creating a queue
3. Starting the Cloudscape database server
4. Creating the J2EE application
5. Packaging the application client
6. Packaging the Equipment message-driven bean
7. Packaging the Office message-driven bean
8. Packaging the Schedule message-driven bean
9. Packaging the entity bean
10. Specifying the entity bean deployment settings
11. Specifying the JNDI names

Step 1, marked with an asterisk (*), is not needed if the server and the deploytool are running.

9.3.1   Starting the J2EE Server and the Deploytool

Before you can create and package the application, you must start the J2EE server and the deploytool. Follow these steps.

1. At the command line prompt, start the J2EE server:

   ```
   j2ee -verbose
   ```

   Wait until the server displays the message "J2EE server startup complete."

   (To stop the server, type j2ee -stop.)

2. At another command line prompt, start the deploytool:

   ```
   deploytool
   ```

   (To access the tool's context-sensitive help, press F1.)

9.3.2   Creating a Queue

For this application, you publish messages by using one of the topics that the J2EE server creates automatically. You create a queue to process the notification that the composite entity bean has aggregated the group of related messages that it was joining. Follow these steps.

1. In the deploytool, select the Tools menu.

2. From the Tools menu, choose Server Configuration.

3. Under the JMS folder, select Destinations.

4. In the JMS Queue Destinations area, click Add.

5. In the text field, enter jms/ScheduleQueue.

6. Click OK.

7. If you wish, you can verify that the queue was created:

   ```
   j2eeadmin -listJmsDestination
   ```

9.3.3   Starting the Cloudscape Database Server

The Cloudscape software is included with the J2EE SDK download bundle. You may also run this example with databases provided by other vendors.

From the command line prompt, run the Cloudscape database server:

```
cloudscape -start
```

9.3.4   Creating the J2EE Application

Create a new J2EE application, called NewHireApp, and store it in the file named NewHireApp.ear. Follow these steps.

1. In the deploytool, select the File menu.

2. From the File menu, choose New → Application.

3. Click Browse next to the Application File Name field, and use the file chooser to locate the directory client_mdb_ent.

4. In the File Name field, enter NewHireApp.

5. Click New Application.

6. Click OK.

A diamond icon labeled NewHireApp appears in the tree view on the left side of the deploytool window. The full path name of NewHireApp.ear appears in the General tabbed pane on the right side.

9.3.5   Packaging the Application Client

In this section, you will run the New Application Client Wizard of the deploytool to package the application client. To start the New Application Client Wizard, follow these steps.

1. In the tree view, select NewHireApp.

2. From the File menu, choose New → Application Client. The wizard displays a series of dialog boxes.

9.3.5.1 Introduction Dialog Box

Click Next.

9.3.5.2 JAR File Contents Dialog Box

1. In the combo box labeled Create Archive Within Application, select `NewHireApp`.

2. Click the Edit button next to the Contents text area.

3. In the dialog box Edit Contents of <Application Client>, choose the `client_mdb_ent` directory. If the directory is not already in the Starting Directory field, type it in the field, or locate it by browsing through the Available Files tree.

4. Select `HumanResourceClient.class` and `HumanResourceClient$HRListener.class` from the Available Files tree area and click Add.

5. Click OK.

6. Click Next.

9.3.5.3 General Dialog Box

1. In the Application Client combo box, select `HumanResourceClient` in the Main Class field, and enter `HumanResourceClient` in the Display Name field.

2. In the Callback Handler Class combo box, verify that container-managed authentication is selected.

3. Click Next.

9.3.5.4 Environment Entries Dialog Box

Click Next.

9.3.5.5 Enterprise Bean References Dialog Box

Click Next.

9.3.5.6 Resource References Dialog Box

In this dialog box, you associate the JNDI API context names for the connection factories in the `HumanResourceClient.java` source file with the names of the `TopicConnectionFactory` and the `QueueConnectionFactory`. You also specify container authentication for the connection factory resources, defining the user name and the password that the user must enter in order to be able to create a connection. Follow these steps.

1. Click Add.

2. In the Coded Name field, enter `jms/TopicConnectionFactory`—the logical name referenced by `HumanResourceClient`.

3. In the Type field, select `javax.jms.TopicConnectionFactory`.

4. In the Authentication field, select Container.

5. In the Sharable field, make sure that the checkbox is selected. This allows the container to optimize connections.

6. In the JNDI Name field, enter `jms/TopicConnectionFactory`.

7. In the User Name field, enter `j2ee`.

8. In the Password field, enter `j2ee`.

9. Click Add.

10. In the Coded Name field, enter `jms/QueueConnectionFactory`—the logical name referenced by `HumanResourceClient`.

11. In the Type field, select `javax.jms.QueueConnectionFactory`.

12. In the Authentication field, select Container.

13. In the Sharable field, make sure that the checkbox is selected.

14. In the JNDI Name field, enter `jms/QueueConnectionFactory`.

15. In the User Name field, enter `j2ee`. (If the user name and the password appear to be filled in already, make sure that you follow the instructions at the end of Section 9.3.5.8 after you exit the Wizard.)

16. In the Password field, enter `j2ee`.

17. Click Next.

9.3.5.7   JMS Destination References Dialog Box

In this dialog box, you associate the JNDI API context name for the topic in the `HumanResourceClient.java` source file with the name of the default topic. You do not specify the queue, because it is a temporary queue created programmatically rather than administratively and does not have to be specified in the deployment descriptor. Follow these steps.

1. Click Add.

2. In the Coded Name field, enter `jms/NewHireTopic`—the logical name for the publisher topic referenced by `HumanResourceClient`.

3. In the Type field, select `javax.jms.Topic`.

4. In the JNDI Name field, enter `jms/Topic` (the default topic).

5. Click Next.

9.3.5.8   Review Settings Dialog Box

1. Check the settings for the deployment descriptor.

2. Click Finish.

    After you exit the Wizard, do the following.

1. Select the `HumanResourceClient` node in the tree.

2. Select the Resource Refs tabbed pane.

3. Select the second entry in the table, `jms/QueueConnectionFactory`.

4. See whether the User Name and Password fields are filled in. If they are blank, enter `j2ee` in each field.

5. Choose Save from the File menu to save the application.

9.3.6   Packaging the Equipment Message-Driven Bean

In this section, you will run the New Enterprise Bean Wizard of the deploytool to package the first message-driven bean. To start the New Enterprise Bean Wizard, follow these steps.

1. In the tree view, select `NewHireApp`.

2. From the File menu, choose New → Enterprise Bean. The wizard displays a series of dialog boxes.

9.3.6.1   Introduction Dialog Box

Click Next.

9.3.6.2   EJB JAR Dialog Box

1. In the combo box labeled JAR File Location, verify that Create New JAR File in Application and `NewHireApp` are selected.

2. In the JAR Display Name field, verify that the name is `Ejb1`, the default display name. Representing the enterprise bean JAR file that contains the bean, this name will be displayed in the tree view.

3. Click the Edit button next to the Contents text area.

4. In the dialog box Edit Contents of Ejb1, choose the `client_mdb_ent` directory. If the directory is not already in the Starting Directory field, type it in the field, or locate it by browsing through the Available Files tree.

5. Select the `ReserveEquipmentMsgBean.class` file from the Available Files tree area and click Add.

6. Click OK.

7. Click Next.

9.3.6.3   General Dialog Box

1. In the Bean Type combo box, select the Message-Driven radio button.

2. Under Enterprise Bean Class, select `ReserveEquipmentMsgBean`.

3. In the Enterprise Bean Name field, enter `EquipmentMDB`.

4. Click Next.

9.3.6.4   Transaction Management Dialog Box

1. Select the Container-Managed radio button.

2. In the Transaction Attribute field opposite the onMessage method, verify that Required is selected.

3. Click Next.

9.3.6.5   Message-Driven Bean Settings Dialog Box

1. In the Destination Type combo box, select Topic.

2. In the Destination field, select jms/Topic.

3. In the Connection Factory field, select jms/TopicConnectionFactory.

4. Click Next.

9.3.6.6   Environment Entries Dialog Box

Click Next.

9.3.6.7   Enterprise Bean References Dialog Box

1. Click Add.

2. In the Coded Name column, enter ejb/MyEjbReference.

3. In the Type column, select Entity.

4. In the Interfaces column, select Local.

5. In the Home Interface column, enter SetupOfficeLocalHome.

6. In the Local/Remote Interface column, enter SetupOffice.

7. In the Deployment Settings combo box, select Enterprise Bean Name. In the Enterprise Bean Name field, enter SetupOfficeEJB.

8. Click Finish. You do not need to enter anything in the other dialog boxes.

9.3.7 Packaging the Office Message-Driven Bean

In this section, you will run the New Enterprise Bean Wizard of the deploytool to package the second message-driven bean. To start the New Enterprise Bean Wizard, follow these steps.

1. In the tree view, select `NewHireApp`.

2. From the File menu, choose New → Enterprise Bean.

9.3.7.1 Introduction Dialog Box

Click Next.

9.3.7.2 EJB JAR Dialog Box

1. In the combo box labeled JAR File Location, select Add to Existing JAR File and select Ejb1 (NewHireApp).

2. Click the Edit button next to the Contents text area.

3. In the dialog box Edit Contents of Ejb1, choose the directory `client_mdb_ent`. If the directory is not already in the Starting Directory field, type it in the field, or locate it by browsing through the Available Files tree.

4. Select the `ReserveOfficeMsgBean.class` file from the Available Files tree area and click Add.

5. Click OK.

6. Click Next.

9.3.7.3 General Dialog Box

1. In the Bean Type combo box, select the Message-Driven radio button.

2. Under Enterprise Bean Class, select `ReserveOfficeMsgBean`. The combo boxes for the local and remote interfaces are grayed out.

3. In the Enterprise Bean Name field, enter `OfficeMDB`. This name will represent the message-driven bean in the tree view.

4. Click Next.

9.3.7.4   Transaction Management Dialog Box

1. Select the Container-Managed radio button.

2. In the Transaction Attribute field opposite the `onMessage` method, verify that Required is selected.

3. Click Next.

9.3.7.5   Message-Driven Bean Settings Dialog Box

1. In the Destination Type combo box, select Topic.

2. In the Destination field, select `jms/Topic`.

3. In the Connection Factory field, select `jms/TopicConnectionFactory`.

4. Click Next.

9.3.7.6   Environment Entries Dialog Box

Click Next.

9.3.7.7   Enterprise Bean References Dialog Box

1. Click Add.

2. In the Coded Name column, enter `ejb/MyEjbReference`.

3. In the Type column, select Entity.

4. In the Interfaces column, select Local.

5. In the Home Interface column, enter `SetupOfficeLocalHome`.

6. In the Local/Remote Interface column, enter `SetupOffice`.

7. In the Deployment Settings combo box, select Enterprise Bean Name. In the Enterprise Bean Name field, enter `SetupOfficeEJB`.

8. Click Finish. You do not need to enter anything in the other dialog boxes.

9.3.8 Packaging the Schedule Message-Driven Bean

In this section, you will run the New Enterprise Bean Wizard of the deploytool to package the third message-driven bean. To start the New Enterprise Bean Wizard, follow these steps.

1. In the tree view, select NewHireApp.

2. From the File menu, choose New → Enterprise Bean.

9.3.8.1 Introduction Dialog Box

Click Next.

9.3.8.2 EJB JAR Dialog Box

1. In the combo box labeled JAR File Location, select Add to Existing JAR File and select Ejb1 (NewHireApp).

2. Click the Edit button next to the Contents text area.

3. In the dialog box Edit Contents of Ejb1, choose the directory client_mdb_ent. If the directory is not already in the Starting Directory field, type it in the field, or locate it by browsing through the Available Files tree.

4. Select the ScheduleMsgBean.class file from the Available Files tree area and click Add.

5. Click OK.

6. Click Next.

9.3.8.3 General Dialog Box

1. In the Bean Type combo box, select the Message-Driven radio button.

2. Under Enterprise Bean Class, select ScheduleMsgBean. The combo boxes for the local and remote interfaces are grayed out.

3. In the Enterprise Bean Name field, enter ScheduleMDB. This name will represent the message-driven bean in the tree view.

4. Click Next.

9.3.8.4   Transaction Management Dialog Box

1. Select the Container-Managed radio button.

2. In the Transaction Attribute field opposite the `onMessage` method, verify that Required is selected.

3. Click Next.

9.3.8.5   Message-Driven Bean Settings Dialog Box

1. In the Destination Type combo box, select Queue.

2. In the Destination field, select `jms/ScheduleQueue`.

3. In the Connection Factory field, select `jms/QueueConnectionFactory`.

4. Click Next.

9.3.8.6   Environment Entries Dialog Box

Click Next.

9.3.8.7   Enterprise Bean References Dialog Box

1. Click Add.

2. In the Coded Name column, enter `ejb/CompositeEjbReference`.

3. In the Type column, select Entity.

4. In the Interfaces column, select Local.

5. In the Home Interface column, enter `SetupOfficeLocalHome`.

6. In the Local/Remote Interface column, enter `SetupOffice`.

7. In the Deployment Settings combo box, select Enterprise Bean Name. In the Enterprise Bean Name field, enter `SetupOfficeEJB`.

8. Click Finish. You do not need to enter anything in the other dialog boxes.

9.3.9   Packaging the Entity Bean

In this section, you will run the New Enterprise Bean Wizard of the deploytool to package the entity bean. To start the New Enterprise Bean Wizard, follow these steps.

1. In the tree view, select `NewHireApp`.

2. From the File menu, choose New → Enterprise Bean.

9.3.9.1   Introduction Dialog Box

Click Next.

9.3.9.2   EJB JAR Dialog Box

1. In the combo box labeled JAR File Location, select Add to Existing JAR File and select Ejb1 (NewHireApp).

2. Click the Edit button next to the Contents text area.

3. In the dialog box Edit Contents of Ejb1, choose the directory `client_mdb_ent`. If the directory is not already in the Starting Directory field, type it in the field, or locate it by browsing through the Available Files tree.

4. Select the following files from the Available Files tree area and click Add: `SetupOfficeLocalHome.class`, `SetupOffice.class`, and `SetupOffice-Bean.class`.

5. Click OK.

6. Click Next.

9.3.9.3   General Dialog Box

1. In the Bean Type combo box, select the Entity radio button.

2. In the Enterprise Bean Class combo box, select `SetupOfficeBean`.

3. In the Enterprise Bean Name field, enter `SetupOfficeEJB`.

4. In the Local Interfaces combo box, select `SetupOfficeLocalHome` for Local Home Interface and `SetupOffice` for Local Interface.

5. Click Next.

9.3.9.4   Entity Settings Dialog Box

1. Select the radio button labeled Container managed persistence (2.0).

2. Select the checkboxes next to all six fields in the Fields To Be Persisted area: `employeeId`, `employeeName`, `equipmentList`, `officeNumber`, `serialized-ReplyDestination`, and `replyCorrelationMsgId`.

3. In the Abstract Schema Name field, enter `SetupOfficeSchema`.

4. In the Primary Key Class field, enter `java.lang.String`.

5. In the Primary Key Field Name field, select `employeeId`.

6. Click Next.

9.3.9.5   Transaction Management Dialog Box

1. Select the Container-Managed radio button.

2. For all methods, verify that Required is set in the Transaction Attribute column opposite the Local and Local Home radio buttons.

3. Click Next.

9.3.9.6   Environment Entries Dialog Box

Click Next.

9.3.9.7   Enterprise Bean References Dialog Box

Click Next.

9.3.9.8   Resource References Dialog Box

In this dialog box, you specify the connection factory for the Schedule queue and for the reply. Follow these steps.

1. Click Add.

2. In the Coded Name field, enter `jms/QueueConnectionFactory`.

3. In the Type field, select `javax.jms.QueueConnectionFactory`.

4. In the Authentication field, select Container.

5. In the Sharable field, make sure that the checkbox is selected.

6. In the JNDI Name field, enter `jms/QueueConnectionFactory`.

7. In the User Name field, enter `j2ee`.

8. In the Password field, enter `j2ee`.

9. Click Next.

9.3.9.9 Resource Environment References Dialog Box

1. Click Add.

2. In the Coded Name field, enter `jms/ScheduleQueue`—the logical name referenced by `SetupOfficeBean`.

3. In the Type field, select `javax.jms.Queue`.

4. In the JNDI Name field, enter `jms/ScheduleQueue`.

5. Click Next.

9.3.9.10 Security Dialog Box

Use the default Security Identity setting for a session or entity bean, Use Caller ID. Click Next.

9.3.9.11 Review Settings Dialog Box

1. Check the settings for the deployment descriptor.

2. Click Finish.

9.3.10   Specifying the Entity Bean Deployment Settings

Generate the SQL for the entity bean and create the table. Follow these steps.

1. In the tree view, select the `SetupOfficeEJB` entity bean.

2. Select the Entity tabbed pane.

3. Click Deployment Settings.

4. In the Deployment Settings dialog box, perform these steps.

    a. In the Database Table combo box, select the two checkboxes labeled Create table on deploy and Delete table on undeploy.

    b. Click Database Settings.

    c. In the Deployment Settings dialog box that appears, enter jdbc/ Cloudscape in the Database JNDI Name field. Do not enter a user name or a password.

    d. Click OK.

    e. Click Generate Default SQL.

    f. When the SQL Generation Complete dialog appears, click OK.

    g. Click OK in the dialog box.

5. Choose Save from the File menu to save the application.

9.3.11 Specifying the JNDI Names

Verify that the JNDI names are correct, and add one for the SetupOfficeEJB component. Follow these steps.

1. In the tree view, select the NewHireApp application.

2. Select the JNDI Names tabbed pane.

3. Make sure that the JNDI names appear as shown in Tables 9.1 and 9.2. You will need to enter SetupOfficeEJB as the JNDI name for the SetupOfficeEJB component.

Table 9.1: Application Pane

Component Type	Component	JNDI Name
EJB	SetupOfficeEJB	SetupOfficeEJB
EJB	EquipmentMDB	jms/Topic
EJB	OfficeMDB	jms/Topic
EJB	ScheduleMDB	jms/ScheduleQueue

Table 9.2: References Pane

Ref. Type	Referenced By	Reference Name	JNDI Name
Resource	SetupOfficeEJB	jms/Queue-ConnectionFactory	jms/Queue-ConnectionFactory
Env Resource	SetupOfficeEJB	jms/ScheduleQueue	jms/ScheduleQueue
Resource	HumanResource-Client	jms/Topic-ConnectionFactory	jms/Topic-ConnectionFactory
Resource	HumanResource-Client	jms/Queue-ConnectionFactory	jms/Queue-ConnectionFactory
Env Resource	HumanResource-Client	jms/NewHireTopic	jms/Topic
Resource	EJB1[CMP]		jdbc/Cloudscape

9.4 Deploying and Running the Application

Deploying and running the application involve several steps:

1. Adding the server, if necessary

2. Deploying the application

3. Running the client

4. Undeploying the application

5. Removing the application and stopping the server

9.4.1 Adding the Server

Before you can deploy the application, you must make available to the deploytool the J2EE server you started in Section 9.3.1 on page 156. Because you started the J2EE server before you started the deploytool, the server, named localhost, probably appears in the tree under Servers. If it does not, do the following.

1. From the File menu, choose Add Server.

2. In the Add Server dialog box, enter localhost in the Server Name field.

3. Click OK. A localhost node appears under Servers in the tree view.

9.4.2   Deploying the Application

To deploy the application, perform the following steps.

1. From the File menu, choose Save to save the application.

2. From the Tools menu, choose Deploy.

3. In the Introduction dialog box, verify that the Object to Deploy selection is
   NewHireApp and that the Target Server selection is localhost.

4. Click Next.

5. In the JNDI Names dialog box, verify that the JNDI names are correct.

6. Click Next.

7. Click Finish.

8. In the Deployment Progress dialog box, click OK when the "Deployment of
   NewHireApp is complete" message appears.

9. In the tree view, expand Servers and select localhost. Verify that
   NewHireApp is deployed.

9.4.3   Running the Client

To run the client, perform the following steps.

1. At the command line prompt, enter the following:

   ```
   runclient -client NewHireApp.ear -name HumanResourceClient -textauth
   ```

2. At the login prompts, enter j2ee as the user name and j2ee as the password.

3. Click OK.

The client program runs in the command window, and output from the application
appears in the window in which you started the J2EE server.

9.4.4 Undeploying the Application

To undeploy the J2EE application, follow these steps.

1. In the tree view, select `localhost`.

2. Select `NewHireApp` in the Deployed Objects area.

3. Click Undeploy.

4. Answer Yes in the confirmation dialog.

9.4.5 Removing the Application and Stopping the Server

To remove the application from the deploytool, follow these steps.

1. Select `NewHireApp` in the tree view.

2. Select Close from the File menu.

To delete the queue you created, enter the following at the command line prompt:

```
j2eeadmin -removeJmsDestination jms/ScheduleQueue
```

To stop the J2EE server, use the following command:

```
j2ee -stop
```

To stop the Cloudscape database server, use the following command:

```
cloudscape -stop
```

To exit the deploytool, choose Exit from the File menu.

An Application Example that Uses Two J2EE Servers

THIS chapter explains how to write, compile, package, deploy, and run a pair of J2EE applications that use the JMS API and run on two J2EE servers. A common practice is to deploy different components of an enterprise application on different systems within a company, and this example illustrates on a small scale how to do this for an application that uses the JMS API.

The applications use the following components:

- An application client that uses two connection factories—one ordinary one and one that is configured to communicate with the remote server—to create two publishers and two subscribers and to publish and to consume messages

- A message-driven bean that is deployed twice—once on the local server and once on the remote one—to process the messages and to send replies

In this chapter, the term *local server* means the server on which the application client is deployed. The term *remote server* means the server on which only the message-driven bean is deployed.

Another possible situation is that an application deployed on a J2EE server must be accessed from another system on which no J2EE server is running. The last section of this chapter discusses how to handle this situation.

The chapter covers the following topics:

- An overview of the applications

- Writing and compiling the application components

- Creating and packaging the applications

- Deploying and running the applications

- Accessing a J2EE application from a remote system that is not running a J2EE server

If you downloaded the tutorial examples as described in the preface, you will find the source code files for this chapter in `jms_tutorial/examples/multi_server` (on UNIX systems) or `jms_tutorial\examples\multi_server` (on Microsoft Windows systems). The directory `ear_files` in the `examples` directory contains two built applications, called `SampleMultiApp.ear` and `SampleReplyBeanApp.ear`. If you run into difficulty at any time, you can open one of these files in the deploytool and compare that file to your own version.

10.1   Overview of the Applications

This pair of applications is somewhat similar to the application in Chapter 7 in that the only components are a client and a message-driven bean. However, the applications here use these components in more complex ways. One application consists of the application client. The other application contains only the message-driven bean and is deployed twice, once on each server.

The basic steps of the applications are as follows.

1. The administrator starts two J2EE servers.

2. On the local server, the administrator creates a connection factory to communicate with the remote server.

3. The application client uses two connection factories—a preconfigured one and the one just created—to create two connections, sessions, publishers, and subscribers. Each publisher publishes five messages.

4. The local and the remote message-driven beans each receive five messages and send replies.

5. The client's message listener consumes the replies.

Figure 10.1 illustrates the structure of this application.

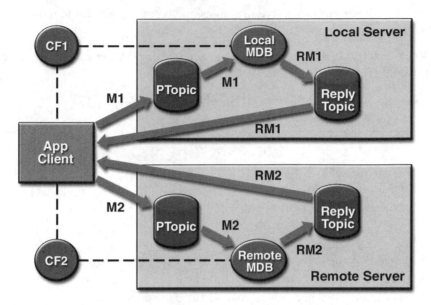

Figure 10.1 A J2EE Two-Server Application

10.2 Writing and Compiling the Application Components

Writing and compiling the components of the applications involve

- Coding the application client
- Coding the message-driven bean
- Compiling the source files

10.2.1 Coding the Application Client: `MultiAppServerRequester.java`

The application client class, `MultiAppServerRequester.java`, does the following.

1. It uses the Java Naming and Directory Interface (JNDI) API naming context `java:comp/env` to look up two connection factories and a topic.

2. For each connection factory, it creates a connection, a publisher session, a publisher, a subscriber session, a subscriber, and a temporary topic for replies.

3. Each subscriber sets its message listener, `ReplyListener`, and starts the connection.

4. Each publisher publishes five messages and creates a list of the messages the listener should expect.

5. When each reply arrives, the message listener displays its contents and removes it from the list of expected messages.

6. When all the messages have arrived, the client exits.

```java
import javax.jms.*;
import javax.naming.*;
import java.util.*;

/**
 * The MultiAppServerRequester class is the client program for
 * this J2EE application.  It publishes a message to two
 * different JMS providers and waits for a reply.
 */
public class MultiAppServerRequester {
    static Object      waitUntilDone = new Object();
    static SortedSet   outstandingRequests1 =
        Collections.synchronizedSortedSet(new TreeSet());
    static SortedSet   outstandingRequests2 =
        Collections.synchronizedSortedSet(new TreeSet());

    public static void main (String[] args) {
        InitialContext          ic = null;
        TopicConnectionFactory  tcf1 = null;  // App Server 1
        TopicConnectionFactory  tcf2 = null;  // App Server 2
        TopicConnection         tc1 = null;
        TopicConnection         tc2 = null;
        TopicSession            pubSession1 = null;
        TopicSession            pubSession2 = null;
        TopicPublisher          topicPublisher1 = null;
        TopicPublisher          topicPublisher2 = null;
        Topic                   pTopic = null;
        TemporaryTopic          replyTopic1 = null;
        TemporaryTopic          replyTopic2 = null;
        TopicSession            subSession1 = null;
        TopicSession            subSession2 = null;
```

```
TopicSubscriber          topicSubscriber1 = null;
TopicSubscriber          topicSubscriber2 = null;
TextMessage              message = null;

/*
 * Create a JNDI API InitialContext object.
 */
try {
    ic = new InitialContext();
} catch (NamingException e) {
    System.err.println("Could not create JNDI API " +
        "context: " + e.toString());
    e.printStackTrace();
    System.exit(1);
}

/*
 * Look up connection factories and topic.  If any do not
 * exist, exit.
 */
try {
    tcf1 = (TopicConnectionFactory)
  ic.lookup("java:comp/env/jms/TopicConnectionFactory1");
    tcf2 = (TopicConnectionFactory)
  ic.lookup("java:comp/env/jms/TopicConnectionFactory2");
  pTopic = (Topic) ic.lookup("java:comp/env/jms/PTopic");
} catch (NamingException e) {
    System.err.println("JNDI API lookup failed: " +
        e.toString());
    e.printStackTrace();
    System.exit(1);
}

try {
    // Create two TopicConnections.
    tc1 = tcf1.createTopicConnection();
    tc2 = tcf2.createTopicConnection();
```

```
// Create TopicSessions for publishers.
pubSession1 =
    tc1.createTopicSession(false,
        Session.AUTO_ACKNOWLEDGE);
pubSession2 =
    tc2.createTopicSession(false,
        Session.AUTO_ACKNOWLEDGE);

// Create temporary topics for replies.
replyTopic1 = pubSession1.createTemporaryTopic();
replyTopic2 = pubSession2.createTemporaryTopic();

// Create TopicSessions for subscribers.
subSession1 =
    tc1.createTopicSession(false,
        Session.AUTO_ACKNOWLEDGE);
subSession2 =
    tc2.createTopicSession(false,
        Session.AUTO_ACKNOWLEDGE);

/*
 * Create subscribers, set message listeners, and
 * start connections.
 */
topicSubscriber1 =
    subSession1.createSubscriber(replyTopic1);
topicSubscriber2 =
    subSession2.createSubscriber(replyTopic2);
topicSubscriber1.setMessageListener(new
    ReplyListener(outstandingRequests1));
topicSubscriber2.setMessageListener(new
    ReplyListener(outstandingRequests2));
tc1.start();
tc2.start();

// Create publishers.
topicPublisher1 =
    pubSession1.createPublisher(pTopic);
```

```
topicPublisher2 =
    pubSession2.createPublisher(pTopic);

/*
 * Create and send two sets of messages, one set to
 * each app server, at 1.5-second intervals.  For
 * each message, set the JMSReplyTo message header to
 * a reply topic, and set an id property.  Add the
 * message ID to the list of outstanding requests for
 * the message listener.
 */
message = pubSession1.createTextMessage();
int id = 1;
for (int i = 0; i < 5; i++) {
    message.setJMSReplyTo(replyTopic1);
    message.setIntProperty("id", id);
    message.setText("text: id=" + id +
        " to local app server");
    topicPublisher1.publish(message);
    System.out.println("Published message: " +
        message.getText());
  outstandingRequests1.add(message.getJMSMessageID());
    id++;
    Thread.sleep(1500);
    message.setJMSReplyTo(replyTopic2);
    message.setIntProperty("id", id);
    message.setText("text: id=" + id +
        " to remote app server");
    try {
        topicPublisher2.publish(message);
    System.out.println("Published message: " +
        message.getText());
  outstandingRequests2.add(message.getJMSMessageID());
    } catch (Exception e) {
        System.err.println("Exception: Caught " +
            "failed publish to " +
            "topicConnectionFactory2");
        e.printStackTrace();
    }
```

```java
            id++;
            Thread.sleep(1500);
        }


        /*
         * Wait for replies.
         */
        System.out.println("Waiting for " +
            outstandingRequests1.size() + " message(s) " +
            "from local app server");
        System.out.println("Waiting for " +
            outstandingRequests2.size() + " message(s) " +
            "from remote app server");
        while (outstandingRequests1.size() > 0 ||
                outstandingRequests2.size() > 0 ) {
            synchronized (waitUntilDone) {
                waitUntilDone.wait();
            }
        }
        System.out.println("Finished");

    } catch (Exception e) {
        System.err.println("Exception occurred: " +
            e.toString());
        e.printStackTrace();
    } finally {
        System.out.println("Closing connection 1");
        if (tc1 != null) {
            try {
                tc1.close();
            } catch (Exception e) {
                System.err.println("Error closing " +
                    "connection 1: " + e.toString());
            }
        }
        System.out.println("Closing connection 2");
        if (tc2 != null) {
            try {
                tc2.close();
```

```java
            } catch (Exception e) {
                System.err.println("Error closing " +
                    "connection 2: " + e.toString());
            }
        }
        System.exit(0);
    }
}

/**
 * The ReplyListener class is instantiated with a set of
 * outstanding requests.
 */
static class ReplyListener implements MessageListener {
    SortedSet outstandingRequests = null;

    /**
     * Constructor for ReplyListener class.
     *
     * @param outstandingRequests    set of outstanding
     *                               requests
     */
    ReplyListener(SortedSet outstandingRequests) {
        this.outstandingRequests = outstandingRequests;
    }

    /**
     * onMessage method, which displays the contents of the
     * id property and text and uses the JMSCorrelationID to
     * remove from the list of outstanding requests the
     * message to which this message is a reply.  If this is
     * the last message, it notifies the client.
     *
     * @param message     the incoming message
     */
    public void onMessage(Message message) {
        TextMessage  tmsg = (TextMessage) message;
        String       txt = null;
```

```
int          id = 0;
String       correlationID = null;

try {
    id = tmsg.getIntProperty("id");
    txt = tmsg.getText();
    correlationID = tmsg.getJMSCorrelationID();
} catch (JMSException e) {
    System.err.println("ReplyListener.onMessage: " +
        "JMSException: " + e.toString());
}
System.out.println("ReplyListener: Received " +
    "message: id=" + id + ", text=" + txt);
outstandingRequests.remove(correlationID);

if (outstandingRequests.size() == 0) {
    synchronized(waitUntilDone) {
        waitUntilDone.notify();
    }
} else {
    System.out.println("ReplyListener: Waiting " +
        "for " + outstandingRequests.size() +
        " message(s)");
}
            }
        }
    }
}
```

Code Example 10.1 `MultiAppServerRequester.java`

10.2.2   Coding the Message-Driven Bean: `ReplyMsgBean.java`

The `onMessage` method of the message-driven bean class, `ReplyMsgBean.java`, does the following:

1. Casts the incoming message to a `TextMessage` and displays the text

2. Creates a connection, session, and publisher for the reply message

3. Publishes the message to the reply topic

4. Closes the connection

```java
import javax.ejb.*;
import javax.naming.*;
import javax.jms.*;

/**
 * The ReplyMsgBean class is a message-driven bean. It
 * implements the javax.ejb.MessageDrivenBean and
 * javax.jms.MessageListener interfaces. It is defined as public
 * (but not final or abstract).  It defines a constructor and the
 * methods ejbCreate, onMessage, setMessageDrivenContext, and
 * ejbRemove.
 */
public class ReplyMsgBean implements MessageDrivenBean,
        MessageListener {

    private transient MessageDrivenContext mdc = null;
    private transient TopicConnectionFactory tcf = null;

    /**
     * Constructor, which is public and takes no arguments.
     */
    public ReplyMsgBean() {
        System.out.println("In " +
            "ReplyMsgBean.ReplyMsgBean()");
    }

    /**
     * setMessageDrivenContext method, declared as public (but
     * not final or static), with a return type of void, and
     * with one argument of type javax.ejb.MessageDrivenContext.
     *
     * @param mdc    the context to set
     */
```

```
public void setMessageDrivenContext(MessageDrivenContext mdc)
{
    System.out.println("In " +
        "ReplyMsgBean.setMessageDrivenContext()");
    this.mdc = mdc;
}


/**
 * ejbCreate method, declared as public (but not final or
 * static), with a return type of void, and with no
 * arguments. It looks up the topic connection factory.
 */
public void ejbCreate() {
    System.out.println("In ReplyMsgBean.ejbCreate()");
    try {
        Context initial = new InitialContext();
        tcf = (TopicConnectionFactory)
  initial.lookup("java:comp/env/jms/TopicConnectionFactory");
    } catch (Exception ex) {
        System.err.println("ReplyMsgBean.ejbCreate: " +
            "Exception: " + ex.toString());
    }
}


/**
 * onMessage method, declared as public (but not final or
 * static), with a return type of void, and with one argument
 * of type javax.jms.Message.
 *
 * It displays the contents of the message and creates a
 * connection, session, and publisher for the reply, using
 * the JMSReplyTo field of the incoming message as the
 * destination.  It creates and publishes a reply message,
 * setting the JMSCorrelationID header field to the message
 * ID of the incoming message, and the id property to that of
 * the incoming message.  It then closes the topic
 * connection.
 *
 * @param inMessagethe incoming message
```

```java
    */
    public void onMessage(Message inMessage) {
        TextMessage msg = null;
        TopicConnection tc = null;
        TopicSession ts = null;
        TopicPublisher tp = null;
        TextMessage replyMsg = null;

        try {
            if (inMessage instanceof TextMessage) {
                msg = (TextMessage) inMessage;
                System.out.println("  ReplyMsgBean: " +
                    "Received message: " + msg.getText());
                tc = tcf.createTopicConnection();
                ts = tc.createTopicSession(true, 0);

                tp =
                  ts.createPublisher((Topic)msg.getJMSReplyTo());
                replyMsg =
                    ts.createTextMessage("ReplyMsgBean " +
                        "processed message: " + msg.getText());
              replyMsg.setJMSCorrelationID(msg.getJMSMessageID());
                replyMsg.setIntProperty("id",
                    msg.getIntProperty("id"));
                tp.publish(replyMsg);
                tc.close();
            } else {
                System.err.println("Message of wrong type: " +
                    inMessage.getClass().getName());
            }
        } catch (JMSException e) {
            System.err.println("ReplyMsgBean.onMessage: " +
                "JMSException: " + e.toString());
        } catch (Throwable te) {
            System.err.println("ReplyMsgBean.onMessage: " +
                "Exception: " + te.toString());
        }
    }
```

```
/**
 * ejbRemove method, declared as public (but not final or
 * static), with a return type of void, and with no
 * arguments.
 */
public void ejbRemove() {
    System.out.println("In ReplyMsgBean.ejbRemove()");
}
}
```

Code Example 10.2 `ReplyMsgBean.java`

10.2.3 Compiling the Source Files

To compile the files in the application, go to the directory `multi_server` and do the following.

1. Make sure that you have set the environment variables shown in Table 4.1 on page 28: `JAVA_HOME`, `J2EE_HOME`, `CLASSPATH`, and `PATH`.

2. At a command line prompt, compile the source files:

```
javac MultiAppServerRequester.java
javac ReplyMsgBean.java
```

10.3 Creating and Packaging the Application

Creating and packaging this application involve several steps:

1. Starting the J2EE servers and the deploytool

2. Creating a connection factory

3. Creating the first J2EE application

4. Packaging the application client

5. Creating the second J2EE application

6. Packaging the message-driven bean

7. Checking the JNDI names

10.3.1   Starting the J2EE Servers and the Deploytool

Before you can create and package the application, you must start the local and remote J2EE servers and the deploytool. Follow these steps.

1. At a command line prompt on the local system, start the J2EE server:

   ```
   j2ee -verbose
   ```

   Wait until the server displays the message "J2EE server startup complete."
   (To stop the server, type `j2ee -stop`.)

2. At another command line prompt on the local system, start the deploytool:

   ```
   deploytool
   ```

   (To access the tool's context-sensitive help, press F1.)

3. At a command line prompt on the remote system, start the J2EE server:

   ```
   j2ee -verbose
   ```

10.3.2   Creating a Connection Factory

For this example, you create on the local system a connection factory that allows the client to communicate with the remote server. If you downloaded the tutorial examples as described in the preface, you will find in the `multi_server` directory a Microsoft Windows script called `setup.bat` and a UNIX script called `setup.sh`. You can use one of these scripts to create the connection factory on the local system. The command in `setup.bat` looks like this:

```
call j2eeadmin -addJmsFactory jms/RemoteTCF topic -props
url=corbaname:iiop:%1:1050#%1
```

The UNIX command in `setup.sh` looks like this:

```
#!/bin/sh -x
j2eeadmin -addJmsFactory jms/RemoteTCF topic -props
url=corbaname:iiop:$1:1050#$1
```

1. To run the script, specify the name of the remote server as an argument. Use the host name that is visible to you on your network; do not use an IP address. For example, if the remote system is named `mars`, enter the following:

```
setup.bat mars
```

or

```
setup.sh mars
```

2. Verify that the connection factory was created:

```
j2eeadmin -listJmsFactory
```

One line of the output looks like this (it appears on one line):

```
< JMS Cnx Factory : jms/RemoteTCF , Topic ,
[ url=corbaname:iiop:mars:1050#mars ] >
```

10.3.3   Creating the First J2EE Application

Create a new J2EE application called `MultiApp` and store it in the file named `MultiApp.ear`. Follow these steps.

1. In the deploytool, select the File menu.

2. From the File menu, choose New → Application.

3. Click Browse next to the Application File Name field, and use the file chooser to locate the directory `multi_server`.

4. In the File Name field, enter `MultiApp`.

5. Click New Application.

6. Click OK.

A diamond icon labeled `MultiApp` appears in the tree view on the left side of the deploytool window. The full path name of `MultiApp.ear` appears in the General tabbed pane on the right side.

10.3.4   Packaging the Application Client

In this section, you will run the New Application Client Wizard of the deploytool to package the application client. To start the New Application Client Wizard, follow these steps.

1. In the tree view, select `MultiApp`.

2. From the File menu, choose New → Application Client. The wizard displays a series of dialog boxes.

10.3.4.1 Introduction Dialog Box

Click Next.

10.3.4.2 JAR File Contents Dialog Box

1. In the combo box labeled Create Archive Within Application, select `MultiApp`.

2. Click the Edit button next to the Contents text area.

3. In the dialog box Edit Contents of <Application Client>, choose the `multi_server` directory. If the directory is not already in the Starting Directory field, type it in the field, or locate it by browsing through the Available Files tree.

4. Select `MultiAppServerRequester.class` and `MultiAppServerRequester$Re-plyListener.class` from the Available Files tree area and click Add.

5. Click OK.

6. Click Next.

10.3.4.3 General Dialog Box

1. In the Application Client combo box, select `MultiAppServerRequester` in the Main Class field, and enter `MultiAppServerRequester` in the Display Name field.

2. In the Callback Handler Class combo box, verify that container-managed authentication is selected.

3. Click Next.

10.3.4.4 Environment Entries Dialog Box

Click Next.

10.3.4.5 Enterprise Bean References Dialog Box

Click Next.

10.3.4.6 Resource References Dialog Box

In this dialog box, you associate the JNDI API context names for the connection factories in the `MultiAppServerRequester.java` source file with the names of the local and remote connection factories. You also specify container authentication for the connection factory resources, defining the user name and the password that the user must enter in order to be able to create a connection. Follow these steps.

1. Click Add.

2. In the Coded Name field, enter `jms/TopicConnectionFactory1`—the first logical name referenced by `MultiAppServerRequester`.

3. In the Type field, select `javax.jms.TopicConnectionFactory`.

4. In the Authentication field, select Container.

5. In the Sharable field, make sure that the checkbox is selected. This allows the container to optimize connections.

6. In the JNDI Name field, enter `jms/TopicConnectionFactory`.

7. In the User Name field, enter `j2ee`.

8. In the Password field, enter `j2ee`.

9. Click Add.

10. In the Coded Name field, enter `jms/TopicConnectionFactory2`—the other logical name referenced by `MultiAppServerRequester`.

11. In the Type field, select `javax.jms.TopicConnectionFactory`.

12. In the Authentication field, select Container.

13. In the Sharable field, make sure that the checkbox is selected.

14. In the JNDI Name field, enter `jms/RemoteTCF`.

15. In the User Name field, enter `j2ee`. (If the user name and the password appear to be filled in already, make sure that you follow the instructions at the end of Section 10.3.4.8 after you exit the Wizard.)

16. In the Password field, enter `j2ee`.

17. Click Next.

10.3.4.7 JMS Destination References Dialog Box

In this dialog box, you associate the JNDI API context name for the topic in the `MultiAppServerRequester.java` source file with the name of the default topic. The client code also uses a reply topic, but it is a temporary topic created programmatically rather than administratively and does not have to be specified in the deployment descriptor. Follow these steps.

1. Click Add.

2. In the Coded Name field, enter `jms/PTopic`—the logical name for the publisher topic referenced by `MultiAppServerRequester`.

3. In the Type field, select `javax.jms.Topic`.

4. In the JNDI Name field, enter `jms/Topic`—the preconfigured topic.

5. Click Next.

10.3.4.8 Review Settings Dialog Box

1. Check the settings for the deployment descriptor.

2. Click Finish.

After you exit the Wizard, do the following.

1. Select the `MultiAppServerRequester` node in the tree.

2. Select the Resource Refs tabbed pane.

3. Select the second entry in the table, `jms/TopicConnectionFactory2`.

4. If the User Name and the Password fields are blank, enter `j2ee` in each field.

5. Choose Save from the File menu to save the application.

10.3.5 Creating the Second J2EE Application

Create a new J2EE application, called `ReplyBeanApp`, and store it in the file named `ReplyBeanApp.ear`. Follow these steps.

1. In the deploytool, select the File menu.

2. From the File menu, choose New → Application.

3. Click Browse next to the Application File Name field, and use the file chooser to locate the directory `multi_server`.

4. In the File Name field, enter `ReplyBeanApp`.

5. Click New Application.

6. Click OK.

A diamond icon labeled `ReplyBeanApp` appears in the tree view on the left side of the deploytool window. The full path name of `ReplyBeanApp.ear` appears in the General tabbed pane on the right side.

10.3.6 Packaging the Message-Driven Bean

In this section, you will run the New Enterprise Bean Wizard of the deploytool to package the message-driven bean. To start the New Enterprise Bean Wizard, follow these steps.

1. In the tree view, select `ReplyBeanApp`.

2. From the File menu, choose New → Enterprise Bean.

10.3.6.1 Introduction Dialog Box

Click Next.

10.3.6.2 EJB JAR Dialog Box

1. In the combo box labeled JAR File Location, verify that Create New JAR File in Application and `ReplyBeanApp` are selected.

2. In the JAR Display Name field, verify that the name is `Ejb1`, the default display name.

3. Click the Edit button next to the Contents text area.

4. In the dialog box Edit Contents of Ejb1, choose the `multi_server` directory. If the directory is not already in the Starting Directory field, type it in the field, or locate it by browsing through the Available Files tree.

5. Select the `ReplyMsgBean.class` file from the Available Files tree area and click Add.

6. Click OK.

7. Click Next.

10.3.6.3 General Dialog Box

1. In the Bean Type combo box, select the Message-Driven radio button.

2. Under Enterprise Bean Class, select `ReplyMsgBean`. The combo boxes for the local and remote interfaces are grayed out.

3. In the Enterprise Bean Name field, enter `ReplyMDB`. This name will represent the message-driven bean in the tree view.

4. Click Next.

10.3.6.4 Transaction Management Dialog Box

1. Select the Container-Managed radio button.

2. In the Transaction Attribute field opposite the `onMessage` method, verify that Required is selected.

3. Click Next.

10.3.6.5 Message-Driven Bean Settings Dialog Box

1. In the Destination Type combo box, select Topic.

2. In the Destination field, select `jms/Topic`.

3. In the Connection Factory field, select `jms/TopicConnectionFactory`.

10.3.6.6 Environment Entries Dialog Box

Click Next.

10.3.6.7 Enterprise Bean References Dialog Box

Click Next.

10.3.6.8 Resource References Dialog Box

1. Click Add.

2. In the Coded Name field, enter `jms/TopicConnectionFactory`.

3. In the Type field, select `javax.jms.TopicConnectionFactory`.

4. In the Authentication field, select Container.

5. In the JNDI Name field, enter `jms/TopicConnectionFactory`.

6. In the User Name field, enter `j2ee`.

7. In the Password field, enter `j2ee`.

8. Click Finish. You do not need to enter anything in the other dialog boxes.

10.3.7   Checking the JNDI Names

Verify that the JNDI names for the application components are correct. To do so, do the following.

1. In the tree view, select the `MultiApp` application.

2. Select the JNDI Names tabbed pane.

3. Verify that the JNDI names appear as shown in Table 10.1.

Table 10.1: References Pane

Ref. Type	Referenced By	Reference Name	JNDI Name
Resource	MultiAppServer-Requester	jms/Topic-ConnectionFactory1	jms/Topic-ConnectionFactory
Resource	MultiAppServer-Requester	jms/Topic-ConnectionFactory2	jms/RemoteTCF
Env Resource	MultiAppServer-Requester	jms/PTopic	jms/Topic

4. In the tree view, select the `ReplyBeanApp` application.

5. Select the JNDI Names tabbed pane.

6. Verify that the JNDI names appear as shown in Tables 10.2 and 10.3.

Table 10.2: Application Pane

Component Type	Component	JNDI Name
EJB	ReplyMDB	jms/Topic

Table 10.3: References Pane

Ref. Type	Referenced By	Reference Name	JNDI Name
Resource	ReplyMDB	jms/Topic-ConnectionFactory	jms/Topic-ConnectionFactory

10.4   Deploying and Running the Applications

Deploying and running this application involve several steps:

1. Adding the server

2. Deploying the applications

3. Running the client

4. Undeploying the applications

5. Removing the applications and stopping the server

10.4.1   Adding the Server

Before you can deploy the application, you must make available to the deploytool both the J2EE servers you started in Section 10.3.1 on page 189. To add the remote server, follow these steps.

1. From the File menu, choose Add Server.

2. In the Add Server dialog box, enter the name of the remote system in the Server Name field. Use the same name you specified when you ran the `setup` script in Section 10.3.2 on page 189.

3. Click OK.

A node with the name of the remote system appears under `Servers` in the tree view.

Because you started the local J2EE server before you started the deploytool, the server, named `localhost`, probably appears in the tree under `Servers`. If it does not, do the following.

1. From the File menu, choose Add Server.

2. In the Add Server dialog box, enter `localhost` in the Server Name field.

3. Click OK.

The `localhost` node appears under `Servers` in the tree view.

10.4.2 Deploying the Applications

To deploy the `MultiApp` application, perform the following steps.

1. In the tree view, select the `MultiApp` application.

2. From the Tools menu, choose Deploy.

3. In the Introduction dialog box, verify that the Object to Deploy selection is `MultiApp`, and select `localhost` as the Target Server.

4. Click Next.

5. In the JNDI Names dialog box, verify that the JNDI names are correct.

6. Click Next.

7. Click Finish.

8. In the Deployment Progress dialog box, click OK when the "Deployment of MultiApp is complete" message appears.

9. In the tree view, expand `Servers` and select the host name. Verify that `MultiApp` is deployed.

To deploy the `ReplyBeanApp` application on the local server, perform the following steps.

1. In the tree view, select the `ReplyBeanApp` application.

2. From the Tools menu, choose Deploy.

3. In the Introduction dialog box, verify that the Object to Deploy selection is `ReplyBeanApp`, and select the local server as the Target Server.

4. Click Next.

5. In the JNDI Names dialog box, verify that the JNDI names are correct.

6. Click Next.

7. Click Finish.

8. In the Deployment Progress dialog box, click OK when the "Deployment of ReplyBeanApp is complete" message appears.

9. In the tree view, expand `Servers` and select the host name. Verify that `ReplyBeanApp` is deployed.

Repeat steps 1–9 for the remote server, selecting the remote server as the Target Server in step 3.

10.4.3 Running the Client

To run the client, perform the following steps.

1. At a command line prompt on the local system, enter the following on one line:

    ```
    runclient -client MultiApp.ear -name MultiAppServerRequester
    -textauth
    ```

2. At the login prompts, enter j2ee as the user name and j2ee as the password.
3. Click OK.

The client program runs in the command window. Output from the message-driven beans appears on both the local and the remote systems, in the windows in which you started each J2EE server.

10.4.4 Undeploying the Applications

To undeploy the J2EE applications, follow these steps.

1. In the tree view, select localhost under Servers.
2. Select MultiApp in the Deployed Objects area.
3. Click Undeploy.
4. Answer Yes in the confirmation dialog.
5. Repeat steps 1–4 for ReplyBeanApp on both the local and the remote servers.

10.4.5   Removing the Applications and Stopping the Servers

To remove the applications from the deploytool, follow these steps.

1. Select `MultiApp` in the tree view.

2. Select Close from the File menu.

3. Repeat these steps for `ReplyBeanApp`.

To delete the connection factory you created, enter the following at a command line prompt on the local system:

```
j2eeadmin -removeJmsFactory jms/RemoteTCF
```

To stop the J2EE servers, use the following command on each system:

```
j2ee -stop
```

To exit the deploytool, choose Exit from the File menu.

10.5   Accessing a J2EE Application from a Remote System that Is Not Running a J2EE Server

To run an application installed on a J2EE server from a system that is not running a J2EE server, you perform tasks similar to those described in Section 4.4.2 on page 52. Again, the J2EE SDK must be installed on both systems. You may also want to use the `runclient` command to run an application client installed on a remote system.

This section describes both of these situations:

- Accessing a J2EE application from a standalone client

- Using `runclient` to access a remote application client

10.5.1   Accessing a J2EE Application from a Standalone Client

You can run a standalone client that uses messages to communicate with a J2EE application. For example, you can use the deploytool to deploy the `ReplyBeanApp` application on a system running the J2EE server, then use a standalone client to publish messages to the topic that the `ReplyMsgBean` is listening on and receive replies on a temporary topic.

For example, suppose that the `ReplyBeanApp` application is deployed on the server running on the system `earth`, and suppose that the standalone client is named `PubSub` and will run on the system `mars`. Section 10.5.1.1 shows the client program.

To specify the remote system on the command line, you use a command line just like the one in Section 4.4.2 (you do so after setting your environment variables as shown in Table 4.1 on page 28).

- On a Microsoft Windows system, type the following command on a single line:

  ```
  java -Djms.properties=%J2EE_HOME%\config\jms_client.properties
  -Dorg.omg.CORBA.ORBInitialHost=earth PubSub jms/Topic
  ```

- On a UNIX system, type the following command on a single line:

  ```
  java -Djms.properties=$J2EE_HOME/config/jms_client.properties
  -Dorg.omg.CORBA.ORBInitialHost=earth PubSub jms/Topic
  ```

If all the remote applications you need to access are deployed on the same server, you can edit the file `%J2EE_HOME%\config\orb.properties` (on Microsoft Windows systems) or `$J2EE_HOME/config/orb.properties` (on UNIX systems) on the local system. The second line of this file looks like this:

```
host=localhost
```

Change `localhost` to the name of the system on which the remote applications are deployed (for example, `earth`):

```
host=earth
```

You can now run the client program as before, but you do not need to specify the option `-Dorg.omg.CORBA.ORBInitialHost`.

10.5.1.1 The Sample Client Program: PubSub.java

The sample client program PubSub.java can publish messages to a topic that the ReplyMsgBean is listening on and receive the message bean's replies.

```java
/**
 * The PubSub class consists of
 *
 *   - A main method, which publishes several messages to a topic
 *     and creates a subscriber and a temporary topic on which
 *     to receive replies
 *   - A TextListener class that receives the replies
 *
 * Run this program in conjunction with ReplyBeanApp.
 * Specify a topic name on the command line when you run the
 * program.  By default, the program sends one message.
 * Specify a number after the topic name to send that number
 * of messages.
 *
 * To end the program, enter Q or q on the command line.
 */
import javax.jms.*;
import javax.naming.*;
import java.io.*;

public class PubSub {

    /**
     * Main method.
     *
     * @param args     the topic used by the example and,
     *                 optionally, the number of messages to send
     */
    public static void main(String[] args) {
        String                 topicName = null;
        Context                jndiContext = null;
        TopicConnectionFactory topicConnectionFactory = null;
        TopicConnection        topicConnection = null;
```

```
TopicSession          topicSession = null;
Topic                 topic = null;
Topic                 replyTopic = null;
TopicPublisher        topicPublisher = null;
TopicSubscriber       topicSubscriber = null;
TextMessage           message = null;
InputStreamReader     inputStreamReader = null;
char                  answer = '\0';
final int             NUM_MSGS;

if ( (args.length < 1) || (args.length > 2) ) {
    System.out.println("Usage: java " +
        "PubSub <topic-name> " +
        "[<number-of-messages>]");
    System.exit(1);
}
topicName = new String(args[0]);
System.out.println("Topic name is " + topicName);
if (args.length == 2){
    NUM_MSGS = (new Integer(args[1])).intValue();
} else {
    NUM_MSGS = 1;
}

/*
 * Create a JNDI API InitialContext object if none exists
 * yet.
 */
try {
    jndiContext = new InitialContext();
} catch (NamingException e) {
    System.out.println("Could not create JNDI API " +
        "context: " + e.toString());
    e.printStackTrace();
    System.exit(1);
}

/*
 * Look up connection factory and topic.  If either does
```

```
 * not exist, exit.
 */
try {
    topicConnectionFactory = (TopicConnectionFactory)
        jndiContext.lookup("jms/TopicConnectionFactory");
    topic = (Topic) jndiContext.lookup(topicName);
} catch (NamingException e) {
    System.out.println("JNDI API lookup failed: " +
        e.toString());
    e.printStackTrace();
    System.exit(1);
}

/*
 * Create connection.
 * Create session from connection; false means session is
 * not transacted.
 * Create publisher, temporary topic, and text message,
 *  setting JMSReplyTo field to temporary topic and
 *  setting an id property.
 * Send messages, varying text slightly.
 * Create subscriber and set message listener to receive
 *  replies.
 * When all messages have been received, enter Q to quit.
 * Finally, close connection.
 */
try {
    topicConnection =
        topicConnectionFactory.createTopicConnection();
    topicSession =
        topicConnection.createTopicSession(false,
            Session.AUTO_ACKNOWLEDGE);
    topicPublisher = topicSession.createPublisher(topic);
    replyTopic = topicSession.createTemporaryTopic();
    message = topicSession.createTextMessage();
    message.setJMSReplyTo(replyTopic);
    int id = 1;
    for (int i = 0; i < NUM_MSGS; i++) {
        message.setText("This is message " + id);
```

```
            message.setIntProperty("id", id);
            System.out.println("Publishing message: " +
                message.getText());
            topicPublisher.publish(message);
            id++;
        }

        topicSubscriber =
            topicSession.createSubscriber(replyTopic);
        topicSubscriber.setMessageListener(new TextListener());
        topicConnection.start();
        System.out.println("To end program, enter Q or q, " +
            "then <return>");
        inputStreamReader = new InputStreamReader(System.in);
        while (!((answer == 'q') || (answer == 'Q'))) {
            try {
                answer = (char) inputStreamReader.read();
            } catch (IOException e) {
                System.out.println("I/O exception: "
                    + e.toString());
            }
        }
    } catch (JMSException e) {
        System.out.println("Exception occurred: " +
            e.toString());
    } finally {
        if (topicConnection != null) {
            try {
                topicConnection.close();
            } catch (JMSException e) {}
        }
    }
}

/**
 * The TextListener class implements the MessageListener
 * interface by defining an onMessage method that displays
 * the contents and id property of a TextMessage.
 *
```

```java
 * This class acts as the listener for the PubSub
 * class.
 */
static class TextListener implements MessageListener {

    /**
     * Casts the message to a TextMessage and displays its
     * text.
     *
     * @param message      the incoming message
     */
    public void onMessage(Message message) {
        TextMessage  msg = null;
        String       txt = null;
        int          id = 0;

        try {
            if (message instanceof TextMessage) {
                msg = (TextMessage) message;
                id = msg.getIntProperty("id");
                txt = msg.getText();
                System.out.println("Reading message: id=" +
                    id + ", text=" + txt);
            } else {
                System.out.println("Message of wrong type: "
                    + message.getClass().getName());
            }
        } catch (JMSException e) {
            System.out.println("JMSException in onMessage():"
                + e.toString());
        } catch (Throwable t) {
            System.out.println("Exception in onMessage():" +
                t.getMessage());
        }
    }
}
```

```
    }
```

_____

Code Example 10.3 PubSub.java

10.5.2 Using runclient to Access a Remote Application Client

If you need to run a J2EE application that contains an application client and that is deployed on a remote system, you can use the runclient command to do so. For example, if you deploy both ReplyBeanApp and MultiApp on the server running on earth, the steps are as follows.

1. Make sure that the multi_server directory on earth is accessible to you via the file system so that the runclient command can find it.

2. Follow the instructions in Section 10.3.2 on page 189 and create on mars a connection factory that will refer to the corresponding connection factory on earth.

3. Set the host property in the orb.properties file in the J2EE SDK on mars, as described in Section 10.5.1, because the runclient command does not allow you to specify the ORBInitialHost value:

   host=earth

4. Go to the multi_server directory on earth—or specify the complete path to the MultiApp.ear file—and issue the runclient command (on one line):

   runclient -client MultiApp.ear -name MultiAppServerRequester
   -textauth

Part Two

PART Two is a reference for the JMS API and contains a chapter for each class and interface used by JMS application programmers. The chapters are arranged alphabetically for easy reference.

Each chapter contains an overview, the definition of the class or the interface, and in-depth descriptions of each constructor, field, and method. The definitions and descriptions also use alphabetical order.

JMS API methods throw a JMSException or one of its subclasses. Exceptions are described in the Throws section of each method description.

The complete JMS API includes interfaces and methods used only by programmers implementing a JMS provider. The complete API is described in the JMS API documentation, which you can download from the JMS API Web site, http://java.sun.com/products/jms/.

The appendix provides several advanced JMS client examples that illustrate the use of durable subscriptions, transactions, and acknowledgment modes.

BytesMessage

11.1 Overview and Related Methods and Interfaces

A BytesMessage object is used to send a message containing a stream of uninterpreted bytes. It inherits from the Message interface and adds a bytes message body. The receiver of the message supplies the interpretation of the bytes.

The BytesMessage methods are based largely on those found in java.io.DataInputStream and java.io.DataOutputStream.

This message type is for client encoding of existing message formats. If possible, one of the other self-defining message types should be used instead.

Although the JMS API allows the use of message properties with byte messages, they are typically not used, since the inclusion of properties may affect the format.

The primitive types can be written explicitly using methods for each type. They may also be written generically as objects. For instance, a call to Bytes-Message.writeInt(6) is equivalent to BytesMessage.writeObject(new Integer(6)). Both forms are provided, because the explicit form is convenient for static programming, and the object form is needed when types are not known at compile time.

When the message is first created, and when clearBody is called, the body of the message is in write-only mode. After the first call to reset has been made, the message body is in read-only mode. After a message has been sent, the client that sent it can retain and modify it without affecting the message that has been sent. The same message object can be sent multiple times. When a message has been received, the provider has called reset so that the message body is in read-only mode for the client.

If clearBody is called on a message in read-only mode, the message body is cleared and the message is in write-only mode.

If a client attempts to read a message in write-only mode, a MessageNot-ReadableException is thrown.

If a client attempts to write a message in read-only mode, a MessageNot-WriteableException is thrown.

The related methods and interfaces are

- Session.createBytesMessage

- MapMessage

- Message

- ObjectMessage

- StreamMessage

- TextMessage

11.2   Interface Definition

```
package javax.jms;
public interface BytesMessage extends Message {
    boolean readBoolean() throws JMSException;
    byte readByte() throws JMSException;
    int readBytes(byte[] value) throws JMSException;
    int readBytes(byte[] value, int length) throws JMSException;
    char readChar() throws JMSException;
    double readDouble() throws JMSException;
    float readFloat() throws JMSException;
    int readInt() throws JMSException;
    long readLong() throws JMSException;
    short readShort() throws JMSException;
    int readUnsignedByte() throws JMSException;
    int readUnsignedShort() throws JMSException;
    String readUTF() throws JMSException;
    void reset() throws JMSException;
    void writeBoolean(boolean value) throws JMSException;
    void writeByte(byte value) throws JMSException;
    void writeBytes(byte[] value) throws JMSException;
```

```
    void writeBytes(byte[] value, int offset, int length)
                                              throws JMSException;
    void writeChar(char value) throws JMSException;
    void writeDouble(double value) throws JMSException;
    void writeFloat(float value) throws JMSException;
    void writeInt(int value) throws JMSException;
    void writeLong(long value) throws JMSException;
    void writeObject(Object value) throws JMSException;
    void writeShort(short value) throws JMSException;
    void writeUTF(String value) throws JMSException;
}
```

11.3 Methods

The BytesMessage interface inherits the fields and the methods of the interface javax.jms.Message. The following methods are defined in the interface javax.jms.BytesMessage.

readBoolean

```
public boolean readBoolean()
```

Reads a boolean from the bytes message stream.

RETURNS:
the boolean value read

THROWS:

JMSException	if the JMS provider fails to read the message due to some internal error
MessageEOFException	if unexpected end of bytes stream has been reached
MessageNotReadableException	if the message is in write-only mode

readByte

```
public byte readByte()
```

Reads a signed 8-bit value from the bytes message stream.

RETURNS:
the next byte from the bytes message stream as a signed 8-bit byte

THROWS:

JMSException	if the JMS provider fails to read the message due to some internal error
MessageEOFException	if unexpected end of bytes stream has been reached
MessageNotReadableException	if the message is in write-only mode

readBytes(byte[])

```
public int readBytes(byte[] value)
```

Reads a byte array from the bytes message stream.

If the length of array value is less than the number of bytes remaining to be read from the stream, the array should be filled. A subsequent call reads the next increment, and so on.

If the number of bytes remaining in the stream is less than the length of array value, the bytes should be read into the array. The return value of the total number of bytes read will be less than the length of the array, indicating that there are no more bytes left to be read from the stream. The next read of the stream returns –1.

PARAMETERS:
value   the buffer into which the data is read

RETURNS:
the total number of bytes read into the buffer, or –1 if there is no more data because the end of the stream has been reached

THROWS:

JMSException	if the JMS provider fails to read the message due to some internal error
MessageNotReadableException	if the message is in write-only mode

readBytes(byte[], int)

```
public int readBytes(byte[] value, int length)
```

Reads a portion of the bytes message stream.

If the length of array `value` is less than the number of bytes remaining to be read from the stream, the array should be filled. A subsequent call reads the next increment, and so on.

If the number of bytes remaining in the stream is less than the length of array `value`, the bytes should be read into the array. The return value of the total number of bytes read will be less than the length of the array, indicating that there are no more bytes left to be read from the stream. The next read of the stream returns −1.

If `length` is negative, or `length` is greater than the length of the array `value`, then an `IndexOutOfBoundsException` is thrown. No bytes will be read from the stream for this exception case.

PARAMETERS:

`value`	the buffer into which the data is read
`length`	the number of bytes to read; must be less than or equal to `value.length`

RETURNS:
the total number of bytes read into the buffer, or −1 if there is no more data because the end of the stream has been reached

THROWS:

`JMSException`	if the JMS provider fails to read the message due to some internal error
`MessageNotReadableException`	if the message is in write-only mode

readChar

```
public char readChar()
```

Reads a Unicode character value from the bytes message stream.

RETURNS:
the next two bytes from the bytes message stream as a Unicode character

THROWS:

`JMSException`	if the JMS provider fails to read the message due to some internal error
`MessageEOFException`	if unexpected end of bytes stream has been reached
`MessageNotReadableException`	if the message is in write-only mode

readDouble

```
public double readDouble()
```

Reads a double from the bytes message stream.

RETURNS:
the next eight bytes from the bytes message stream, interpreted as a double

THROWS:

JMSException	if the JMS provider fails to read the message due to some internal error
MessageEOFException	if unexpected end of bytes stream has been reached
MessageNotReadableException	if the message is in write-only mode

readFloat

```
public float readFloat()
```

Reads a float from the bytes message stream.

RETURNS:
the next four bytes from the bytes message stream, interpreted as a float

THROWS:

JMSException	if the JMS provider fails to read the message due to some internal error
MessageEOFException	if unexpected end of bytes stream has been reached
MessageNotReadableException	if the message is in write-only mode

readInt

```
public int readInt()
```

Reads a signed 32-bit integer from the bytes message stream.

RETURNS:
the next four bytes from the bytes message stream, interpreted as an int

THROWS:

JMSException	if the JMS provider fails to read the message due to some internal error

MessageEOFException	if unexpected end of bytes stream has been reached
MessageNotReadableException	if the message is in write-only mode

readLong

```
public long readLong()
```

Reads a signed 64-bit integer from the bytes message stream.

RETURNS:
the next eight bytes from the bytes message stream, interpreted as a `long`

THROWS:

JMSException	if the JMS provider fails to read the message due to some internal error
MessageEOFException	if unexpected end of bytes stream has been reached
MessageNotReadableException	if the message is in write-only mode

readShort

```
public short readShort()
```

Reads a signed 16-bit number from the bytes message stream.

RETURNS:
the next two bytes from the bytes message stream, interpreted as a signed 16-bit number

THROWS:

JMSException	if the JMS provider fails to read the message due to some internal error
MessageEOFException	if unexpected end of bytes stream has been reached
MessageNotReadableException	if the message is in write-only mode

readUnsignedByte

```
public int readUnsignedByte()
```

Reads an unsigned 8-bit number from the bytes message stream.

RETURNS:
the next byte from the bytes message stream, interpreted as an unsigned 8-bit number

THROWS:

JMSException	if the JMS provider fails to read the message due to some internal error
MessageEOFException	if unexpected end of bytes stream has been reached
MessageNotReadableException	if the message is in write-only mode

readUnsignedShort

```
public int readUnsignedShort()
```

Reads an unsigned 16-bit number from the bytes message stream.

RETURNS:
the next two bytes from the bytes message stream, interpreted as an unsigned 16-bit integer

THROWS:

JMSException	if the JMS provider fails to read the message due to some internal error
MessageEOFException	if unexpected end of bytes stream has been reached
MessageNotReadableException	if the message is in write-only mode

readUTF

```
public java.lang.String readUTF()
```

Reads a string that has been encoded using a modified UTF-8 format from the bytes message stream.

For more information on the UTF-8 format, see "File System Safe UCS Transformation Format (FSS_UTF)", X/Open Preliminary Specification, X/Open Company Ltd., Document Number: P316. This information also appears in ISO/IEC 10646, Annex P.

RETURNS:
a Unicode string from the bytes message stream

THROWS:

`JMSException`	if the JMS provider fails to read the message due to some internal error
`MessageEOFException`	if unexpected end of bytes stream has been reached
`MessageNotReadableException`	if the message is in write-only mode

reset

`public void `**`reset`**`()`

Puts the message body in read-only mode and repositions the stream of bytes to the beginning.

THROWS:

`JMSException`	if the JMS provider fails to reset the message due to some internal error
`MessageFormatException`	if the message has an invalid format

writeBoolean

`public void `**`writeBoolean`**`(boolean `*`value`*`)`

Writes a `boolean` to the bytes message stream as a 1-byte value. The value `true` is written as the value `(byte)1`; the value `false` is written as the value `(byte)0`.

PARAMETERS:

`value`	the `boolean` value to be written

THROWS:

`JMSException`	if the JMS provider fails to write the message due to some internal error
`MessageNotWriteableException`	if the message is in read-only mode

writeByte

`public void `**`writeByte`**`(byte `*`value`*`)`

Writes a `byte` to the bytes message stream as a 1-byte value.

PARAMETERS:

value   the byte value to be written

THROWS:

JMSException   if the JMS provider fails to write the message due to some internal error

MessageNotWriteableException if the message is in read-only mode

writeBytes(byte[])

```
public void writeBytes(byte[] value)
```

Writes a byte array to the bytes message stream.

PARAMETERS:

value   the byte array to be written

THROWS:

JMSException   if the JMS provider fails to write the message due to some internal error

MessageNotWriteableException if the message is in read-only mode

writeBytes(byte[], int, int)

```
public void writeBytes(byte[] value, int offset, int length)
```

Writes a portion of a byte array to the bytes message stream.

PARAMETERS:

value   the byte array value to be written
offset   the initial offset within the byte array
length   the number of bytes to use

THROWS:

JMSException   if the JMS provider fails to write the message due to some internal error

MessageNotWriteableException if the message is in read-only mode

writeChar

```
public void writeChar(char value)
```

Writes a char to the bytes message stream as a 2-byte value, high byte first.

PARAMETERS:
value   the char value to be written

THROWS:
JMSException   if the JMS provider fails to write the message due to some internal error
MessageNotWriteableException if the message is in read-only mode

writeDouble

```
public void writeDouble(double value)
```

Converts the double argument to a long using the doubleToLongBits method in class Double, and then writes that long value to the bytes message stream as an 8-byte quantity, high byte first.

PARAMETERS:
value   the double value to be written

THROWS:
JMSException   if the JMS provider fails to write the message due to some internal error
MessageNotWriteableException if the message is in read-only mode

writeFloat

```
public void writeFloat(float value)
```

Converts the float argument to an int using the floatToIntBits method in class Float, and then writes that int value to the bytes message stream as a 4-byte quantity, high byte first.

PARAMETERS:
value   the float value to be written

THROWS:

JMSException   if the JMS provider fails to write the mes-
                                                     sage due to some internal error

MessageNotWriteableException if the message is in read-only mode

writeInt

```
public void writeInt(int value)
```

Writes an int to the bytes message stream as four bytes, high byte first.

PARAMETERS:

value   the int to be written

THROWS:

JMSException   if the JMS provider fails to write the mes-
                                                     sage due to some internal error

MessageNotWriteableException if the message is in read-only mode

writeLong

```
public void writeLong(long value)
```

Writes a long to the bytes message stream as eight bytes, high byte first.

PARAMETERS:

value   the long to be written

THROWS:

JMSException   if the JMS provider fails to write the mes-
                                                     sage due to some internal error

MessageNotWriteableException if the message is in read-only mode

writeObject

```
public void writeObject(java.lang.Object value)
```

Writes an object to the bytes message stream.

This method works only for the objectified primitive object types
(Integer, Double, Long ...), String objects, and byte arrays.

PARAMETERS:

value	the object in the Java programming language ("Java object") to be written; it must not be null

THROWS:

JMSException	if the JMS provider fails to write the message due to some internal error
MessageFormatException	if the object is of an invalid type
MessageNotWriteableException	if the message is in read-only mode
java.lang.NullPointerException	if the parameter value is null

writeShort

```
public void writeShort(short value)
```

Writes a short to the bytes message stream as two bytes, high byte first.

PARAMETERS:

value	the short to be written

THROWS:

JMSException	if the JMS provider fails to write the message due to some internal error
MessageNotWriteableException	if the message is in read-only mode

writeUTF

```
public void writeUTF(java.lang.String value)
```

Writes a string to the bytes message stream using UTF-8 encoding in a machine-independent manner.

For more information on the UTF-8 format, see "File System Safe UCS Transformation Format (FSS_UTF)", X/Open Preliminary Specification, X/Open Company Ltd., Document Number: P316. This information also appears in ISO/IEC 10646, Annex P.

PARAMETERS:

value   the String value to be written

THROWS:

JMSException   if the JMS provider fails to write the mes-
                               sage due to some internal error

MessageNotWriteableExceptionif the message is in read-only mode

CHAPTER **12**

Connection

12.1 Overview and Related Interfaces

A `Connection` object is a client's active connection to its JMS provider. It typically allocates provider resources outside the Java virtual machine (JVM).

Connections support concurrent use.

A connection serves several purposes:

- It encapsulates an open connection with a JMS provider. It typically represents an open TCP/IP socket between a client and a provider service daemon.

- Its creation is where client authentication takes place.

- It can specify a unique client identifier.

- It provides a `ConnectionMetaData` object.

- It supports an optional `ExceptionListener` object.

Because the creation of a connection involves setting up authentication and communication, a connection is a relatively heavyweight object. Most clients will do all their messaging with a single connection. Other more advanced applications may use several connections. The JMS API does not architect a reason for using multiple connections; however, there may be operational reasons for doing so.

A JMS client typically creates a connection, one or more sessions, and a number of message producers and consumers. When a connection is created, it is in stopped mode. That means that no messages are being delivered.

It is typical to leave the connection in stopped mode until setup is complete (that is, until all message consumers have been created). At that point, the client calls the connection's `start` method, and messages begin arriving at the connection's consumers. This setup convention minimizes any client confusion that may result from asynchronous message delivery while the client is still in the process of setting itself up.

A connection can be started immediately, and the setup can be done afterwards. Clients that do this must be prepared to handle asynchronous message delivery while they are still in the process of setting up.

A message producer can send messages while a connection is stopped.

The related interfaces are

- ConnectionFactory

- QueueConnection

- TopicConnection

12.2   Interface Definition

```
package javax.jms;
public interface Connection {
    void close() throws JMSException;
    String getClientID() throws JMSException;
    ExceptionListener getExceptionListener() throws JMSException;
    ConnectionMetaData getMetaData() throws JMSException;
    void setClientID(String clientID) throws JMSException;
    void setExceptionListener(ExceptionListener listener)
                                              throws JMSException;
    void start() throws JMSException;
    void stop() throws JMSException;
}
```

12.3 Methods

The following methods are defined in the interface `javax.jms.Connection`.

close

```
public void close()
```

Closes the connection.

Since a provider typically allocates significant resources outside the JVM on behalf of a connection, clients should close these resources when they are not needed. Relying on garbage collection to eventually reclaim these resources may not be timely enough.

There is no need to close the sessions, producers, and consumers of a closed connection.

Closing a connection causes all temporary destinations to be deleted.

When this method is invoked, it should not return until message processing has been shut down in an orderly fashion. This means that all message listeners that may have been running have returned, and that all pending receives have returned. A close terminates all pending message receives on the connection's sessions' consumers. The receives may return with a message or with null, depending on whether there was a message available at the time of the close. If one or more of the connection's sessions' message listeners is processing a message at the time when connection `close` is invoked, all the facilities of the connection and its sessions must remain available to those listeners until they return control to the JMS provider.

Closing a connection causes any of its sessions' transactions in progress to be rolled back. In the case where a session's work is coordinated by an external transaction manager, a session's `commit` and `rollback` methods are not used and the result of a closed session's work is determined later by the transaction manager. Closing a connection does NOT force an acknowledgment of client-acknowledged sessions.

Invoking the `acknowledge` method of a received message from a closed connection's session must throw an `IllegalStateException`. Closing a closed connection must *not* throw an exception.

THROWS:

JMSException	if the JMS provider fails to close the connection due to some internal error. For example, a failure to release resources or to close a

socket connection can cause this exception to be thrown

getClientID

```
public java.lang.String getClientID()
```

Gets the client identifier for this connection.

This value is specific to the JMS provider. It is either preconfigured by an administrator in a `ConnectionFactory` object or assigned dynamically by the application by calling the `setClientID` method.

RETURNS:
the unique client identifier

THROWS:

JMSException   if the JMS provider fails to return the client ID for this connection due to some internal error

getExceptionListener

```
public ExceptionListener getExceptionListener()
```

Gets the `ExceptionListener` object for this connection.

RETURNS:
the `ExceptionListener` for this connection

THROWS:

JMSException   if the JMS provider fails to get the `ExceptionListener` for this connection

getMetaData

```
public ConnectionMetaData getMetaData()
```

Gets the metadata for this connection.

RETURNS:
the connection metadata

THROWS:

JMSException   if the JMS provider fails to get the connec-
                                            tion metadata for this connection

SEE ALSO:

ConnectionMetaData

setClientID

```
public void setClientID(java.lang.String clientID)
```

Sets the client identifier for this connection.

The preferred way to assign a JMS client's client identifier is for it to be configured in a client-specific ConnectionFactory object and transparently assigned to the Connection object it creates. See Section 5.2.1 on page 61 for details.

Alternatively, a client can set a connection's client identifier using a provider-specific value. The facility to set a connection's client identifier explicitly is not a mechanism for overriding the identifier that has been administratively configured. It is provided for the case where no administratively specified identifier exists. If one does exist, an attempt to change it by setting it must throw an IllegalStateException. If a client sets the client identifier explicitly, it must do so immediately after it creates the connection and before any other action on the connection is taken. After this point, setting the client identifier is a programming error that should throw an IllegalStateException.

The purpose of the client identifier is to associate a connection and its objects with a state maintained on behalf of the client by a provider. The only such state identified by the JMS API is that required to support durable subscriptions.

If another connection with the same clientID is already running when this method is called, the JMS provider should detect the duplicate ID and throw an InvalidClientIDException.

PARAMETERS:

clientID   the unique client identifier

THROWS:

JMSException   if the JMS provider fails to set the client ID
                                            for this connection due to some internal error

InvalidClientException   if the JMS client specifies an invalid or du-
                                            plicate client ID

| IllegalStateException | if the JMS client attempts to set a connection's client ID at the wrong time or when it has been administratively configured |

setExceptionListener

```
public void setExceptionListener(ExceptionListener listener)
```

Sets an exception listener for this connection.

If a JMS provider detects a serious problem with a connection, it informs the connection's ExceptionListener, if one has been registered. It does this by calling the listener's onException method, passing it a JMSException object describing the problem.

An exception listener allows a client to be notified of a problem asynchronously. Some connections only consume messages, so they would have no other way to learn their connection has failed.

A connection serializes execution of its ExceptionListener.

A JMS provider should attempt to resolve connection problems itself before it notifies the client of them.

PARAMETERS:

| listener | the exception listener |

THROWS:

| JMSException | if the JMS provider fails to set the exception listener for this connection |

start

```
public void start()
```

Starts (or restarts) a connection's delivery of incoming messages. A call to start on a connection that has already been started is ignored.

THROWS:

| JMSException | if the JMS provider fails to start message delivery due to some internal error |

SEE ALSO:
stop

stop

```
public void stop()
```

Temporarily stops a connection's delivery of incoming messages. Delivery can be restarted using the connection's `start` method. When the connection is stopped, delivery to all the connection's message consumers is inhibited: Synchronous receives block, and messages are not delivered to message listeners.

This call blocks until receives and/or message listeners in progress have completed.

Stopping a connection has no effect on its ability to send messages. A call to `stop` on a connection that has already been stopped is ignored.

A call to `stop` must not return until delivery of messages has paused. This means that a client can rely on the fact that none of its message listeners will be called and that all threads of control waiting for `receive` calls to return will not return with a message until the connection is restarted. The receive timers for a stopped connection continue to advance, so receives may time out while the connection is stopped.

If message listeners are running when `stop` is invoked, the `stop` call must wait until all of them have returned before it may return. While these message listeners are completing, they must have the full services of the connection available to them.

THROWS:

JMSException   if the JMS provider fails to stop message delivery due to some internal error

SEE ALSO:

start

CHAPTER 13

ConnectionFactory

13.1 Overview and Related Interfaces

A ConnectionFactory object encapsulates a set of connection configuration parameters that has been defined by an administrator. A client uses it to create a connection with a JMS provider.

ConnectionFactory objects support concurrent use.

A ConnectionFactory object is a JMS administered object.

JMS administered objects are objects containing configuration information that are created by an administrator and later used by JMS clients. They make it practical to administer the JMS API in the enterprise.

Although the interfaces for administered objects do not explicitly depend on the Java Naming and Directory Interface (JNDI) API, the JMS API establishes the convention that JMS clients find administered objects by looking them up in a JNDI API namespace.

An administrator can place an administered object anywhere in a namespace. The JMS API does not define a naming policy.

It is expected that JMS providers will provide the tools an administrator needs to create and configure administered objects in a JNDI API namespace. JMS provider implementations of administered objects should be both javax.jndi.Referenceable and java.io.Serializable so that they can be stored in all JNDI API naming contexts. In addition, it is recommended that these implementations follow the JavaBeans™ design patterns.

This strategy provides several benefits:

- It hides provider-specific details from JMS clients.

- It abstracts administrative information into objects in the Java programming language ("Java objects") that are easily organized and administered from a common management console.

- Since there will be JNDI API providers for all popular naming services, this means that JMS providers can deliver one implementation of administered objects that will run everywhere.

An administered object should not hold on to any remote resources. Its lookup should not use remote resources other than those used by the JNDI API itself.

Clients should think of administered objects as local Java objects. Looking them up should not have any hidden side effects or use surprising amounts of local resources.

The related interfaces are

- QueueConnectionFactory

- TopicConnectionFactory

13.2   Interface Definition

```
package javax.jms;
public interface ConnectionFactory {
}
```

CHAPTER 14

ConnectionMetaData

14.1 Overview

A ConnectionMetaData object provides information describing the Connection object.

14.2 Interface Definition

```
package javax.jms;
public interface ConnectionMetaData {
    int getJMSMajorVersion() throws JMSException;
    int getJMSMinorVersion() throws JMSException;
    String getJMSProviderName() throws JMSException;
    String getJMSVersion() throws JMSException;
    Enumeration getJMSXPropertyNames() throws JMSException;
    int getProviderMajorVersion() throws JMSException;
    int getProviderMinorVersion() throws JMSException;
    String getProviderVersion() throws JMSException;
}
```

14.3   Methods

The following methods are defined in the interface `javax.jms.Connection-`
`MetaData`.

getJMSMajorVersion

`public int getJMSMajorVersion()`

Gets the JMS major version number.

RETURNS:
the JMS API major version number

THROWS:
JMSException   if the JMS provider fails to retrieve the meta-
                                    data due to some internal error

getJMSMinorVersion

`public int getJMSMinorVersion()`

Gets the JMS minor version number.

RETURNS:
the JMS API minor version number

THROWS:
JMSException   if the JMS provider fails to retrieve the meta-
                                    data due to some internal error

getJMSProviderName

`public java.lang.String getJMSProviderName()`

Gets the JMS provider name.

RETURNS:
the JMS provider name

THROWS:
JMSException   if the JMS provider fails to retrieve the meta-
                                    data due to some internal error

getJMSVersion

```
public java.lang.String getJMSVersion()
```

Gets the JMS API version.

RETURNS:
the JMS API version

THROWS:

JMSException   if the JMS provider fails to retrieve the meta-
                                data due to some internal error

getJMSXPropertyNames

```
public java.util.Enumeration getJMSXPropertyNames()
```

Gets an enumeration of the JMSX property names.

RETURNS:
an Enumeration of JMSX property names

THROWS:

JMSException   if the JMS provider fails to retrieve the meta-
                                data due to some internal error

getProviderMajorVersion

```
public int getProviderMajorVersion()
```

Gets the JMS provider major version number.

RETURNS:
the JMS provider major version number

THROWS:

JMSException   if the JMS provider fails to retrieve the meta-
                                data due to some internal error

getProviderMinorVersion

```
public int getProviderMinorVersion()
```

Gets the JMS provider minor version number.

RETURNS:
the JMS provider minor version number

THROWS:

JMSException   if the JMS provider fails to retrieve the meta-
                                          data due to some internal error

getProviderVersion

```
public java.lang.String getProviderVersion()
```

Gets the JMS provider version.

RETURNS:
the JMS provider version

THROWS:

JMSException   if the JMS provider fails to retrieve the meta-
                                          data due to some internal error

CHAPTER 15

DeliveryMode

15.1 Overview

The delivery modes supported by the JMS API are PERSISTENT and NON_PERSISTENT.

A client marks a message as persistent if it feels that the application will have problems if the message is lost in transit. A client marks a message as nonpersistent if an occasional lost message is tolerable. Clients use delivery mode to tell a JMS provider how to balance message transport reliability with throughput.

Delivery mode covers only the transport of the message to its destination. Retention of a message at the destination until its receipt is acknowledged is not guaranteed by a PERSISTENT delivery mode. Clients should assume that message retention policies are set administratively. Message retention policy governs the reliability of message delivery from destination to message consumer. For example, if a client's message storage space is exhausted, some messages may be dropped in accordance with a site-specific message retention policy.

A message is guaranteed to be delivered once and only once by a JMS provider if the delivery mode of the message is PERSISTENT and if the destination has a sufficient message retention policy.

15.2 Interface Definition

```
package javax.jms;
public interface DeliveryMode {
    static final int NON_PERSISTENT = 1;
    static final int PERSISTENT     = 2;
}
```

15.3 Fields

Two fields are defined in the interface `javax.jms.DeliveryMode`.

NON_PERSISTENT

`public static final int NON_PERSISTENT`

This is the lowest-overhead delivery mode because it does not require that the message be logged to stable storage. The level of JMS provider failure that causes a `NON_PERSISTENT` message to be lost is not defined.

A JMS provider must deliver a `NON_PERSISTENT` message with an at-most-once guarantee. This means that it may lose the message, but it must not deliver it twice.

PERSISTENT

`public static final int PERSISTENT`

This delivery mode instructs the JMS provider to log the message to stable storage as part of the client's send operation. Only a hard media failure should cause a `PERSISTENT` message to be lost.

CHAPTER 16

Destination

16.1 Overview and Related Interfaces

A Destination object encapsulates a provider-specific address. The JMS API does not define a standard address syntax. Although a standard address syntax was considered, it was decided that the differences in address semantics between existing message-oriented middleware (MOM) products were too wide to bridge with a single syntax.

Since Destination is an administered object, it may contain provider-specific configuration information in addition to its address.

The JMS API also supports a client's use of provider-specific address names.

Destination objects support concurrent use.

A Destination object is a JMS administered object.

JMS administered objects are objects containing configuration information that are created by an administrator and later used by JMS clients. They make it practical to administer the JMS API in the enterprise.

Although the interfaces for administered objects do not explicitly depend on the Java Naming and Directory Interface (JNDI) API, the JMS API establishes the convention that JMS clients find administered objects by looking them up in a JNDI API namespace.

An administrator can place an administered object anywhere in a namespace. The JMS API does not define a naming policy.

It is expected that JMS providers will provide the tools an administrator needs to create and configure administered objects in a JNDI API namespace. JMS provider implementations of administered objects should implement the javax.naming.Referenceable and java.io.Serializable interfaces so that they can be stored in all JNDI API naming contexts. In addition, it is recommended that these implementations follow the JavaBeans design patterns.

This strategy provides several benefits:

- It hides provider-specific details from JMS clients.

- It abstracts JMS administrative information into objects in the Java programming language ("Java objects") that are easily organized and administered from a common management console.

- Since there will be JNDI API providers for all popular naming services, JMS providers can deliver one implementation of administered objects that will run everywhere.

An administered object should not hold on to any remote resources. Its lookup should not use remote resources other than those used by the JNDI API itself.

Clients should think of administered objects as local Java objects. Looking them up should not have any hidden side effects or use surprising amounts of local resources.

The related interfaces are

- Queue

- Topic

16.2 Interface Definition

```
package javax.jms;
public interface Destination {
}
```

CHAPTER 17

ExceptionListener

17.1 Overview and Related Method

If a JMS provider detects a serious problem with a Connection object, it informs the Connection object's ExceptionListener, if one has been registered. It does this by calling the listener's onException method, passing it a JMSException argument describing the problem.

An exception listener allows a client to be notified of a problem asynchronously. Some connections only consume messages, so they would have no other way to learn that their connection has failed.

A JMS provider should attempt to resolve connection problems itself before it notifies the client of them.

The related method is Connection.setExceptionListener.

17.2 Interface Definition

```
package javax.jms;
public interface ExceptionListener {
    void onException(JMSException exception);
}
```

17.3   Methods

The following method is defined in the interface javax.jms.ExceptionListener.

onException

public void **onException**(JMSException exception)

Notifies user of a JMS exception.

PARAMETERS:

exception   the JMS exception

IllegalStateException

18.1 Overview

This exception is thrown when a method is invoked at an illegal or inappropriate time or if the provider is not in an appropriate state for the requested operation. For example, this exception must be thrown if Session.commit is called on a non-transacted session.

The IllegalStateException class inherits the methods of the class javax.jms.JMSException.

18.2 Class Definition

```
package javax.jms;
public class IllegalStateException extends JMSException {
    public IllegalStateException(String reason);
    public IllegalStateException(String reason, String errorCode);
}
```

18.3 Constructors

The following constructors are defined by the class `javax.jms.IllegalState-Exception`.

IllegalStateException(String)

public **IllegalStateException**(java.lang.String *reason*)

Constructs an `IllegalStateException` with the specified reason. The error code defaults to null.

PARAMETERS:

reason   a description of the exception

IllegalStateException(String, String)

public **IllegalStateException**(java.lang.String *reason*,
                                        java.lang.String *errorCode*)

Constructs an `IllegalStateException` with the specified reason and error code.

PARAMETERS:

reason   a description of the exception
errorCode   a string specifying the vendor-specific error
                                  code

CHAPTER 19

InvalidClientIDException

19.1   Overview

This exception must be thrown when a client attempts to set a connection's client ID to a value that is rejected by a provider.

The `InvalidClientIDException` class inherits the methods of the class `javax.jms.JMSException`.

19.2   Class Definition

```
package javax.jms;
public class InvalidClientIDException extends JMSException {
    public InvalidClientIDException(String reason);
    public InvalidClientIDException(String reason, String errorCode);
}
```

19.3   Constructors

The following constructors are defined by the class `javax.jms.InvalidClientID-Exception`.

InvalidClientIDException(String)

---

public **InvalidClientIDException**(java.lang.String *reason*)

Constructs an `InvalidClientIDException` with the specified reason. The error code defaults to null.

PARAMETERS:

reason   a description of the exception

InvalidClientIDException(String, String)

---

public **InvalidClientIDException**(java.lang.String *reason*,
                                              java.lang.String *errorCode*)

Constructs an `InvalidClientIDException` with the specified reason and error code.

PARAMETERS:

reason   a description of the exception
errorCode   a string specifying the vendor-specific error
                                             code

CHAPTER 20

InvalidDestinationException

20.1 Overview

This exception must be thrown when a destination either is not understood by a provider or is no longer valid.

The `InvalidDestinationException` class inherits the methods of the class `javax.jms.JMSException`.

20.2 Class Definition

```
package javax.jms;
public class InvalidDestinationException extends JMSException {
    public InvalidDestinationException(String reason);
    public InvalidDestinationException(String reason,
                                                String errorCode);
}
```

20.3 Constructors

The following constructors are defined by the class `javax.jms.Invalid-DestinationException`.

InvalidDestinationException(String)

```
public InvalidDestinationException(java.lang.String reason)
```

  Constructs an `InvalidDestinationException` with the specified reason. The error code defaults to null.

  PARAMETERS:
reason   a description of the exception

InvalidDestinationException(String, String)

```
public InvalidDestinationException(java.lang.String reason,
                                   java.lang.String errorCode)
```

  Constructs an `InvalidDestinationException` with the specified reason and error code.

  PARAMETERS:
reason   a description of the exception
errorCode   a string specifying the vendor-specific error code

CHAPTER 21

InvalidSelectorException

21.1 Overview

This exception must be thrown when a JMS client attempts to give a provider a message selector with invalid syntax.

The `InvalidSelectorException` class inherits the methods of the class `javax.jms.JMSException`.

21.2 Class Definition

```
package javax.jms;
public class InvalidSelectorException extends JMSException {
    public InvalidSelectorException(String reason);
    public InvalidSelectorException(String reason, String errorCode);
}
```

21.3   Constructors

The following constructors are defined by the class `javax.jms.InvalidSelector-Exception`.

InvalidSelectorException(String)

```
public InvalidSelectorException(java.lang.String reason)
```

Constructs an `InvalidSelectorException` with the specified reason. The error code defaults to null.

PARAMETERS:

reason   a description of the exception

InvalidSelectorException(String, String)

```
public InvalidSelectorException(java.lang.String reason,
                                 java.lang.String errorCode)
```

Constructs an `InvalidSelectorException` with the specified reason and error code.

PARAMETERS:

reason   a description of the exception

errorCode   a string specifying the vendor-specific error code

CHAPTER 22

JMSException

22.1 Overview

The JMSException class is the root class of all JMS API exceptions. It provides the following information:

- A provider-specific string describing the error. This string is the standard exception message and is available via the getMessage method.

- A provider-specific string error code.

- A reference to another exception. Often a JMS API exception will be the result of a lower-level problem. If appropriate, this lower-level exception can be linked to the JMS API exception.

    The JMSException subclasses are as follows:

- IllegalStateException

- InvalidClientIDException

- InvalidDestinationException

- InvalidSelectorException

- JMSSecurityException

- MessageEOFException

- MessageFormatException

- MessageNotReadableException

- MessageNotWriteableException

- ResourceAllocationException

- TransactionInProgressException

- TransactionRolledBackException

22.2   Class Definition

```
package javax.jms;
public class JMSException {
    public JMSException(String reason);
    public JMSException(String reason, String errorCode);
    public String getErrorCode();
    public Exception getLinkedException();
    public synchronized void setLinkedException(Exception ex);
}
```

22.3   Constructors

The following constructors are defined by the class javax.jms.JMSException.

JMSException(String)

```
public JMSException(java.lang.String reason)
```

Constructs a JMSException with the specified reason. The error code defaults to null.

PARAMETERS:
reason   a description of the exception

JMSException(String, String)

```
public JMSException(java.lang.String reason,
                                        java.lang.String errorCode)
```

Constructs a JMSException with the specified reason and error code.

PARAMETERS:

reason	a description of the exception
errorCode	a string specifying the vendor-specific error code

22.4 Methods

The following methods are defined in the class javax.jms.JMSException.

getErrorCode

public java.lang.String **getErrorCode**()

Gets the vendor-specific error code.

RETURNS:
a string specifying the vendor-specific error code

getLinkedException

public java.lang.Exception **getLinkedException**()

Gets the exception linked to this one.

RETURNS:
the linked Exception, null if none

setLinkedException

public synchronized void **setLinkedException**(java.lang.Exception *ex*)

Adds a linked Exception.

PARAMETERS:

ex	the linked Exception

CHAPTER 23

JMSSecurityException

23.1 Overview

This exception must be thrown when a provider rejects a user name/password submitted by a client. It may also be thrown for any case where a security restriction prevents a method from completing.

The JMSSecurityException class inherits the methods of the class javax.jms.JMSException.

23.2 Class Definition

```
package javax.jms;
public class JMSSecurityException extends JMSException {
    public JMSSecurityException(String reason);
    public JMSSecurityException(String reason, String errorCode);
}
```

23.3 Constructors

The following constructors are defined by the class `javax.jms.JMSSecurity-Exception`.

JMSSecurityException(String)

```
public JMSSecurityException(java.lang.String reason)
```

Constructs a `JMSSecurityException` with the specified reason. The error code defaults to null.

PARAMETERS:

reason   a description of the exception

JMSSecurityException(String, String)

```
public JMSSecurityException(java.lang.String reason,
                                 java.lang.String errorCode)
```

Constructs a `JMSSecurityException` with the specified reason and error code.

PARAMETERS:

reason   a description of the exception

errorCode   a string specifying the vendor-specific error code

CHAPTER 24

MapMessage

24.1 Overview and Related Methods and Interfaces

A `MapMessage` object is used to send a set of name/value pairs. The names are `String` objects, and the values are primitive data types in the Java programming language. The entries can be accessed sequentially or randomly by name. The order of the entries is undefined. `MapMessage` inherits from the `Message` interface and adds a message body that contains a Map.

The primitive types can be read or written explicitly using methods for each type. They may also be read or written generically as objects. For instance, a call to `MapMessage.setInt("foo", 6)` is equivalent to `MapMessage.setObject("foo", new Integer(6))`. Both forms are provided, because the explicit form is convenient for static programming, and the object form is needed when types are not known at compile time.

When a client receives a `MapMessage`, it is in read-only mode. If a client attempts to write to the message at this point, a `MessageNotWriteableException` is thrown. If `clearBody` is called, the message can now be both read from and written to.

`MapMessage` objects support the conversions shown in Table 24.1. The marked cases must be supported. The unmarked cases must throw a `JMSException`. The `String`-to-primitive conversions may throw a runtime exception if the primitive's `valueOf` method does not accept it as a valid `String` representation of the primitive.

A value written as the row type can be read as the column type.

Table 24.1: MapMessage Conversions

	boolean	byte	short	char	int	long	float	double	String	Byte[]
boolean	X								X	
byte		X	X		X	X			X	
short			X		X	X			X	
char				X					X	
int					X	X			X	
long						X			X	
float							X	X	X	
double								X	X	
String	X	X	X		X	X	X	X	X	
byte[]										X

Attempting to read a null value as a primitive type must be treated as calling the primitive's corresponding `valueOf(String)` conversion method with a null value. Since `char` does not support a `String` conversion, attempting to read a null value as a `char` must throw a `NullPointerException`.

The related methods and interfaces are

- `Session.createMapMessage`

- `BytesMessage`

- `Message`

- `ObjectMessage`

- `StreamMessage`

- `TextMessage`

24.2 Interface Definition

```
package javax.jms;
    public interface MapMessage extends Message {
    boolean getBoolean(String name) throws JMSException;
    byte getByte(String name) throws JMSException;
    byte[] getBytes(String name) throws JMSException;
    char getChar(String name) throws JMSException;
    double getDouble(String name) throws JMSException;
    float getFloat(String name) throws JMSException;
    int getInt(String name) throws JMSException;
    long getLong(String name) throws JMSException;
    Enumeration getMapNames() throws JMSException;
    Object getObject(String name) throws JMSException;
    short getShort(String name) throws JMSException;
    String getString(String name) throws JMSException;
    boolean itemExists(String name) throws JMSException;
    void setBoolean(String name, boolean value) throws JMSException;
    void setByte(String name, byte value) throws JMSException;
    void setBytes(String name, byte[] value) throws JMSException;
    void setBytes(String name, byte[] value, int offset, int length)
                                        throws JMSException;
    void setChar(String name, char value) throws JMSException;
    void setDouble(String name, double value) throws JMSException;
    void setFloat(String name, float value) throws JMSException;
    void setInt(String name, int value) throws JMSException;
    void setLong(String name, long value) throws JMSException;
    void setObject(String name, Object value) throws JMSException;
    void setShort(String name, short value) throws JMSException;
    void setString(String name, String value) throws JMSException;
}
```

24.3 Methods

The MapMessage interface inherits the fields and the methods of the interface javax.jms.Message. The following methods are defined in the interface javax.jms.MapMessage.

getBoolean

```
public boolean getBoolean(java.lang.String name)
```

Returns the boolean value with the specified name.

PARAMETERS:
name   the name of the boolean

RETURNS:
the boolean value with the specified name

THROWS:
JMSException   if the JMS provider fails to read the message
                                due to some internal error
MessageFormatException   if this type conversion is invalid

getByte

```
public byte getByte(java.lang.String name)
```

Returns the byte value with the specified name.

PARAMETERS:
name   the name of the byte

RETURNS:
the byte value with the specified name

THROWS:
JMSException   if the JMS provider fails to read the message
                                due to some internal error
MessageFormatException   if this type conversion is invalid

getBytes

```
public byte[] getBytes(java.lang.String name)
```

Returns the byte array value with the specified name.

PARAMETERS:
name   the name of the byte array

RETURNS:
a copy of the byte array value with the specified name; if there is no item by this name, a null value is returned

THROWS:

JMSException	if the JMS provider fails to read the message due to some internal error
MessageFormatException	if this type conversion is invalid

getChar

```
public char getChar(java.lang.String name)
```

Returns the Unicode character value with the specified name.

PARAMETERS:

name	the name of the Unicode character

RETURNS:
the Unicode character value with the specified name

THROWS:

JMSException	if the JMS provider fails to read the message due to some internal error
MessageFormatException	if this type conversion is invalid

getDouble

```
public double getDouble(java.lang.String name)
```

Returns the double value with the specified name.

PARAMETERS:

name	the name of the double

RETURNS:
the double value with the specified name

THROWS:

JMSException	if the JMS provider fails to read the message due to some internal error
MessageFormatException	if this type conversion is invalid

getFloat

```
public float getFloat(java.lang.String name)
```

Returns the float value with the specified name.

PARAMETERS:

name   the name of the float

RETURNS:

the float value with the specified name

THROWS:

JMSException   if the JMS provider fails to read the message
                                  due to some internal error

MessageFormatException   if this type conversion is invalid

getInt

```
public int getInt(java.lang.String name)
```

Returns the int value with the specified name.

PARAMETERS:

name   the name of the int

RETURNS:

the int value with the specified name

THROWS:

JMSException   if the JMS provider fails to read the message
                                  due to some internal error

MessageFormatException   if this type conversion is invalid

getLong

```
public long getLong(java.lang.String name)
```

Returns the long value with the specified name.

PARAMETERS:

name   the name of the long

RETURNS:

the long value with the specified name

THROWS:

JMSException	if the JMS provider fails to read the message due to some internal error
MessageFormatException	if this type conversion is invalid

getMapNames

```
public java.util.Enumeration getMapNames()
```

Returns an `Enumeration` of all the names in the `MapMessage` object.

RETURNS:
an enumeration of all the names in this `MapMessage`

THROWS:

JMSException	if the JMS provider fails to read the message due to some internal error

getObject

```
public java.lang.Object getObject(java.lang.String name)
```

Returns the value of the object with the specified name.

This method can be used to return, in objectified format, an object in the Java programming language ("Java object") that had been stored in the Map with the equivalent `setObject` method call, or its equivalent primitive `settype` method.

Note that byte values are returned as `byte[]`, not `Byte[]`.

PARAMETERS:

name	the name of the Java object

RETURNS:
a copy of the Java object value with the specified name, in objectified format (for example, if the object was set as an `int`, an `Integer` is returned); if there is no item by this name, a null value is returned

THROWS:

JMSException	if the JMS provider fails to read the message due to some internal error

getShort

```
public short getShort(java.lang.String name)
```

Returns the short value with the specified name.

PARAMETERS:

name   the name of the short

RETURNS:

the short value with the specified name

THROWS:

JMSException   if the JMS provider fails to read the message
                                due to some internal error

MessageFormatException   if this type conversion is invalid

getString

```
public java.lang.String getString(java.lang.String name)
```

Returns the String value with the specified name.

PARAMETERS:

name   the name of the String

RETURNS:

the String value with the specified name; if there is no item by this name, a
null value is returned

THROWS:

JMSException   if the JMS provider fails to read the message
                                due to some internal error

MessageFormatException   if this type conversion is invalid

itemExists

```
public boolean itemExists(java.lang.String name)
```

Indicates whether an item exists in this MapMessage object.

PARAMETERS:

name   the name of the item to test

RETURNS:
true if the item exists

THROWS:

JMSException   if the JMS provider fails to determine if the item exists due to some internal error

setBoolean

```
public void setBoolean(java.lang.String name, boolean value)
```

Sets a boolean value with the specified name into the Map.

PARAMETERS:
name   the name of the boolean
value   the boolean value to set in the Map

THROWS:

JMSException   if the JMS provider fails to write the message due to some internal error
MessageNotWriteableException if the message is in read-only mode

setByte

```
public void setByte(java.lang.String name, byte value)
```

Sets a byte value with the specified name into the Map.

PARAMETERS:
name   the name of the byte
value   the byte value to set in the Map

THROWS:

JMSException   if the JMS provider fails to write the message due to some internal error
MessageNotWriteableException if the message is in read-only mode

setBytes(String, byte[])

```
public void setBytes(java.lang.String name, byte[] value)
```

Sets a byte array value with the specified name into the Map.

PARAMETERS:

name	the name of the byte array
value	the byte array value to set in the Map; the array is copied so that the value for name will not be altered by future modifications

THROWS:

JMSException   if the JMS provider fails to write the message due to some internal error

MessageNotWriteableException if the message is in read-only mode

setBytes(String, byte[], int, int)

```
public void setBytes(java.lang.String name, byte[] value, int offset,
                                                int length)
```

Sets a portion of the byte array value with the specified name into the Map.

PARAMETERS:

name	the name of the byte array
value	the byte array value to set in the Map
offset	the initial offset within the byte array
length	the number of bytes to use

THROWS:

JMSException   if the JMS provider fails to write the message due to some internal error

MessageNotWriteableException if the message is in read-only mode

setChar

```
public void setChar(java.lang.String name, char value)
```

Sets a Unicode character value with the specified name into the Map.

PARAMETERS:

name	the name of the Unicode character
value	the Unicode character value to set in the Map

THROWS:

JMSException   if the JMS provider fails to write the message due to some internal error

MessageNotWriteableException if the message is in read-only mode.

setDouble

```
public void setDouble(java.lang.String name, double value)
```

Sets a double value with the specified name into the Map.

PARAMETERS:

name   the name of the double

value   the double value to set in the Map

THROWS:

JMSException   if the JMS provider fails to write the message due to some internal error

MessageNotWriteableException if the message is in read-only mode

setFloat

```
public void setFloat(java.lang.String name, float value)
```

Sets a float value with the specified name into the Map.

PARAMETERS:

name   the name of the float

value   the float value to set in the Map

THROWS:

JMSException   if the JMS provider fails to write the message due to some internal error

MessageNotWriteableException if the message is in read-only mode

setInt

```
public void setInt(java.lang.String name, int value)
```

Sets an int value with the specified name into the Map.

PARAMETERS:

name   the name of the `int`
value   the `int` value to set in the Map

THROWS:

`JMSException`   if the JMS provider fails to write the mes-
                                        sage due to some internal error

`MessageNotWriteableException` if the message is in read-only mode

setLong

```
public void setLong(java.lang.String name, long value)
```

Sets a `long` value with the specified name into the Map.

PARAMETERS:

name   the name of the `long`
value   the `long` value to set in the Map

THROWS:

`JMSException`   if the JMS provider fails to write the mes-
                                        sage due to some internal error

`MessageNotWriteableException` if the message is in read-only mode

setObject

```
public void setObject(java.lang.String name, java.lang.Object value)
```

Sets an object value with the specified name into the Map.

This method works only for the objectified primitive object types
(`Integer`, `Double`, `Long` ...), `String` objects, and byte arrays.

PARAMETERS:

name   the name of the Java object
value   the Java object value to set in the Map

THROWS:

`JMSException`   if the JMS provider fails to write the mes-
                                        sage due to some internal error

`MessageFormatException`   if the object is invalid

`MessageNotWriteableException` if the message is in read-only mode

setShort

```
public void setShort(java.lang.String name, short value)
```

Sets a short value with the specified name into the Map.

PARAMETERS:

name	the name of the short
value	the short value to set in the Map

THROWS:

JMSException   if the JMS provider fails to write the mes-
                                     sage due to some internal error

MessageNotWriteableException if the message is in read-only mode

setString

```
public void setString(java.lang.String name, java.lang.String value)
```

Sets a String value with the specified name into the Map.

PARAMETERS:

name	the name of the String
value	the String value to set in the Map

THROWS:

JMSException   if the JMS provider fails to write the mes-
                                     sage due to some internal error

MessageNotWriteableException if the message is in read-only mode

CHAPTER 25

Message

25.1 Overview

The `Message` interface is the root interface of all JMS messages. It defines the message header and the `acknowledge` method used for all messages.

Most message-oriented middleware (MOM) products treat messages as lightweight entities that consist of a header and a payload. The header contains fields used for message routing and identification; the payload contains the application data being sent.

Within this general form, the definition of a message varies significantly across products. It would be quite difficult for the JMS API to support all of these message models.

With this in mind, the JMS message model has the following goals:

- Provide a single, unified message API

- Provide an API suitable for creating messages that match the format used by provider-native messaging applications

- Support the development of heterogeneous applications that span operating systems, machine architectures, and computer languages

- Support messages containing objects in the Java programming language ("Java objects")

- Support messages containing Extensible Markup Language (XML) pages

JMS messages are composed of the following parts:

- **Header.** All messages support the same set of header fields. Header fields contain values used by both clients and providers to identify and route messages.

- **Properties.** Each message contains a built-in facility for supporting application-defined property values. Properties provide an efficient mechanism for supporting application-defined message filtering.

- **Body.** The JMS API defines several types of message body, which cover the majority of messaging styles currently in use.

25.1.1 Message Bodies

The JMS API defines five types of message body:

- **Stream.** A `StreamMessage` object's message body contains a stream of primitive values in the Java programming language ("Java primitives"). It is filled and read sequentially.

- **Map.** A `MapMessage` object's message body contains a set of name/value pairs, where names are `String` objects, and values are Java primitives. The entries can be accessed sequentially or randomly by name. The order of the entries is undefined.

- **Text.** A `TextMessage` object's message body contains a `java.lang.String` object. The inclusion of this message type is based on our presumption that XML will likely become a popular mechanism for representing content of all kinds, including the content of JMS messages.

- **Object.** An `ObjectMessage` object's message body contains a `Serializable` Java object.

- **Bytes.** A `BytesMessage` object's message body contains a stream of uninterpreted bytes. This message type is for literally encoding a body to match an existing message format. In many cases, it is possible to use one of the other body types, which are easier to use. Although the JMS API allows the use of message properties with byte messages, they are typically not used, since the inclusion of properties may affect the format.

25.1.2 Message Headers

The `JMSCorrelationID` header field is used for linking one message with another. It typically links a reply message with its requesting message.

`JMSCorrelationID` can hold a provider-specific message ID, an application-specific `String` object, or a provider-native `byte[]` value.

25.1.3 Message Properties

A `Message` object contains a built-in facility for supporting application-defined property values. In effect, this provides a mechanism for adding application-specific header fields to a message.

Properties allow an application, via message selectors, to have a JMS provider select, or filter, messages on its behalf using application-specific criteria.

Property names must obey the rules for a message selector identifier.

Property values can be `boolean`, `byte`, `short`, `int`, `long`, `float`, `double`, and `String`.

Property values are set prior to sending a message. When a client receives a message, its properties are in read-only mode. If a client attempts to set properties at this point, a `MessageNotWriteableException` is thrown. If `clearProperties` is called, the properties can now be both read from and written to. Note that header fields are distinct from properties. Header fields are never in read-only mode.

A property value may duplicate a value in a message's body, or it may not. Although JMS does not define a policy for what should or should not be made a property, application developers should note that JMS providers will likely handle data in a message's body more efficiently than data in a message's properties. For best performance, applications should use message properties only when they need to customize a message's header. The primary reason for doing this is to support customized message selection.

Message properties support the conversions shown in Table 25.1. The marked cases must be supported. The unmarked cases must throw a `JMSException`. The `String`-to-primitive conversions may throw a runtime exception if the primitive's `valueOf` method does not accept the `String` as a valid representation of the primitive.

A value written as the row type can be read as the column type.

Table 25.1: Message Property Conversions

	boolean	byte	short	char	int	long	float	double	String
boolean	X								X
byte		X	X		X	X			X
short			X		X	X			X
char				X					X
int					X	X			X
long						X			X
float							X	X	X
double								X	X
String	X	X	X		X	X	X	X	X

In addition to the type-specific set/get methods for properties, JMS provides the setObjectProperty and getObjectProperty methods. These support the same set of property types using the objectified primitive values. Their purpose is to allow the decision of property type to made at execution time rather than at compile time. They support the same property value conversions.

The setObjectProperty method accepts values of class Boolean, Byte, Short, Integer, Long, Float, Double, and String. An attempt to use any other class must throw a JMSException.

The getObjectProperty method only returns values of class Boolean, Byte, Short, Integer, Long, Float, Double, and String.

The order of property values is not defined. To iterate through a message's property values, use getPropertyNames to retrieve a property name enumeration and then use the various property get methods to retrieve their values.

A message's properties are deleted by the clearProperties method. This leaves the message with an empty set of properties.

Getting a property value for a name which has not been set returns a null value. Only the getStringProperty and getObjectProperty methods can return a null value. Attempting to read a null value as a primitive type must be treated as calling the primitive's corresponding `valueOf(String)` conversion method with a null value.

The JMS API reserves the `JMSX` property name prefix for JMS defined properties. The full set of these properties is defined in the Java Message Service Specification. New JMS defined properties may be added in later versions of the JMS API. Support for these properties is optional. The `String[]` `Connection-MetaData.getJMSXPropertyNames` method returns the names of the `JMSX` properties supported by a connection.

`JMSX` properties may be referenced in message selectors whether or not they are supported by a connection. If they are not present in a message, they are treated like any other absent property.

`JMSX` properties defined in the Specification as "set by provider on send" are available to both the producer and the consumers of the message. `JMSX` properties defined in the Specification as "set by provider on receive" are available only to the consumers.

`JMSXGroupID` and `JMSXGroupSeq` are standard properties that clients should use if they want to group messages. All providers must support them. Unless specifically noted, the values and semantics of the `JMSX` properties are undefined.

The JMS API reserves the `JMS_vendor_name` property name prefix for provider-specific properties. Each provider defines its own value for `vendor_name`. This is the mechanism a JMS provider uses to make its special per-message services available to a JMS client.

The purpose of provider-specific properties is to provide special features needed to integrate JMS clients with provider-native clients in a single JMS application. They should not be used for messaging between JMS clients.

25.1.4 Provider Implementations of JMS Message Interfaces

The JMS API provides a set of message interfaces that define the JMS message model. It does not provide implementations of these interfaces.

Each JMS provider supplies a set of message factories with its `Session` object for creating instances of messages. This allows a provider to use message implementations tailored to its specific needs.

A provider must be prepared to accept message implementations that are not its own. They may not be handled as efficiently as its own implementation; however, they must be handled.

Note the following exception case when a provider is handling a foreign message implementation. If the foreign message implementation contains a `JMSReplyTo` header field that is set to a foreign destination implementation, the provider is not required to handle or preserve the value of this header field.

25.1.5 Message Selectors

A JMS message selector allows a client to specify, by header field references and property references, the messages it is interested in. Only messages whose header and property values match the selector are delivered. What it means for a message not to be delivered depends on the `MessageConsumer` being used (see `QueueReceiver` and `TopicSubscriber`).

Message selectors cannot reference message body values.

A message selector matches a message if the selector evaluates to true when the message's header field values and property values are substituted for their corresponding identifiers in the selector.

A message selector is a `String` whose syntax is based on a subset of the SQL92 conditional expression syntax. If the value of a message selector is an empty string, the value is treated as a null and indicates that there is no message selector for the message consumer.

The order of evaluation of a message selector is from left to right within precedence level. Parentheses can be used to change this order.

Predefined selector literals and operator names are shown here in uppercase; however, they are case insensitive.

A selector can contain:

- Literals:

  - A string literal is enclosed in single quotes, with a single quote represented by doubled single quote; for example, `'literal'` and `'literal''s'`. Like string literals in the Java programming language, these use the Unicode character encoding.

  - An exact numeric literal is a numeric value without a decimal point, such as 57, -957, and +62; numbers in the range of `long` are supported. Exact numeric literals use the integer literal syntax of the Java programming language.

  - An approximate numeric literal is a numeric value in scientific notation, such as 7E3 and -57.9E2, or a numeric value with a decimal, such as 7., -95.7, and +6.2; numbers in the range of `double` are supported.

Approximate literals use the floating-point literal syntax of the Java programming language.

- The boolean literals TRUE and FALSE.

- Identifiers:

  - An identifier is an unlimited-length sequence of letters and digits, the first of which must be a letter. A letter is any character for which the method Character.isJavaLetter returns true. This includes '_' and '$'. A letter or digit is any character for which the method Character.isJavaLetterOrDigit returns true.

  - Identifiers cannot be the names NULL, TRUE, and FALSE.

  - Identifiers cannot be NOT, AND, OR, BETWEEN, LIKE, IN, IS, or ESCAPE.

  - Identifiers are either header field references or property references. The type of a property value in a message selector corresponds to the type used to set the property. If a property that does not exist in a message is referenced, its value is NULL.

  - The conversions that apply to the get methods for properties do not apply when a property is used in a message selector expression. For example, suppose you set a property as a string value, as in the following:

    ```
    myMessage.setStringProperty("NumberOfOrders", "2");
    ```

    The following expression in a message selector would evaluate to false, because a string cannot be used in an arithmetic expression:

    ```
    "NumberOfOrders > 1"
    ```

  - Identifiers are case-sensitive.

  - Message header field references are restricted to JMSDeliveryMode, JMSPriority, JMSMessageID, JMSTimestamp, JMSCorrelationID, and JMSType. JMSMessageID, JMSCorrelationID, and JMSType values may be null and if so are treated as a NULL value.

  - Any name beginning with 'JMSX' is a JMS defined property name.

  - Any name beginning with 'JMS_' is a provider-specific property name.

  - Any name that does not begin with 'JMS' is an application-specific property name.

- White space is the same as that defined for the Java programming language: space, horizontal tab, form feed, and line terminator.

- Expressions:

  - A selector is a conditional expression; a selector that evaluates to `true` matches; a selector that evaluates to `false` or unknown does not match.

  - Arithmetic expressions are composed of themselves, arithmetic operations, identifiers (whose value is treated as a numeric literal), and numeric literals.

  - Conditional expressions are composed of themselves, comparison operations, and logical operations.

- Standard bracketing () for ordering expression evaluation is supported.

- Logical operators in precedence order: `NOT`, `AND`, `OR`

- Comparison operators: =, >, >=, <, <=, <> (not equal)

  - Only like type values can be compared. One exception is that it is valid to compare exact numeric values and approximate numeric values; the type conversion required is defined by the rules of numeric promotion in the Java programming language. If the comparison of non-like type values is attempted, the value of the expression is false. If either of the type values evaluates to `NULL`, the value of the expression is unknown.

  - String and boolean comparison is restricted to = and <>. Two strings are equal if and only if they contain the same sequence of characters.

- Arithmetic operators in precedence order:

  - +, – (unary)

  - *, / (multiplication and division)

  - +, – (addition and subtraction)

  - Arithmetic operations must use numeric promotion in the Java programming language.

- `arithmetic-expr1 [NOT] BETWEEN arithmetic-expr2 AND arithmetic-expr3` (comparison operator)

  - "`age BETWEEN 15 AND 19`" is equivalent to "`age >= 15 AND age <= 19`"

  - "`age NOT BETWEEN 15 AND 19`" is equivalent to "`age < 15 OR age > 19`"

- `identifier [NOT] IN (string-literal1, string-literal2,...)` (comparison operator where `identifier` has a `String` or `NULL` value)

  - `"Country IN (' UK', 'US', 'France')"` is true for `'UK'` and false for `'Peru'`; it is equivalent to the expression `"(Country = ' UK') OR (Country = ' US') OR (Country = ' France')"`

  - `"Country NOT IN (' UK', 'US', 'France')"` is false for `'UK'` and true for `'Peru'`; it is equivalent to the expression `"NOT ((Country = ' UK') OR (Country = ' US') OR (Country = ' France'))"`

  - If identifier of an `IN` or `NOT IN` operation is `NULL`, the value of the operation is unknown.

- `identifier [NOT] LIKE pattern-value [ESCAPE escape-character]` (comparison operator, where `identifier` has a `String` value; `pattern-value` is a string literal where `'_'` stands for any single character; `'%'` stands for any sequence of characters, including the empty sequence; and all other characters stand for themselves. The optional `escape-character` is a single-character string literal whose character is used to escape the special meaning of the `'_'` and `'%'` in `pattern-value`.)

  - `"phone LIKE '12%3'"` is true for `'123'` or `'12993'` and false for `'1234'`

  - `"word LIKE 'l_se'"` is true for `'lose'` and false for `'loose'`

  - `"underscored LIKE '\_%' ESCAPE '\'"` is true for `'_foo'` and false for `'bar'`

  - `"phone NOT LIKE '12%3'"` is false for `'123'` or `'12993'` and true for `'1234'`

  - If `identifier` of a `LIKE` or `NOT LIKE` operation is `NULL`, the value of the operation is unknown.

- `identifier IS NULL` (comparison operator that tests for a null header field value or a missing property value)

  - `"prop_name IS NULL"`

- `identifier IS NOT NULL` (comparison operator that tests for the existence of a non-null header field value or a property value)

  - `"prop_name IS NOT NULL"`

JMS providers are required to verify the syntactic correctness of a message selector at the time it is presented. A method that provides a syntactically incorrect selector must result in a `JMSException`.

The following message selector selects messages with a message type of car and color of blue and weight greater than 2500 pounds:

```
"JMSType = 'car' AND color = 'blue' AND weight > 2500"
```

25.1.5.1 Null Values in Message Selectors

As noted above, property values may be NULL. The evaluation of selector expressions containing NULL values is defined by SQL92 NULL semantics. A brief description of these semantics is provided here.

SQL treats a NULL value as unknown. Comparison or arithmetic with an unknown value always yields an unknown value.

The IS NULL and IS NOT NULL operators convert an unknown value into the respective TRUE and FALSE values.

25.1.5.2 Boolean Operators in Message Selectors

The Boolean operators use three-valued logic as defined by Tables 25.2, 25.3, and 25.4.

Table 25.2: The AND Operator

AND	T	F	U
T	T	F	U
F	F	F	F
U	U	F	U

Table 25.3: The OR Operator

OR	T	F	U
T	T	T	T
F	T	F	U
U	T	U	U

Table 25.4: The NOT Operator

NOT	
T	F
F	T
U	U

25.1.5.3 Special Notes on Message Selectors

- When used in a message selector, the JMSDeliveryMode header field is treated as having the values PERSISTENT and NON_PERSISTENT.

- Date and time values should use the standard long millisecond value. When a date or time literal is included in a message selector, it should be an integer literal for a millisecond value. The standard way to produce millisecond values is to use java.util.Calendar.

- Although SQL supports fixed decimal comparison and arithmetic, JMS message selectors do not. This is the reason for restricting exact numeric literals to those without a decimal (and the addition of numerics with a decimal as an alternate representation for approximate numeric values).

- SQL comments are not supported.

25.1.6 Related Methods and Interfaces

- MessageConsumer.receive()

- MessageConsumer.receive(long)

- MessageConsumer.receiveNoWait

- MessageListener.onMessage

- BytesMessage

- MapMessage

- ObjectMessage

- StreamMessage

- TextMessage

25.2   Interface Definition

```
package javax.jms;
public interface Message {
    // Fields
    static final int DEFAULT_DELIVERY_MODE = DeliveryMode.PERSISTENT;
    static final int DEFAULT_PRIORITY      = 4;
    static final long DEFAULT_TIME_TO_LIVE = 0;
    // Methods
    void acknowledge() throws JMSException;
    void clearBody() throws JMSException;
    void clearProperties() throws JMSException;
    boolean getBooleanProperty(String name) throws JMSException;
    byte getByteProperty(String name) throws JMSException;
    double getDoubleProperty(String name) throws JMSException;
    float getFloatProperty(String name) throws JMSException;
    int getIntProperty(String name) throws JMSException;
    String getJMSCorrelationID() throws JMSException;
    byte [] getJMSCorrelationIDAsBytes() throws JMSException;
    int getJMSDeliveryMode() throws JMSException;
    Destination getJMSDestination() throws JMSException;
    long getJMSExpiration() throws JMSException;
    String getJMSMessageID() throws JMSException;
    int getJMSPriority() throws JMSException;
    boolean getJMSRedelivered() throws JMSException;
    Destination getJMSReplyTo() throws JMSException;
    long getJMSTimestamp() throws JMSException;
    String getJMSType() throws JMSException;
    long getLongProperty(String name) throws JMSException;
    Object getObjectProperty(String name) throws JMSException;
    Enumeration getPropertyNames() throws JMSException;
    short getShortProperty(String name) throws JMSException;
    String getStringProperty(String name) throws JMSException;
    boolean propertyExists(String name) throws JMSException;
    void setBooleanProperty(String name, boolean value)
                                        throws JMSException;
```

```
void setByteProperty(String name, byte value) throws JMSException;
void setDoubleProperty(String name, double value)
                                            throws JMSException;
void setFloatProperty(String name, float value)
                                            throws JMSException;
void setIntProperty(String name, int value) throws JMSException;
void setJMSCorrelationID(String correlationID) throws JMSException;
void setJMSCorrelationIDAsBytes(byte[] correlationID)
                                            throws JMSException;
void setJMSDeliveryMode(int deliveryMode) throws JMSException;
void setJMSDestination(Destination destination)
                                            throws JMSException;
void setJMSExpiration(long expiration) throws JMSException;
void setJMSMessageID(String id) throws JMSException;
void setJMSPriority(int priority) throws JMSException;
void setJMSRedelivered(boolean redelivered) throws JMSException;
void setJMSReplyTo(Destination replyTo) throws JMSException;
void setJMSTimestamp(long timestamp) throws JMSException;
void setJMSType(String type) throws JMSException;
void setLongProperty(String name, long value) throws JMSException;
void setObjectProperty(String name, Object value)
                                            throws JMSException;
void setShortProperty(String name, short value)
                                            throws JMSException;
void setStringProperty(String name, String value)
                                            throws JMSException;
}
```

25.3 Fields

The following fields are defined in the interface javax.jms.Message.

DEFAULT_DELIVERY_MODE

```
public static final int DEFAULT_DELIVERY_MODE
```

The message producer's default delivery mode is PERSISTENT.

SEE ALSO:
DeliveryMode.PERSISTENT

DEFAULT_PRIORITY

```
public static final int DEFAULT_PRIORITY
```

The message producer's default priority is 4.

DEFAULT_TIME_TO_LIVE

```
public static final long DEFAULT_TIME_TO_LIVE
```

The message producer's default time to live is unlimited; the message never expires.

25.4 Methods

The following methods are defined in the interface `javax.jms.Message`.

acknowledge

```
public void acknowledge()
```

Acknowledges all consumed messages of the session of this consumed message.

All consumed JMS messages support the `acknowledge` method for use when a client has specified that its JMS session's consumed messages are to be explicitly acknowledged. By invoking `acknowledge` on a consumed message, a client acknowledges all messages consumed by the session that the message was delivered to.

Calls to `acknowledge` are ignored for both transacted sessions and sessions specified to use implicit acknowledgement modes.

A client may individually acknowledge each message as it is consumed, or it may choose to acknowledge messages as an application-defined group (which is done by calling `acknowledge` on the last received message of the group, thereby acknowledging all messages consumed by the session.)

Messages that have been received but not acknowledged may be redelivered.

THROWS:

JMSException	if the JMS provider fails to acknowledge the messages due to some internal error
IllegalStateException	if this method is called on a closed session

SEE ALSO:
Session.CLIENT_ACKNOWLEDGE

clearBody

```
public void clearBody()
```

Clears out the message body. Clearing a message's body does not clear its header values or property entries.

If this message body was read-only, calling this method leaves the message body in the same state as an empty body in a newly created message.

THROWS:

JMSException	if the JMS provider fails to clear the message body due to some internal error

clearProperties

```
public void clearProperties()
```

Clears a message's properties.
The message's header fields and body are not cleared.

THROWS:

JMSException	if the JMS provider fails to clear the message properties due to some internal error

getBooleanProperty

```
public boolean getBooleanProperty(java.lang.String name)
```

Returns the value of the boolean property with the specified name.

PARAMETERS:

name	the name of the boolean property

RETURNS:
the boolean property value for the specified name

THROWS:

JMSException	if the JMS provider fails to get the property value due to some internal error
MessageFormatException	if this type conversion is invalid

getByteProperty

```
public byte getByteProperty(java.lang.String name)
```

Returns the value of the byte property with the specified name.

PARAMETERS:

name   the name of the byte property

RETURNS:
the byte property value for the specified name

THROWS:

JMSException	if the JMS provider fails to get the property value due to some internal error
MessageFormatException	if this type conversion is invalid

getDoubleProperty

```
public double getDoubleProperty(java.lang.String name)
```

Returns the value of the double property with the specified name.

PARAMETERS:

name   the name of the double property

RETURNS:
the double property value for the specified name

THROWS:

JMSException	if the JMS provider fails to get the property value due to some internal error
MessageFormatException	if this type conversion is invalid

getFloatProperty

```
public float getFloatProperty(java.lang.String name)
```

Returns the value of the `float` property with the specified name.

PARAMETERS:
name   the name of the `float` property

RETURNS:
the `float` property value for the specified name

THROWS:
JMSException   if the JMS provider fails to get the property
                                          value due to some internal error
MessageFormatException   if this type conversion is invalid

getIntProperty

```
public int getIntProperty(java.lang.String name)
```

Returns the value of the `int` property with the specified name.

PARAMETERS:
name   the name of the `int` property

RETURNS:
the `int` property value for the specified name

THROWS:
JMSException   if the JMS provider fails to get the property
                                          value due to some internal error
MessageFormatException   if this type conversion is invalid

getJMSCorrelationID

```
public java.lang.String getJMSCorrelationID()
```

Gets the correlation ID for the message.

The `JMSCorrelationID` header field is used for linking one message with another. It typically links a reply message with its requesting message.

This method is used to return correlation ID values that are either provider-specific message IDs or application-specific `String` values.

RETURNS:
the correlation ID of a message as a `String`

THROWS:

`JMSException`	if the JMS provider fails to get the correlation ID due to some internal error

SEE ALSO:
`setJMSCorrelationID`
`getJMSCorrelationIDAsBytes`
`setJMSCorrelationIDAsBytes`

getJMSCorrelationIDAsBytes

`public byte[] getJMSCorrelationIDAsBytes()`

Gets the correlation ID as an array of bytes for the message.
The use of a `byte[]` value for `JMSCorrelationID` is non-portable.

RETURNS:
the correlation ID of a message as an array of bytes

THROWS:

`JMSException`	if the JMS provider fails to get the correlation ID due to some internal error

SEE ALSO:
`setJMSCorrelationID`
`getJMSCorrelationID`
`setJMSCorrelationIDAsBytes`

getJMSDeliveryMode

`public int getJMSDeliveryMode()`

Gets the `DeliveryMode` value specified for this message.

RETURNS:
the delivery mode for this message

THROWS:

`JMSException`	if the JMS provider fails to get the delivery mode due to some internal error

SEE ALSO:
setJMSDeliveryMode
DeliveryMode

getJMSDestination

public Destination **getJMSDestination**()

Gets the Destination object for this message.

The JMSDestination header field contains the destination to which the message is being sent.

When a message is sent, this field is ignored. After completion of the send or publish method, the field holds the destination specified by the method.

When a message is received, its JMSDestination value must be equivalent to the value assigned when it was sent.

RETURNS:
the destination of this message

THROWS:

JMSException   if the JMS provider fails to get the destination due to some internal error

SEE ALSO:
setJMSDestination

getJMSExpiration

public long **getJMSExpiration**()

Gets the message's expiration value.

When a message is sent, the JMSExpiration header field is left unassigned. After completion of the send or publish method, it holds the expiration time of the message. This is the sum of the time-to-live value specified by the client and the GMT at the time of the send or publish.

If the time-to-live is specified as zero, JMSExpiration is set to zero to indicate that the message does not expire.

When a message's expiration time is reached, a provider should discard it. The JMS API does not define any form of notification of message expiration.

Clients should not receive messages that have expired; however, the JMS API does not guarantee that this will not happen.

RETURNS:

the time the message expires, which is the sum of the time-to-live value specified by the client and the GMT at the time of the send

THROWS:

JMSException   if the JMS provider fails to get the message
                                          expiration due to some internal error

SEE ALSO:

setJMSExpiration

getJMSMessageID

```
public java.lang.String getJMSMessageID()
```

Gets the message ID.

The JMSMessageID header field contains a value that uniquely identifies each message sent by a provider.

When a message is sent, JMSMessageID can be ignored. When the send or publish method returns, it contains a provider-assigned value.

A JMSMessageID is a String value that should function as a unique key for identifying messages in a historical repository. The exact scope of uniqueness is provider-defined. It should at least cover all messages for a specific installation of a provider, where an installation is some connected set of message routers.

All JMSMessageID values must start with the prefix 'ID:'. Uniqueness of message ID values across different providers is not required.

Since message IDs take some effort to create and increase a message's size, some JMS providers may be able to optimize message overhead if they are given a hint that the message ID is not used by an application. By calling the MessageProducer.setDisableMessageID method, a JMS client enables this potential optimization for all messages sent by that message producer. If the JMS provider accepts this hint, these messages must have the message ID set to null; if the provider ignores the hint, the message ID must be set to its normal unique value.

RETURNS:

the message ID

THROWS:

JMSException   if the JMS provider fails to get the message
                                          ID due to some internal error

getJMSPriority

```
public int getJMSPriority()
```

Gets the message priority level.

The JMS API defines ten levels of priority value, with 0 as the lowest priority and 9 as the highest. In addition, clients should consider priorities 0–4 as gradations of normal priority and priorities 5–9 as gradations of expedited priority.

The JMS API does not require that a provider strictly implement priority ordering of messages; however, it should do its best to deliver expedited messages ahead of normal messages.

RETURNS:
the default message priority

THROWS:

JMSException   if the JMS provider fails to get the message priority due to some internal error

SEE ALSO:
setJMSPriority

getJMSRedelivered

```
public boolean getJMSRedelivered()
```

Gets an indication of whether this message is being redelivered.

If a client receives a message with the JMSRedelivered field set, it is likely, but not guaranteed, that this message was delivered earlier but that its receipt was not acknowledged at that time.

RETURNS:
true if this message is being redelivered

THROWS:

JMSException   if the JMS provider fails to get the redelivered state due to some internal error

SEE ALSO:
setJMSRedelivered

getJMSReplyTo

public Destination **getJMSReplyTo**()

Gets the `Destination` object to which a reply to this message should be sent.

RETURNS:
`Destination` to which to send a response to this message

THROWS:

JMSException	if the JMS provider fails to get the JMSReplyTo destination due to some internal error

SEE ALSO:
setJMSReplyTo

getJMSTimestamp

public long **getJMSTimestamp**()

Gets the message timestamp.

The JMSTimestamp header field contains the time a message was handed off to a provider to be sent. It is not the time the message was actually transmitted, because the actual send may occur later due to transactions or other client-side queueing of messages.

When a message is sent, JMSTimestamp is ignored. When the send or publish method returns, it contains a time value somewhere in the interval between the call and the return. The value is in the format of a normal millisecond time value in the Java programming language.

Since timestamps take some effort to create and increase a message's size, some JMS providers may be able to optimize message overhead if they are given a hint that the timestamp is not used by an application. By calling the MessageProducer.setDisableMessageTimestamp method, a JMS client enables this potential optimization for all messages sent by that message producer. If the JMS provider accepts this hint, these messages must have the timestamp set to zero; if the provider ignores the hint, the timestamp must be set to its normal value.

RETURNS:
the message timestamp

THROWS:

`JMSException`	if the JMS provider fails to get the timestamp due to some internal error

SEE ALSO:
`setJMSTimestamp`
`setDisableMessageTimestamp`

getJMSType

```
public java.lang.String getJMSType()
```

Gets the message type identifier supplied by the client when the message was sent.

RETURNS:
the message type

THROWS:

`JMSException`	if the JMS provider fails to get the message type due to some internal error

SEE ALSO:
`setJMSType`

getLongProperty

```
public long getLongProperty(java.lang.String name)
```

Returns the value of the `long` property with the specified name.

PARAMETERS:

name	the name of the `long` property

RETURNS:
the `long` property value for the specified name

THROWS:

`JMSException`	if the JMS provider fails to get the property value due to some internal error
`MessageFormatException`	if this type conversion is invalid

getObjectProperty

```
public java.lang.Object getObjectProperty(java.lang.String name)
```

Returns the value of the Java object property with the specified name.

This method can be used to return, in objectified format, an object that has been stored as a property in the message with the equivalent setObject-Property method call, or its equivalent primitive set*type*Property method.

PARAMETERS:

name   the name of the Java object property

RETURNS:

the Java object property value with the specified name, in objectified format (for example, if the property was set as an int, an Integer is returned); if there is no property by this name, a null value is returned

THROWS:

JMSException   if the JMS provider fails to get the property value due to some internal error

getPropertyNames

```
public java.util.Enumeration getPropertyNames()
```

Returns an Enumeration of all the property names.

Note that JMS standard header fields are not considered properties and are not returned in this enumeration.

RETURNS:

an enumeration of all the names of property values

THROWS:

JMSException   if the JMS provider fails to get the property names due to some internal error

getShortProperty

```
public short getShortProperty(java.lang.String name)
```

Returns the value of the short property with the specified name.

PARAMETERS:

name   the name of the short property

RETURNS:
the short property value for the specified name

THROWS:

JMSException	if the JMS provider fails to get the property value due to some internal error
MessageFormatException	if this type conversion is invalid

getStringProperty

```
public java.lang.String getStringProperty(java.lang.String name)
```

Returns the value of the String property with the specified name.

PARAMETERS:

name	the name of the String property

RETURNS:
the String property value for the specified name; if there is no property by this name, a null value is returned

THROWS:

JMSException	if the JMS provider fails to get the property value due to some internal error
MessageFormatException	if this type conversion is invalid

propertyExists

```
public boolean propertyExists(java.lang.String name)
```

Indicates whether a property value exists.

PARAMETERS:

name	the name of the property to test

RETURNS:
true if the property exists

THROWS:

JMSException	if the JMS provider fails to determine if the property exists due to some internal error

setBooleanProperty

```
public void setBooleanProperty(java.lang.String name, boolean value)
```

Sets a boolean property value with the specified name into the message.

PARAMETERS:

name   the name of the boolean property

value   the boolean property value to set

THROWS:

JMSException   if the JMS provider fails to set the property
                            due to some internal error

MessageNotWriteableException if properties are read-only

setByteProperty

```
public void setByteProperty(java.lang.String name, byte value)
```

Sets a byte property value with the specified name into the message.

PARAMETERS:

name   the name of the byte property

value   the byte property value to set

THROWS:

JMSException   if the JMS provider fails to set the property
                            due to some internal error

MessageNotWriteableException if properties are read-only

setDoubleProperty

```
public void setDoubleProperty(java.lang.String name, double value)
```

Sets a double property value with the specified name into the message.

PARAMETERS:

name   the name of the double property

value   the double property value to set

THROWS:

JMSException   if the JMS provider fails to set the property
                            due to some internal error

MessageNotWriteableException if properties are read-only

setFloatProperty

```
public void setFloatProperty(java.lang.String name, float value)
```

Sets a float property value with the specified name into the message.

PARAMETERS:

name	the name of the float property
value	the float property value to set

THROWS:

JMSException   if the JMS provider fails to set the property due to some internal error

MessageNotWriteableException if properties are read-only

setIntProperty

```
public void setIntProperty(java.lang.String name, int value)
```

Sets an int property value with the specified name into the message.

PARAMETERS:

name	the name of the int property
value	the int property value to set

THROWS:

JMSException   if the JMS provider fails to set the property due to some internal error

MessageNotWriteableException if properties are read-only

setJMSCorrelationID

```
public void setJMSCorrelationID(java.lang.String correlationID)
```

Sets the correlation ID for the message.

A client can use the JMSCorrelationID header field to link one message with another. A typical use is to link a response message with its request message.

JMSCorrelationID can hold one of the following:

- A provider-specific message ID

- An application-specific String

- A provider-native byte[] value

Since each message sent by a JMS provider is assigned a message ID value, it is convenient to link messages via message ID. All message ID values must start with the 'ID:' prefix.

In some cases, an application (made up of several clients) needs to use an application-specific value for linking messages. For instance, an application may use JMSCorrelationID to hold a value referencing some external information. Application-specified values must not start with the 'ID:' prefix; this is reserved for provider-generated message ID values.

If a provider supports the native concept of correlation ID, a JMS client may need to assign specific JMSCorrelationID values to match those expected by clients that do not use the JMS API. A byte[] value is used for this purpose. JMS providers without native correlation ID values are not required to support byte[] values. The use of a byte[] value for JMSCorrelationID is non-portable.

PARAMETERS:

correlationID   the message ID of a message being referred to

THROWS:

JMSException   if the JMS provider fails to set the correlation ID due to some internal error

SEE ALSO:

getJMSCorrelationID
getJMSCorrelationIDAsBytes
setJMSCorrelationIDAsBytes

setJMSCorrelationIDAsBytes

public void **setJMSCorrelationIDAsBytes**(byte[] *correlationID*)

Sets the correlation ID as an array of bytes for the message.

The array is copied before the method returns, so future modifications to the array will not alter this message header.

If a provider supports the native concept of correlation ID, a JMS client may need to assign specific `JMSCorrelationID` values to match those expected by native messaging clients. JMS providers without native correlation ID values are not required to support this method and its corresponding get method; their implementation may throw a `java.lang.UnsupportedOperationException`.

The use of a `byte[]` value for `JMSCorrelationID` is non-portable.

PARAMETERS:

correlationID   the correlation ID value as an array of bytes

THROWS:

JMSException   if the JMS provider fails to set the correlation ID due to some internal error

SEE ALSO:

setJMSCorrelationID
getJMSCorrelationID
getJMSCorrelationIDAsBytes

setJMSDeliveryMode

```
public void setJMSDeliveryMode(int deliveryMode)
```

Sets the `DeliveryMode` value for this message.

JMS providers set this field when a message is sent. This method is not ordinarily used by clients, but it can be used to change the value for a message that has been received.

PARAMETERS:

deliveryMode   the delivery mode for this message

THROWS:

JMSException   if the JMS provider fails to set the delivery mode due to some internal error

SEE ALSO:

getJMSDeliveryMode
DeliveryMode

setJMSDestination

```
public void setJMSDestination(Destination destination)
```

Sets the `Destination` object for this message.

JMS providers set this field when a message is sent. This method is not ordinarily used by clients, but it can be used to change the value for a message that has been received.

PARAMETERS:

`destination`   the destination for this message

THROWS:

`JMSException`   if the JMS provider fails to set the destination due to some internal error

SEE ALSO:
`getJMSDestination`

setJMSExpiration

```
public void setJMSExpiration(long expiration)
```

Sets the message's expiration value.

JMS providers set this field when a message is sent. This method is not ordinarily used by clients, but it can be used to change the value for a message that has been received.

PARAMETERS:

`expiration`   the message's expiration time

THROWS:

`JMSException`   if the JMS provider fails to set the message expiration due to some internal error

SEE ALSO:
`getJMSExpiration`

setJMSMessageID

```
public void setJMSMessageID(java.lang.String id)
```

Sets the message ID.

JMS providers set this field when a message is sent. This method is not ordinarily used by clients, but it can be used to change the value for a message that has been received.

PARAMETERS:

`id`	the ID of the message

THROWS:

`JMSException`	if the JMS provider fails to set the message ID due to some internal error

SEE ALSO:
`getJMSMessageID`

setJMSPriority

```
public void setJMSPriority(int priority)
```

Sets the priority level for this message.

JMS providers set this field when a message is sent. This method is not ordinarily used by clients, but it can be used to change the value for a message that has been received.

PARAMETERS:

`priority`	the priority of this message

THROWS:

`JMSException`	if the JMS provider fails to set the message priority due to some internal error

SEE ALSO:
`getJMSPriority`

setJMSRedelivered

```
public void setJMSRedelivered(boolean redelivered)
```

Specifies whether this message is being redelivered.

This field is set at the time the message is delivered. This method is not ordinarily used by clients, but it can be used to change the value for a message that has been received.

PARAMETERS:

redelivered   an indication of whether this message is being redelivered

THROWS:

JMSException   if the JMS provider fails to set the redelivered state due to some internal error

SEE ALSO:

getJMSRedelivered

setJMSReplyTo

```
public void setJMSReplyTo(Destination replyTo)
```

Sets the `Destination` object to which a reply to this message should be sent.

The `JMSReplyTo` header field contains the destination where a reply to the current message should be sent. If it is null, no reply is expected. The destination may be either a `Queue` object or a `Topic` object.

Messages sent with a null `JMSReplyTo` value may be a notification of some event, or they may just be some data the sender thinks is of interest.

Messages with a `JMSReplyTo` value typically expect a response. A response is optional; it is up to the client to decide. These messages are called requests. A message sent in response to a request is called a reply.

In some cases a client may wish to match a request it sent earlier with a reply it has just received. The client can use the `JMSCorrelationID` header field for this purpose.

PARAMETERS:

replyTo   Destination to which to send a response to this message

THROWS:

JMSException

if the JMS provider fails to set the JMSReplyTo destination due to some internal error

SEE ALSO:
getJMSReplyTo

setJMSTimestamp

```
public void setJMSTimestamp(long timestamp)
```

Sets the message timestamp.

JMS providers set this field when a message is sent. This method is not ordinarily used by clients, but it can be used to change the value for a message that has been received.

PARAMETERS:

timestamp

the timestamp for this message

THROWS:

JMSException

if the JMS provider fails to set the timestamp due to some internal error

SEE ALSO:
getJMSTimestamp

setJMSType

```
public void setJMSType(java.lang.String type)
```

Sets the message type.

Some JMS providers use a message repository that contains the definitions of messages sent by applications. The JMSType header field may reference a message's definition in the provider's repository.

The JMS API does not define a standard message definition repository, nor does it define a naming policy for the definitions it contains.

Some messaging systems require that a message type definition for each application message be created and that each message specify its type. In order to work with such JMS providers, JMS clients should assign a value to JMSType, whether the application makes use of it or not. This ensures that the field is properly set for those providers that require it.

To ensure portability, JMS clients should use symbolic values for JMSType that can be configured at installation time to the values defined in the current provider's message repository. If string literals are used, they may not be valid type names for some JMS providers.

PARAMETERS:

type   the message type

THROWS:

JMSException   if the JMS provider fails to set the message type due to some internal error

SEE ALSO:

getJMSType

setLongProperty

```
public void setLongProperty(java.lang.String name, long value)
```

Sets a long property value with the specified name into the message.

PARAMETERS:

name   the name of the long property

value   the long property value to set

THROWS:

JMSException   if the JMS provider fails to set the property due to some internal error

MessageNotWriteableException if properties are read-only

setObjectProperty

```
public void setObjectProperty(java.lang.String name,
                                     java.lang.Object value)
```

Sets a Java object property value with the specified name into the message.

Note that this method works only for the objectified primitive object types (Integer, Double, Long ...) and String objects.

PARAMETERS:

name   the name of the Java object property

value   the Java object property value to set

THROWS:

JMSException	if the JMS provider fails to set the property due to some internal error
MessageFormatException	if the object is invalid
MessageNotWriteableException	if properties are read-only

setShortProperty

```
public void setShortProperty(java.lang.String name, short value)
```

Sets a short property value with the specified name into the message.

PARAMETERS:

name	the name of the short property
value	the short property value to set

THROWS:

JMSException	if the JMS provider fails to set the property due to some internal error
MessageNotWriteableException	if properties are read-only

setStringProperty

```
public void setStringProperty(java.lang.String name,
                              java.lang.String value)
```

Sets a String property value with the specified name into the message.

PARAMETERS:

name	the name of the String property
value	the String property value to set

THROWS:

JMSException	if the JMS provider fails to set the property due to some internal error
MessageNotWriteableException	if properties are read-only

CHAPTER 26

MessageConsumer

26.1 Overview and Related Interfaces

A client uses a MessageConsumer object to receive messages from a destination. A MessageConsumer object is created by passing a Destination object to a message-consumer creation method supplied by a session.

MessageConsumer is the parent interface for all message consumers.

A message consumer can be created with a message selector. A message selector allows the client to restrict the messages delivered to the message consumer to those that match the selector.

A client may either synchronously receive a message consumer's messages or have the consumer asynchronously deliver them as they arrive.

For synchronous receipt, a client can request the next message from a message consumer using one of its receive methods. There are several variations of receive that allow a client to poll or wait for the next message.

For asynchronous delivery, a client can register a MessageListener object with a message consumer. As messages arrive at the message consumer, it delivers them by calling the MessageListener's onMessage method.

It is a client programming error for a MessageListener to throw an exception.

The related interfaces are

- QueueReceiver

- TopicSubscriber

- Session

26.2   Interface Definition

```
package javax.jms;
public interface MessageConsumer {
    void close() throws JMSException;
    MessageListener getMessageListener() throws JMSException;
    String getMessageSelector() throws JMSException;
    Message receive() throws JMSException;
    Message receive(long timeout) throws JMSException;
    Message receiveNoWait() throws JMSException;
    void setMessageListener(MessageListener listener)
                                                throws JMSException;
}
```

26.3   Methods

The following methods are defined in the interface javax.jms.MessageConsumer.

close

```
public void close()
```

Closes the message consumer.

Since a provider may allocate some resources on behalf of a Message-Consumer outside the Java virtual machine, clients should close them when they are not needed. Relying on garbage collection to eventually reclaim these resources may not be timely enough.

This call blocks until a receive or message listener in progress has completed. A blocked message consumer receive call returns null when this message consumer is closed.

THROWS:

JMSException   if the JMS provider fails to close the consumer due to some internal error

getMessageListener

```
public MessageListener getMessageListener()
```

Gets the message consumer's `MessageListener`.

RETURNS:
the listener for the message consumer, or null if no listener is set

THROWS:

`JMSException`   if the JMS provider fails to get the message listener due to some internal error.

SEE ALSO:
`setMessageListener`

getMessageSelector

```
public java.lang.String getMessageSelector()
```

Gets this message consumer's message selector expression.

RETURNS:
this message consumer's message selector, or null if no message selector exists for the message consumer (that is, if the message selector was not set or was set to null or the empty string)

THROWS:

`JMSException`   if the JMS provider fails to get the message selector due to some internal error

receive()

```
public Message receive()
```

Receives the next message produced for this message consumer.

This call blocks indefinitely until a message is produced or until this message consumer is closed.

If this `receive` is done within a transaction, the consumer retains the message until the transaction commits.

RETURNS:
the next message produced for this message consumer, or null if this message consumer is concurrently closed

THROWS:

JMSException   if the JMS provider fails to receive the next message due to some internal error

receive(long)

```
public Message receive(long timeout)
```

Receives the next message that arrives within the specified timeout interval.

This call blocks until a message arrives, the timeout expires, or this message consumer is closed. A timeout of zero never expires, and the call blocks indefinitely.

PARAMETERS:

timeout   the timeout value (in milliseconds)

RETURNS:

the next message produced for this message consumer, or null if the timeout expires or this message consumer is concurrently closed

THROWS:

JMSException   if the JMS provider fails to receive the next message due to some internal error

receiveNoWait

```
public Message receiveNoWait()
```

Receives the next message if one is immediately available.

RETURNS:

the next message produced for this message consumer, or null if one is not available

THROWS:

JMSException   if the JMS provider fails to receive the next message due to some internal error

setMessageListener

```
public void setMessageListener(MessageListener listener)
```

Sets the message consumer's `MessageListener`.

Setting the message listener to null is the equivalent of unsetting the message listener for the message consumer.

The effect of calling `MessageConsumer.setMessageListener` while messages are being consumed by an existing listener or the consumer is being used to consume messages synchronously is undefined.

PARAMETERS:

listener   the listener to which the messages are to be delivered

THROWS:

JMSException   if the JMS provider fails to set the message listener due to some internal error

SEE ALSO:

getMessageListener

CHAPTER 27

MessageEOFException

27.1 Overview

This exception must be thrown when an unexpected end of stream has been reached when a StreamMessage or BytesMessage is being read.

The MessageEOFException class inherits the methods of the class javax.jms.JMSException.

27.2 Class Definition

```
package javax.jms;
public class MessageEOFException extends JMSException {
    public MessageEOFException(String reason);
    public MessageEOFException(String reason, String errorCode);
}
```

27.3 Constructors

The following constructors are defined by the class `javax.jms.MessageEOF-Exception`.

MessageEOFException(String)

public **MessageEOFException**(java.lang.String *reason*)

Constructs a `MessageEOFException` with the specified reason. The error code defaults to null.

PARAMETERS:

reason   a description of the exception

MessageEOFException(String, String)

public **MessageEOFException**(java.lang.String *reason*,

java.lang.String *errorCode*)

Constructs a `MessageEOFException` with the specified reason and error code.

PARAMETERS:

reason   a description of the exception

errorCode   a string specifying the vendor-specific error code

CHAPTER 28

MessageFormatException

28.1 Overview

This exception must be thrown when a JMS client attempts to use a data type not supported by a message or attempts to read data in a message as the wrong type. It must also be thrown when equivalent type errors are made with message property values. For example, this exception must be thrown if `StreamMessage.writeObject` is given an unsupported class or if `StreamMessage.readShort` is used to read a `boolean` value. Note that the special case of a failure caused by an attempt to read improperly formatted `String` data as numeric values must throw the `java.lang.NumberFormatException`.

The `MessageFormatException` class inherits the methods of the class `javax.jms.JMSException`.

28.2 Class Definition

```
package javax.jms;
public class MessageFormatException extends JMSException {
    public MessageFormatException(String reason);
    public MessageFormatException(String reason, String errorCode);
}
```

28.3   Constructors

The following constructors are defined by the class javax.jms.MessageFormat-Exception.

MessageFormatException(String)

```
public MessageFormatException(java.lang.String reason)
```

Constructs a MessageFormatException with the specified reason. The error code defaults to null.

PARAMETERS:

reason   a description of the exception

MessageFormatException(String, String)

```
public MessageFormatException(java.lang.String reason,
                              java.lang.String errorCode)
```

Constructs a MessageFormatException with the specified reason and error code.

PARAMETERS:

reason   a description of the exception
errorCode   a string specifying the vendor-specific error code

CHAPTER 29

MessageListener

29.1 Overview

A `MessageListener` object is used to receive asynchronously delivered messages.

Each session must insure that it passes messages serially to the listener. This means that a listener assigned to one or more consumers of the same session can assume that the `onMessage` method is not called with the next message until the session has completed the last call.

29.2 Interface Definition

```
package javax.jms;
public interface MessageListener {
    void onMessage(Message message);
}
```

29.3 Methods

The following method is defined in the interface javax.jms.MessageListener.

onMessage

public void **onMessage**(Message *message*)

    Passes a message to the listener.

PARAMETERS:

message   the message passed to the listener

CHAPTER 30

MessageNotReadable-Exception

30.1 Overview

This exception must be thrown when a JMS client attempts to read a write-only message.

The MessageNotReadableException class inherits the methods of the class javax.jms.JMSException.

30.2 Class Definition

```
package javax.jms;
public class MessageNotReadableException extends JMSException {
    public MessageNotReadableException(String reason);
    public MessageNotReadableException(String reason,
                                                String errorCode);
}
```

30.3   Constructors

The following constructors are defined by the class `javax.jms.MessageNot-ReadableException`.

MessageNotReadableException(String)

public **MessageNotReadableException**(java.lang.String *reason*)

Constructs a `MessageNotReadableException` with the specified reason. The error code defaults to null.

PARAMETERS:

reason   a description of the exception

MessageNotReadableException(String, String)

public **MessageNotReadableException**(java.lang.String *reason*,
                                    java.lang.String *errorCode*)

Constructs a `MessageNotReadableException` with the specified reason and error code.

PARAMETERS:

reason   a description of the exception
errorCode   a string specifying the vendor-specific error
                            code

CHAPTER 31

MessageNotWriteable-Exception

31.1 Overview

This exception must be thrown when a JMS client attempts to write to a read-only message.

The `MessageNotWriteableException` class inherits the methods of the class `javax.jms.JMSException`.

31.2 Class Definition

```
package javax.jms;
public class MessageNotWriteableException extends JMSException {
    public MessageNotWriteableException(String reason);
    public MessageNotWriteableException(String reason,
                                                String errorCode);
}
```

31.3 Constructors

The following constructors are defined by the class `javax.jms.MessageNot-WriteableException`.

MessageNotWriteableException(String)

public **MessageNotWriteableException**(java.lang.String *reason*)

Constructs a `MessageNotWriteableException` with the specified reason. The error code defaults to null.

PARAMETERS:

reason	a description of the exception

MessageNotWriteableException(String, String)

public **MessageNotWriteableException**(java.lang.String *reason*,
                                        java.lang.String *errorCode*)

Constructs a `MessageNotWriteableException` with the specified reason and error code.

PARAMETERS:

reason	a description of the exception
errorCode	a string specifying the vendor-specific error code

MessageProducer

32.1 Overview and Related Interfaces

A client uses a `MessageProducer` object to send messages to a destination. A `MessageProducer` object is created by passing a `Destination` object to a message-producer creation method supplied by a session.

`MessageProducer` is the parent interface for all message producers.

A client also has the option of creating a message producer without supplying a destination. In this case, a destination must be provided with every send operation. A typical use for this kind of message producer is to send replies to requests using the request's `JMSReplyTo` destination.

A client can specify a default delivery mode, priority, and time to live for messages sent by a message producer. It can also specify the delivery mode, priority, and time to live for an individual message.

A client can specify a time-to-live value in milliseconds for each message it sends. This value defines a message expiration time that is the sum of the message's time-to-live and the GMT when it is sent (for transacted sends, this is the time the client sends the message, not the time the transaction is committed).

A JMS provider should do its best to expire messages accurately; however, the JMS API does not define the accuracy provided.

The related interfaces are

- `TopicPublisher`
- `QueueSender`
- `Session`

32.2 Interface Definition

```
package javax.jms;
public interface MessageProducer {
    void close() throws JMSException;
    int getDeliveryMode() throws JMSException;
    boolean getDisableMessageID() throws JMSException;
    boolean getDisableMessageTimestamp() throws JMSException;
    int getPriority() throws JMSException;
    long getTimeToLive() throws JMSException;
    void setDeliveryMode(int deliveryMode) throws JMSException;
    void setDisableMessageID(boolean value) throws JMSException;
    void setDisableMessageTimestamp(boolean value) throws JMSException;
    void setPriority(int defaultPriority) throws JMSException;
    void setTimeToLive(long timeToLive) throws JMSException;
}
```

32.3 Methods

The following methods are defined in the interface javax.jms.MessageProducer.

close

```
public void close()
```

Closes the message producer.

Since a provider may allocate some resources on behalf of a Message-Producer outside the Java virtual machine, clients should close them when they are not needed. Relying on garbage collection to eventually reclaim these resources may not be timely enough.

THROWS:

JMSException   if the JMS provider fails to close the producer due to some internal error

getDeliveryMode

```
public int getDeliveryMode()
```

Gets the producer's default delivery mode.

RETURNS:
the message delivery mode for this message producer

THROWS:

JMSException   if the JMS provider fails to get the delivery
                                      mode due to some internal error

SEE ALSO:
setDeliveryMode

getDisableMessageID

```
public boolean getDisableMessageID()
```

Gets an indication of whether message IDs are disabled.

RETURNS:
an indication of whether message IDs are disabled

THROWS:

JMSException   if the JMS provider fails to determine if mes-
                                      sage IDs are disabled due to some internal
                                      error

getDisableMessageTimestamp

```
public boolean getDisableMessageTimestamp()
```

Gets an indication of whether message timestamps are disabled.

RETURNS:
an indication of whether message timestamps are disabled

THROWS:

JMSException   if the JMS provider fails to determine if
                                      timestamps are disabled due to some internal
                                      error

getPriority

```
public int getPriority()
```

Gets the producer's default priority.

RETURNS:
the message priority for this message producer

THROWS:

JMSException   if the JMS provider fails to get the priority
                                    due to some internal error

SEE ALSO:
setPriority

getTimeToLive

```
public long getTimeToLive()
```

Gets the default length of time in milliseconds from its dispatch time that
a produced message should be retained by the message system.

RETURNS:
the message time to live in milliseconds; zero is unlimited

THROWS:

JMSException   if the JMS provider fails to get the time to
                                    live due to some internal error

SEE ALSO:
setTimeToLive

setDeliveryMode

```
public void setDeliveryMode(int deliveryMode)
```

Sets the producer's default delivery mode.
Delivery mode is set to PERSISTENT by default.

PARAMETERS:

deliveryMode   the message delivery mode for this message
                                    producer; legal values are Delivery-
                                    Mode.NON_PERSISTENT and Delivery-
                                    Mode.PERSISTENT

THROWS:

JMSException   if the JMS provider fails to set the delivery
                                mode due to some internal error

SEE ALSO:

getDeliveryMode
DeliveryMode.NON_PERSISTENT
DeliveryMode.PERSISTENT
Message.DEFAULT_DELIVERY_MODE

setDisableMessageID

```
public void setDisableMessageID(boolean value)
```

Sets whether message IDs are disabled.

Since message IDs take some effort to create and increase a message's size, some JMS providers may be able to optimize message overhead if they are given a hint that the message ID is not used by an application. By calling the setDisableMessageID method on this message producer, a JMS client enables this potential optimization for all messages sent by this message producer. If the JMS provider accepts this hint, these messages must have the message ID set to null; if the provider ignores the hint, the message ID must be set to its normal unique value.

Message IDs are enabled by default.

PARAMETERS:

value   indicates if message IDs are disabled

THROWS:

JMSException   if the JMS provider fails to set message ID to
                                disabled due to some internal error

setDisableMessageTimestamp

```
public void setDisableMessageTimestamp(boolean value)
```

Sets whether message timestamps are disabled.

Since timestamps take some effort to create and increase a message's size, some JMS providers may be able to optimize message overhead if they are given a hint that the timestamp is not used by an application. By calling the setDisableMessageTimestamp method on this message producer, a JMS client enables this potential optimization for all messages sent by this message producer. If the JMS provider accepts this hint, these messages must have the timestamp set to zero; if the provider ignores the hint, the timestamp must be set to its normal value.

Message timestamps are enabled by default.

PARAMETERS:

value   indicates if message timestamps are disabled

THROWS:

JMSException   if the JMS provider fails to set timestamps to disabled due to some internal error

setPriority

```
public void setPriority(int defaultPriority)
```

Sets the producer's default priority.

The JMS API defines ten levels of priority value, with 0 as the lowest priority and 9 as the highest. Clients should consider priorities 0–4 as gradations of normal priority and priorities 5–9 as gradations of expedited priority. Priority is set to 4 by default.

PARAMETERS:

defaultPriority   the message priority for this message producer; must be a value between 0 and 9

THROWS:

JMSException   if the JMS provider fails to set the priority due to some internal error

SEE ALSO:

getPriority
Message.DEFAULT_PRIORITY

setTimeToLive

```
public void setTimeToLive(long timeToLive)
```

Sets the default length of time in milliseconds from its dispatch time that a produced message should be retained by the message system.

Time to live is set to zero by default.

PARAMETERS:

timeToLive   the message time to live in milliseconds; zero is unlimited

THROWS:

JMSException   if the JMS provider fails to set the time to live due to some internal error

SEE ALSO:

getTimeToLive

Message.DEFAULT_TIME_TO_LIVE

CHAPTER 33

ObjectMessage

33.1 Overview and Related Methods and Interfaces

An `ObjectMessage` object is used to send a message that contains a serializable object in the Java programming language ("Java object"). It inherits from the `Message` interface and adds a body containing a single reference to an object. Only `Serializable` Java objects can be used.

If a collection of Java objects must be sent, one of the `Collection` classes provided since version 1.2 of the J2SE SDK can be used.

When a client receives an `ObjectMessage`, it is in read-only mode. If a client attempts to write to the message at this point, a `MessageNotWriteableException` is thrown. If `clearBody` is called, the message can now be both read from and written to.

The related methods and interfaces are

- `Session.createObjectMessage()`

- `Session.createObjectMessage(Serializable)`

- `BytesMessage`

- `MapMessage`

- `Message`

- `StreamMessage`

- `TextMessage`

33.2   Interface Definition

```
package javax.jms;
public interface ObjectMessage extends Message {
    Serializable getObject() throws JMSException;
    void setObject(Serializable object) throws JMSException;
}
```

33.3   Methods

The ObjectMessage interface inherits the fields and the methods of the interface javax.jms.Message. The following methods are defined in the interface javax.jms.ObjectMessage.

getObject

```
public java.io.Serializable getObject()
```

Gets the serializable object containing this message's data. The default value is null.

RETURNS:
the serializable object containing this message's data

THROWS:

JMSException	if the JMS provider fails to get the object due to some internal error
MessageFormatException	if object deserialization fails

setObject

```
public void setObject(java.io.Serializable object)
```

Sets the serializable object containing this message's data. It is important to note that an ObjectMessage contains a snapshot of the object at the time setObject is called; subsequent modifications of the object will have no effect on the ObjectMessage body.

PARAMETERS:

object	the message's data

THROWS:

`JMSException`	if the JMS provider fails to set the object due to some internal error
`MessageFormatException`	if object serialization fails
`MessageNotWriteableException`	if the message is in read-only mode

CHAPTER 34

Queue

34.1 Overview and Related Methods and Interfaces

A Queue object encapsulates a provider-specific queue name. It is the way a client specifies the identity of a queue to JMS API methods.

The actual length of time messages are held by a queue and the consequences of resource overflow are not defined by the JMS API.

The related methods and interfaces are

- QueueSession.createQueue

- TemporaryQueue

- Destination

- Topic

34.2 Interface Definition

```
package javax.jms;
public interface Queue extends Destination {
    String getQueueName() throws JMSException;
    String toString();
}
```

34.3   Methods

The `Queue` interface inherits from the interface `javax.jms.Destination`, which has no fields or methods. The following methods are defined in the interface `javax.jms.Queue`.

getQueueName

```
public java.lang.String getQueueName()
```

>   Gets the name of this queue.
>   Clients that depend upon the name are not portable.

>   **RETURNS:**
>   the queue name

>   **THROWS:**
>   JMSException   if the JMS provider implementation of Queue
>   fails to return the queue name due to some
>   internal error

toString

```
public java.lang.String toString()
```

>   Returns a string representation of this object.

>   **OVERRIDES:**
>   java.lang.Object.toString() in class java.lang.Object

>   **RETURNS:**
>   the provider-specific identity values for this queue

CHAPTER 35

QueueBrowser

35.1 Overview and Related Methods and Interfaces

A client uses a `QueueBrowser` object to look at messages on a queue without removing them.

The `getEnumeration` method returns a `java.util.Enumeration` that is used to scan the queue's messages. It may be an enumeration of the entire content of a queue, or it may contain only the messages matching a message selector.

Messages may be arriving and expiring while the scan is done. The JMS API does not require the content of an enumeration to be a static snapshot of queue content. Whether these changes are visible or not depends on the JMS provider.

The related methods and interfaces are

- `QueueSession.createBrowser(Queue)`

- `QueueSession.createBrowser(Queue, String)`

- `QueueReceiver`

35.2 Interface Definition

```
package javax.jms;
public interface QueueBrowser {
    void close() throws JMSException;
    Enumeration getEnumeration() throws JMSException;
    String getMessageSelector() throws JMSException;
    Queue getQueue() throws JMSException;
}
```

35.3 Methods

The following methods are defined in the interface `javax.jms.QueueBrowser`.

close

```
public void close()
```

Closes the QueueBrowser.

Since a provider may allocate some resources on behalf of a Queue-Browser outside the Java virtual machine, clients should close them when they are not needed. Relying on garbage collection to eventually reclaim these resources may not be timely enough.

THROWS:

JMSException   if the JMS provider fails to close this browser due to some internal error

getEnumeration

```
public java.util.Enumeration getEnumeration()
```

Gets an enumeration for browsing the current queue messages in the order they would be received.

RETURNS:
an enumeration for browsing the messages

THROWS:

JMSException   if the JMS provider fails to get the enumeration for this browser due to some internal error

getMessageSelector

```
public java.lang.String getMessageSelector()
```

Gets this queue browser's message selector expression.

RETURNS:
this queue browser's message selector, or null if no message selector exists for the message consumer (that is, if the message selector was not set or was set to null or the empty string)

THROWS:

JMSException	if the JMS provider fails to get the message selector for this browser due to some internal error

getQueue

```
public Queue getQueue()
```

Gets the queue associated with this queue browser.

RETURNS:
the queue

THROWS:

JMSException	if the JMS provider fails to get the queue associated with this browser due to some internal error

CHAPTER 36

QueueConnection

36.1 Overview and Related Interfaces

A QueueConnection object is an active connection to a point-to-point JMS provider. A client uses a QueueConnection object to create one or more QueueSession objects for producing and consuming messages.

The related interfaces are

- Connection
- QueueConnectionFactory

36.2 Interface Definition

```
package javax.jms;
public interface QueueConnection extends Connection {
    QueueSession createQueueSession(boolean transacted,
                                    int acknowledgeMode)
                                            throws JMSException;
}
```

36.3 Methods

The QueueConnection interface inherits the methods of the interface javax.jms.Connection. The following method is defined in the interface javax.jms.QueueConnection.

createQueueSession

```
public QueueSession createQueueSession(boolean transacted,
                                          int acknowledgeMode)
```

Creates a QueueSession object.

PARAMETERS:

transacted   indicates whether the session is transacted

acknowledgeMode   indicates whether the consumer or the client
                                  will acknowledge any messages it receives;
                                  ignored if the session is transacted. Legal
                                  values are:

                                  Session.AUTO_ACKNOWLEDGE
                                  Session.CLIENT_ACKNOWLEDGE
                                  Session.DUPS_OK_ACKNOWLEDGE

RETURNS:
a newly created queue session

THROWS:

JMSException   if the QueueConnection object fails to create
                                  a session due to some internal error or lack
                                  of support for the specific transaction and ac-
                                  knowledgement mode

SEE ALSO:
Session.AUTO_ACKNOWLEDGE
Session.CLIENT_ACKNOWLEDGE
Session.DUPS_OK_ACKNOWLEDGE

CHAPTER 37

QueueConnectionFactory

37.1 Overview and Related Interfaces

A client uses a QueueConnectionFactory object to create QueueConnection objects with a point-to-point JMS provider.

The related interfaces are

- ConnectionFactory

- QueueConnection

37.2 Interface Definition

```
package javax.jms;
public interface QueueConnectionFactory extends ConnectionFactory {
    QueueConnection createQueueConnection() throws JMSException;
    QueueConnection createQueueConnection(String userName,
                                          String password)
                                                  throws JMSException;
}
```

37.3 Methods

The QueueConnectionFactory interface inherits from the interface javax.jms.ConnectionFactory, which has no fields or methods. The following methods are defined in the interface javax.jms.QueueConnectionFactory.

createQueueConnection()

```
public QueueConnection createQueueConnection()
```

Creates a queue connection with the default user identity. The connection is created in stopped mode. No messages will be delivered until the `Connection.start` method is explicitly called.

RETURNS:
a newly created queue connection

THROWS:

JMSException	if the JMS provider fails to create the queue connection due to some internal error
JMSSecurityException	if client authentication fails due to an invalid user name or password

createQueueConnection(String, String)

```
public QueueConnection createQueueConnection(java.lang.String userName,
                                             java.lang.String password)
```

Creates a queue connection with the specified user identity. The connection is created in stopped mode. No messages will be delivered until the `Connection.start` method is explicitly called.

PARAMETERS:

userName	the caller's user name
password	the caller's password

RETURNS:
a newly created queue connection

THROWS:

JMSException	if the JMS provider fails to create the queue connection due to some internal error
JMSSecurityException	if client authentication fails due to an invalid user name or password

CHAPTER 38

QueueReceiver

38.1 Overview and Related Methods and Interfaces

A client uses a QueueReceiver object to receive messages that have been delivered to a queue.

Although it is possible to have multiple QueueReceiver objects for the same queue, the JMS API does not define how messages are distributed between the QueueReceiver objects.

If a QueueReceiver specifies a message selector, the messages that are not selected remain on the queue. By definition, a message selector allows a Queue-Receiver to skip messages. This means that when the skipped messages are eventually read, the total ordering of the reads does not retain the partial order defined by each message producer. Only QueueReceiver objects without a message selector will read messages in message producer order.

The related methods and interfaces are

- QueueSession.createReceiver(Queue, String)

- QueueSession.createReceiver(Queue)

- MessageConsumer

38.2 Interface Definition

```
package javax.jms;
public interface QueueReceiver extends MessageConsumer {
    Queue getQueue() throws JMSException;
}
```

38.3 Methods

The `QueueReceiver` interface inherits the methods of the interface `javax.jms.MessageConsumer`. The following method is defined in the interface `javax.jms.QueueReceiver`.

getQueue

`public Queue getQueue()`

Gets the `Queue` associated with this queue receiver.

RETURNS:
this receiver's `Queue`

THROWS:
`JMSException`   if the JMS provider fails to get the queue for this queue receiver due to some internal error

CHAPTER 39

QueueRequestor

39.1 Overview and Related Interfaces

The QueueRequestor helper class simplifies making service requests.

The QueueRequestor constructor is given a non-transacted QueueSession and a destination Queue. It creates a TemporaryQueue for the responses and provides a request method that sends the request message and waits for its reply.

This is a basic request/reply abstraction that should be sufficient for most uses. JMS providers and clients are free to create more sophisticated versions.

The related interface is TopicRequestor.

39.2 Class Definition

```
package javax.jms;
public class QueueRequestor extends java.lang.Object {
    public QueueRequestor(QueueSession session, Queue queue)
                                                throws JMSException;
    public void close() throws JMSException;
    public Message request(Message message) throws JMSException;
}
```

39.3 Constructor

The following constructor is defined by the class `javax.jms.QueueRequestor`.

QueueRequestor

`public QueueRequestor(QueueSession session, Queue queue)`

Constructor for the `QueueRequestor` class.

This implementation assumes the session parameter to be non-transacted, with a delivery mode of either `AUTO_ACKNOWLEDGE` or `DUPS_OK_ACKNOWLEDGE`.

PARAMETERS:

`session`	the `QueueSession` the queue belongs to
`queue`	the queue to perform the request/reply call on

THROWS:

`JMSException`	if the JMS provider fails to create the `QueueRequestor` due to some internal error
`InvalidDestinationException`	if an invalid queue is specified

39.4 Methods

The `QueueRequestor` interface inherits the methods of the class `java.lang.Object`. The following methods are defined in the class `javax.jms.QueueRequestor`.

close

`public void close()`

Closes the `QueueRequestor` and its session.

Since a provider may allocate some resources on behalf of a `QueueRequestor` outside the Java virtual machine, clients should close them when they are not needed. Relying on garbage collection to eventually reclaim these resources may not be timely enough.

Note that this method closes the `QueueSession` object passed to the `QueueRequestor` constructor.

THROWS:

JMSException — if the JMS provider fails to close the Queue-Requestor due to some internal error

request

```
public Message request(Message message)
```

Sends a request and waits for a reply. The temporary queue is used for the JMSReplyTo destination, and only one reply per request is expected.

PARAMETERS:

message — the message to send

RETURNS:

the reply message

THROWS:

JMSException — if the JMS provider fails to complete the request due to some internal error

CHAPTER 40

QueueSender

40.1 Overview and Related Methods and Interfaces

A client uses a `QueueSender` object to send messages to a queue.

Normally, the `Queue` is specified when a `QueueSender` is created. In this case, an attempt to use the `send` methods for an unidentified `QueueSender` will throw a `java.lang.UnsupportedOperationException`.

If the `QueueSender` is created with an unidentified `Queue`, an attempt to use the `send` methods that assume that the `Queue` has been identified will throw a `java.lang.UnsupportedOperationException`.

During the execution of its `send` method, a message must not be changed by other threads within the client. If the message is modified, the result of the `send` is undefined.

After sending a message, a client may retain and modify it without affecting the message that has been sent. The same message object may be sent multiple times.

The following message headers are set as part of sending a message: `JMSDestination`, `JMSDeliveryMode`, `JMSExpiration`, `JMSPriority`, `JMSMessageID` and `JMSTimeStamp`. When the message is sent, the values of these headers are ignored. After the completion of the `send`, the headers hold the values specified by the method sending the message. It is possible for the `send` method not to set `JMSMessageID` and `JMSTimeStamp` if the setting of these headers is explicitly disabled by the `MessageProducer.setDisableMessageID` or `MessageProducer.set-DisableMessageTimestamp` method.

The related methods and interfaces are

- `QueueSession.createSender`

- `MessageProducer`

40.2   Interface Definition

```
package javax.jms;
public interface QueueSender extends MessageProducer {
    Queue getQueue() throws JMSException;
    void send(Message message) throws JMSException;
    void send(Message message, int deliveryMode, int priority,
                            long timeToLive) throws JMSException;
    void send(Queue queue, Message message) throws JMSException;
    void send(Queue queue, Message message, int deliveryMode,
                          int priority, long timeToLive)
                                             throws JMSException;
}
```

40.3   Methods

The `QueueSender` interface inherits the methods of the interface `javax.jms.MessageProducer`. The following methods are defined in the interface `javax.jms.QueueSender`.

getQueue

```
public Queue getQueue()
```

Gets the queue associated with this `QueueSender`.

RETURNS:
this sender's queue

THROWS:

`JMSException`   if the JMS provider fails to get the queue for this `QueueSender` due to some internal error

send(Message)

```
public void send(Message message)
```

Sends a message to the queue. Uses the `QueueSender`'s default delivery mode, priority, and time to live.

PARAMETERS:

message	the message to send

THROWS:

JMSException	if the JMS provider fails to send the message due to some internal error
MessageFormatException	if an invalid message is specified
InvalidDestinationException	if a client uses this method with a Queue-Sender with an invalid queue
java.lang.UnsupportedOperationException	
	if a client uses this method with a Queue-Sender that did not specify a queue at creation time

SEE ALSO:

MessageProducer.getDeliveryMode
MessageProducer.getTimeToLive
MessageProducer.getPriority

send(Message, int, int, long)

```
public void send(Message message, int deliveryMode, int priority,
                                              long timeToLive)
```

Sends a message to the queue, specifying delivery mode, priority, and time to live.

PARAMETERS:

message	the message to send
deliveryMode	the delivery mode to use
priority	the priority for this message
timeToLive	the message's lifetime (in milliseconds)

THROWS:

JMSException	if the JMS provider fails to send the message due to some internal error
MessageFormatException	if an invalid message is specified

InvalidDestinationException if a client uses this method with a `Queue-Sender` with an invalid queue

java.lang.UnsupportedOperationException

if a client uses this method with a `Queue-Sender` that did not specify a queue at creation time

send(Queue, Message)

```
public void send(Queue queue, Message message)
```

Sends a message to a queue for an unidentified message producer. Uses the `QueueSender`'s default delivery mode, priority, and time to live.

Typically, a message producer is assigned a queue at creation time; however, the JMS API also supports unidentified message producers, which require that the queue be supplied every time a message is sent.

PARAMETERS:

queue	the queue to send this message to
message	the message to send

THROWS:

JMSException	if the JMS provider fails to send the message due to some internal error
MessageFormatException	if an invalid message is specified
InvalidDestinationException	if a client uses this method with an invalid queue

SEE ALSO:

MessageProducer.getDeliveryMode
MessageProducer.getTimeToLive
MessageProducer.getPriority

send(Queue, Message, int, int, long)

```
public void send(Queue queue, Message message, int deliveryMode,
                                int priority, long timeToLive)
```

Sends a message to a queue for an unidentified message producer, specifying delivery mode, priority and time to live.

Typically, a message producer is assigned a queue at creation time; however, the JMS API also supports unidentified message producers, which require that the queue be supplied every time a message is sent.

PARAMETERS:

queue	the queue to send this message to
message	the message to send
deliveryMode	the delivery mode to use
priority	the priority for this message
timeToLive	the message's lifetime (in milliseconds)

THROWS:

JMSException	if the JMS provider fails to send the message due to some internal error
MessageFormatException	if an invalid message is specified
InvalidDestinationException	if a client uses this method with an invalid queue

CHAPTER 41

QueueSession

41.1   Overview and Related Methods and Interfaces

A QueueSession object provides methods for creating QueueReceiver, Queue-Sender, QueueBrowser, and TemporaryQueue objects.

If there are messages that have been received but not acknowledged when a QueueSession terminates, these messages will be retained and redelivered when a consumer next accesses the queue.

The related methods and interfaces are

* QueueConnection.createQueueSession

* Session

41.2   Interface Definition

```
package javax.jms;
public interface QueueSession extends Session {
    QueueBrowser createBrowser(Queue queue) throws JMSException;
    QueueBrowser createBrowser(Queue queue, String messageSelector)
                                            throws JMSException;
    Queue createQueue(String queueName) throws JMSException;
    QueueReceiver createReceiver(Queue queue) throws JMSException;
    QueueReceiver createReceiver(Queue queue, String messageSelector)
                                            throws JMSException;
    QueueSender createSender(Queue queue) throws JMSException;
    TemporaryQueue createTemporaryQueue() throws JMSException;
}
```

41.3 Methods

The `QueueSession` interface inherits the fields and the methods of the interface `javax.jms.Session`. The following methods are defined in the interface `javax.jms.QueueSession`.

createBrowser(Queue)

```
public QueueBrowser createBrowser(Queue queue)
```

Creates a `QueueBrowser` object to peek at the messages on the specified queue.

PARAMETERS:

queue   the Queue to access

THROWS:

JMSException   if the session fails to create a browser due to some internal error

InvalidDestinationException   if an invalid queue is specified

createBrowser(Queue, String)

```
public QueueBrowser createBrowser(Queue queue,
                            java.lang.String messageSelector)
```

Creates a `QueueBrowser` object to peek at the messages on the specified queue using a message selector.

PARAMETERS:

queue   the Queue to access

messageSelector   only messages with properties matching the message selector expression are delivered. A value of null or an empty string indicates that there is no message selector for the message consumer.

THROWS:

JMSException   if the session fails to create a browser due to some internal error

InvalidDestinationException   if an invalid queue is specified

InvalidSelectorException   if the message selector is invalid

createQueue

```
public Queue createQueue(java.lang.String queueName)
```

Creates a queue identity given a Queue name.

This facility is provided for the rare cases where clients need to dynamically manipulate queue identity. It allows the creation of a queue identity with a provider-specific name. Clients that depend on this ability are not portable.

Note that this method is not for creating the physical queue. The physical creation of queues is an administrative task and is not to be initiated by the JMS API. The one exception is the creation of temporary queues, which is accomplished with the createTemporaryQueue method.

PARAMETERS:

queueName   the name of this Queue

RETURNS:
a Queue with the given name

THROWS:

JMSException   if the session fails to create a queue due to some internal error

createReceiver(Queue)

```
public QueueReceiver createReceiver(Queue queue)
```

Creates a QueueReceiver object to receive messages from the specified queue.

PARAMETERS:

queue   the Queue to access

THROWS:

JMSException   if the session fails to create a receiver due to some internal error

InvalidDestinationException if an invalid queue is specified

createReceiver(Queue, String)

```
public QueueReceiver createReceiver(Queue queue,
                              java.lang.String messageSelector)
```

Creates a `QueueReceiver` object to receive messages from the specified queue using a message selector.

PARAMETERS:

queue	the `Queue` to access
messageSelector	only messages with properties matching the message selector expression are delivered. A value of null or an empty string indicates that there is no message selector for the message consumer.

THROWS:

JMSException	if the session fails to create a receiver due to some internal error
InvalidDestinationException	if an invalid queue is specified
InvalidSelectorException	if the message selector is invalid

createSender

```
public QueueSender createSender(Queue queue)
```

Creates a `QueueSender` object to send messages to the specified queue.

PARAMETERS:

queue	the `Queue` to access, or null if this is an unidentified producer

THROWS:

JMSException	if the session fails to create a sender due to some internal error
InvalidDestinationException	if an invalid queue is specified

createTemporaryQueue

```
public TemporaryQueue createTemporaryQueue()
```

Creates a `TemporaryQueue` object. Its lifetime will be that of the `QueueConnection` unless it is deleted earlier.

RETURNS:
a temporary queue identity

THROWS:

JMSException   if the session fails to create a temporary
                                      queue due to some internal error

CHAPTER 42

ResourceAllocationException

42.1 Overview

This exception is thrown when a provider is unable to allocate the resources required by a method. For example, this exception should be thrown when a call to `TopicConnectionFactory.createTopicConnection` fails due to a lack of JMS provider resources.

The `ResourceAllocationException` class inherits the methods of the class `javax.jms.JMSException`.

42.2 Class Definition

```
package javax.jms;
public class ResourceAllocationException extends JMSException {
    public ResourceAllocationException(String reason);
    public ResourceAllocationException(String reason,
                                                String errorCode);
}
```

42.3   Constructors

The following constructors are defined by the class `javax.jms.ResourceAllocationException`.

ResourceAllocationException(String)

public **ResourceAllocationException**(java.lang.String *reason*)

Constructs a `ResourceAllocationException` with the specified reason. The error code defaults to null.

PARAMETERS:

reason   a description of the exception

ResourceAllocationException(String, String)

public **ResourceAllocationException**(java.lang.String *reason*,
                                       java.lang.String *errorCode*)

Constructs a `ResourceAllocationException` with the specified reason and error code.

PARAMETERS:

reason   a description of the exception

errorCode   a string specifying the vendor-specific error code

CHAPTER 43

Session

43.1 Overview and Related Interfaces

A `Session` object is a single-threaded context for producing and consuming messages. Although it may allocate provider resources outside the Java virtual machine (JVM), it is considered a lightweight JMS object.

A session serves several purposes:

- It is a factory for its message producers and consumers.

- It supplies provider-optimized message factories.

- It supports a single series of transactions that combine work spanning its producers and consumers into atomic units.

- It defines a serial order for the messages it consumes and the messages it produces.

- It retains messages it consumes until they have been acknowledged.

- It serializes execution of message listeners registered with its message consumers.

A session can create and service multiple message producers and consumers.

One typical use is to have a thread block on a synchronous `MessageConsumer` until a message arrives. The thread may then use one or more of the `Session`'s `MessageProducers`.

If a client desires to have one thread produce messages while others consume them, the client should use a separate session for its producing thread.

Once a connection has been started, any session with one or more registered message listeners is dedicated to the thread of control that delivers messages to it. It is erroneous for client code to use this session or any of its constituent objects from another thread of control. The only exception to this rule is the use of the session or connection `close` method.

It should be easy for most clients to partition their work naturally into sessions. This model allows clients to start simply and incrementally add message processing complexity as their need for concurrency grows.

The `close` method is the only session method that can be called while some other session method is being executed in another thread.

A session may be specified as transacted. Each transacted session supports a single series of transactions. Each transaction groups a set of message sends and a set of message receives into an atomic unit of work. In effect, transactions organize a session's input message stream and output message stream into series of atomic units. When a transaction commits, its atomic unit of input is acknowledged and its associated atomic unit of output is sent. If a transaction rollback is done, the transaction's sent messages are destroyed and the session's input is automatically recovered.

The content of a transaction's input and output units is simply those messages that have been produced and consumed within the session's current transaction.

A transaction is completed using either its session's `commit` method or its session's `rollback` method. The completion of a session's current transaction automatically begins the next. The result is that a transacted session always has a current transaction within which its work is done.

The Java Transaction Service (JTS) or some other transaction monitor may be used to combine a session's transaction with transactions on other resources (databases, other JMS sessions, and so on). Since Java distributed transactions are controlled via the Java Transaction API (JTA), use of the session's `commit` and `rollback` methods in this context is prohibited.

The JMS API does not require support for JTA; however, it does define how a provider supplies this support.

Although it is also possible for a JMS client to handle distributed transactions directly, it is unlikely that many JMS clients will do this. Support for JTA in the JMS API is targeted at systems vendors who will be integrating the JMS API into their application server products.

The related interfaces are

- QueueSession

- TopicSession

43.2 Interface Definition

```
package javax.jms;
public interface Session extends java.lang.Runnable {
    static final int AUTO_ACKNOWLEDGE       = 1;
    static final int CLIENT_ACKNOWLEDGE     = 2;
    static final int DUPS_OK_ACKNOWLEDGE    = 3;
    void close() throws JMSException;
    void commit() throws JMSException;
    BytesMessage createBytesMessage() throws JMSException;
    MapMessage createMapMessage() throws JMSException;
    Message createMessage() throws JMSException;
    ObjectMessage createObjectMessage() throws JMSException;
    ObjectMessage createObjectMessage(Serializable object)
                                            throws JMSException;
    StreamMessage createStreamMessage() throws JMSException;
    TextMessage createTextMessage() throws JMSException;
    TextMessage createTextMessage(String text) throws JMSException;
    boolean getTransacted() throws JMSException;
    void recover() throws JMSException;
    void rollback() throws JMSException;
}
```

43.3   Fields

The following fields are defined in the interface `javax.jms.Session`.

AUTO_ACKNOWLEDGE

`public static final int AUTO_ACKNOWLEDGE`

    With this acknowledgment mode, the session automatically acknowledges a client's receipt of a message either when the session has successfully returned from a call to `receive` or when the message listener the session has called to process the message successfully returns.

CLIENT_ACKNOWLEDGE

`public static final int CLIENT_ACKNOWLEDGE`

    With this acknowledgment mode, the client acknowledges a consumed message by calling the message's `acknowledge` method. Acknowledging a consumed message acknowledges all messages that the session has consumed.

    When client acknowledgment mode is used, a client may build up a large number of unacknowledged messages while attempting to process them. A JMS provider should provide administrators with a way to limit client overrun so that clients are not driven to resource exhaustion and ensuing failure when some resource they are using is temporarily blocked.

SEE ALSO:
`Message.acknowledge`

DUPS_OK_ACKNOWLEDGE

`public static final int DUPS_OK_ACKNOWLEDGE`

    This acknowledgment mode instructs the session to lazily acknowledge the delivery of messages. This is likely to result in the delivery of some duplicate messages if the JMS provider fails, so it should only be used by consumers that can tolerate duplicate messages. Use of this mode can reduce session overhead by minimizing the work the session does to prevent duplicates.

43.4 Methods

The following methods are defined in the interface `javax.jms.Session`.

close

```
public void close()
```

Closes the session.

Since a provider may allocate some resources on behalf of a session outside the JVM, clients should close the resources when they are not needed. Relying on garbage collection to eventually reclaim these resources may not be timely enough.

There is no need to close the producers and consumers of a closed session.

This call will block until a `receive` call or message listener in progress has completed. A blocked message consumer `receive` call returns `null` when this session is closed.

Closing a transacted session must roll back the transaction in progress.

This method is the only `Session` method that can be called concurrently.

Invoking any other `Session` method on a closed session must throw a `JMSException.IllegalStateException`. Closing a closed session must *not* throw an exception.

THROWS:

JMSException   if the JMS provider fails to close the session due to some internal error

commit

```
public void commit()
```

Commits all messages done in this transaction and releases any locks currently held.

THROWS:

JMSException   if the JMS provider fails to commit the transaction due to some internal error

TransactionRolledBackException if the transaction is rolled back due to some internal error during commit

IllegalStateException   if the method is not called by a transacted
                                   session

createBytesMessage

public BytesMessage **createBytesMessage**()

    Creates a BytesMessage object. A BytesMessage object is used to send a
message containing a stream of uninterpreted bytes.

THROWS:
JMSException   if the JMS provider fails to create this mes-
                                   sage due to some internal error

createMapMessage

public MapMessage **createMapMessage**()

    Creates a MapMessage object. A MapMessage object is used to send a self-
defining set of name/value pairs, where names are String objects and values
are primitive values in the Java programming language.

THROWS:
JMSException   if the JMS provider fails to create this mes-
                                   sage due to some internal error

createMessage

public Message **createMessage**()

    Creates a Message object. The Message interface is the root interface of all
JMS messages. A Message object holds all the standard message header information. It can be sent when a message containing only header information is
sufficient.

THROWS:
JMSException   if the JMS provider fails to create this mes-
                                   sage due to some internal error

createObjectMessage()

```
public ObjectMessage createObjectMessage()
```

Creates an `ObjectMessage` object. An `ObjectMessage` object is used to send a message that contains a serializable Java object.

THROWS:

JMSException   if the JMS provider fails to create this message due to some internal error

createObjectMessage(Serializable)

```
public ObjectMessage createObjectMessage(java.io.Serializable object)
```

Creates an initialized `ObjectMessage` object. An `ObjectMessage` object is used to send a message that contains a serializable Java object.

PARAMETERS:

object   the object to use to initialize this message

THROWS:

JMSException   if the JMS provider fails to create this message due to some internal error

createStreamMessage

```
public StreamMessage createStreamMessage()
```

Creates a `StreamMessage` object. A `StreamMessage` object is used to send a self-defining stream of primitive values in the Java programming language.

THROWS:

JMSException   if the JMS provider fails to create this message due to some internal error

createTextMessage()

```
public TextMessage createTextMessage()
```

Creates a `TextMessage` object. A `TextMessage` object is used to send a message containing a `String` object.

THROWS:

JMSException   if the JMS provider fails to create this mes-
                                                sage due to some internal error

createTextMessage(String)

```
public TextMessage createTextMessage(java.lang.String text)
```

Creates an initialized `TextMessage` object. A `TextMessage` object is used
to send a message containing a `String`.

PARAMETERS:

text   the string used to initialize this message

THROWS:

JMSException   if the JMS provider fails to create this mes-
                                                sage due to some internal error

getTransacted

```
public boolean getTransacted()
```

Indicates whether the session is in transacted mode.

RETURNS:

true if the session is in transacted mode

THROWS:

JMSException   if the JMS provider fails to return the trans-
                                                action mode due to some internal error

recover

```
public void recover()
```

Stops message delivery in this session, and restarts message delivery with
the oldest unacknowledged message.

All consumers deliver messages in a serial order. Acknowledging a
received message automatically acknowledges all messages that have been
delivered to the client.

Restarting a session causes it to take the following actions:

- Stop message delivery.

- Mark all messages that might have been delivered but not acknowledged as "redelivered."

- Restart the delivery sequence including all unacknowledged messages that had been previously delivered. Redelivered messages do not have to be delivered in exactly their original delivery order.

THROWS:

JMSException	if the JMS provider fails to stop and restart message delivery due to some internal error
IllegalStateException	if the method is called by a transacted session

rollback

```
public void rollback()
```

Rolls back any messages done in this transaction and releases any locks currently held.

THROWS:

JMSException	if the JMS provider fails to roll back the transaction due to some internal error
IllegalStateException	if the method is not called by a transacted session

CHAPTER 44

StreamMessage

44.1 Overview and Related Methods and Interfaces

A StreamMessage object is used to send a stream of primitive types in the Java programming language. It is filled and read sequentially. It inherits from the Message interface and adds a stream message body. Its methods are based largely on those found in java.io.DataInputStream and java.io.DataOutputStream.

The primitive types can be read or written explicitly using methods for each type. They may also be read or written generically as objects. For instance, a call to StreamMessage.writeInt(6) is equivalent to StreamMessage.writeObject(new Integer(6)). Both forms are provided, because the explicit form is convenient for static programming, and the object form is needed when types are not known at compile time.

When the message is first created, and when clearBody is called, the body of the message is in write-only mode. After the first call to reset has been made, the message body is in read-only mode. After a message has been sent, the client that sent it can retain and modify it without affecting the message that has been sent. The same message object can be sent multiple times. When a message has been received, the provider has called reset so that the message body is in read-only mode for the client.

If clearBody is called on a message in read-only mode, the message body is cleared and the message body is in write-only mode.

If a client attempts to read a message in write-only mode, a MessageNot-ReadableException is thrown.

If a client attempts to write a message in read-only mode, a MessageNot-WriteableException is thrown.

StreamMessage objects support the conversions shown in Table 44.1. The marked cases must be supported. The unmarked cases must throw a JMSException. The String-to-primitive conversions may throw a runtime exception if the primitive's valueOf method does not accept it as a valid String representation of the primitive.

A value written as the row type can be read as the column type.

Table 44.1: StreamMessage Conversions

	boolean	byte	short	char	int	long	float	double	String	Byte[]
boolean	X								X	
byte		X	X		X	X			X	
short			X		X	X			X	
char				X					X	
int					X	X			X	
long						X			X	
float							X	X	X	
double								X	X	
String	X	X	X		X	X	X	X	X	
byte[]										X

Attempting to read a null value as a primitive type must be treated as calling the primitive's corresponding valueOf(String) conversion method with a null value. Since char does not support a String conversion, attempting to read a null value as a char must throw a NullPointerException.

The related methods and interfaces are

- Session.createStreamMessage

- BytesMessage

- MapMessage

- Message

- ObjectMessage

- TextMessage

44.2   Interface Definition

```
package javax.jms;
public interface StreamMessage extends Message {
    boolean readBoolean() throws JMSException;
    byte readByte() throws JMSException;
    int readBytes(byte[] value) throws JMSException;
    char readChar() throws JMSException;
    double readDouble() throws JMSException;
    float readFloat() throws JMSException;
    int readInt() throws JMSException;
    long readLong() throws JMSException;
    Object readObject() throws JMSException;
    short readShort() throws JMSException;
    String readString() throws JMSException;
    void reset() throws JMSException;
    void writeBoolean(boolean value) throws JMSException;
    void writeByte(byte value) throws JMSException;
    void writeBytes(byte[] value) throws JMSException;
    void writeBytes(byte[] value, int offset, int length)
                                           throws JMSException;
    void writeChar(char value) throws JMSException;
    void writeDouble(double value) throws JMSException;
    void writeFloat(float value) throws JMSException;
    void writeInt(int value) throws JMSException;
    void writeLong(long value) throws JMSException;
    void writeObject(Object value) throws JMSException;
    void writeShort(short value) throws JMSException;
    void writeString(String value) throws JMSException;
}
```

44.3 Methods

The `StreamMessage` interface inherits the fields and the methods of the interface `javax.jms.Message`. The following methods are defined in the interface `javax.jms.StreamMessage`.

readBoolean

```
public boolean readBoolean()
```

Reads a `boolean` from the stream message.

RETURNS:
the `boolean` value read

THROWS:

JMSException	if the JMS provider fails to read the message due to some internal error
MessageEOFException	if unexpected end of message stream has been reached
MessageFormatException	if this type conversion is invalid
MessageNotReadableException	if the message is in write-only mode

readByte

```
public byte readByte()
```

Reads a `byte` value from the stream message.

RETURNS:
the next byte from the stream message as a 8-bit `byte`

THROWS:

JMSException	if the JMS provider fails to read the message due to some internal error
MessageEOFException	if unexpected end of message stream has been reached
MessageFormatException	if this type conversion is invalid
MessageNotReadableException	if the message is in write-only mode

readBytes

```
public int readBytes(byte[] value)
```

Reads a byte array field from the stream message into the specified `byte[]` object (the read buffer).

To read the field value, `readBytes` should be successively called until it returns a value less than the length of the read buffer. The value of the bytes in the buffer following the last byte read is undefined.

If `readBytes` returns a value equal to the length of the buffer, a subsequent `readBytes` call must be made. If there are no more bytes to be read, this call returns −1.

If the byte array field value is null, `readBytes` returns −1.

If the byte array field value is empty, `readBytes` returns 0.

Once the first `readBytes` call on a `byte[]` field value has been made, the full value of the field must be read before it is valid to read the next field. An attempt to read the next field before that has been done will throw a `Message-FormatException`.

To read the byte field value into a new `byte[]` object, use the `readObject` method.

PARAMETERS:

value   the buffer into which the data is read

RETURNS:

the total number of bytes read into the buffer, or −1 if there is no more data because the end of the byte field has been reached

THROWS:

`JMSException`	if the JMS provider fails to read the message due to some internal error
`MessageEOFException`	if unexpected end of message stream has been reached
`MessageFormatException`	if this type conversion is invalid
`MessageNotReadableException`	if the message is in write-only mode

SEE ALSO:

`readObject`

readChar

```
public char readChar()
```

Reads a Unicode character value from the stream message.

RETURNS:
a Unicode character from the stream message

THROWS:

JMSException	if the JMS provider fails to read the message due to some internal error
MessageEOFException	if unexpected end of message stream has been reached
MessageFormatException	if this type conversion is invalid
MessageNotReadableException	if the message is in write-only mode

readDouble

```
public double readDouble()
```

Reads a double from the stream message.

RETURNS:
a double value from the stream message

THROWS:

JMSException	if the JMS provider fails to read the message due to some internal error
MessageEOFException	if unexpected end of message stream has been reached
MessageFormatException	if this type conversion is invalid
MessageNotReadableException	if the message is in write-only mode

readFloat

```
public float readFloat()
```

Reads a float from the stream message.

RETURNS:
a float value from the stream message

THROWS:

JMSException	if the JMS provider fails to read the message due to some internal error
MessageEOFException	if unexpected end of message stream has been reached
MessageFormatException	if this type conversion is invalid
MessageNotReadableException	if the message is in write-only mode

readInt

```
public int readInt()
```

Reads a 32-bit integer from the stream message.

RETURNS:

a 32-bit integer value from the stream message, interpreted as an `int`

THROWS:

JMSException	if the JMS provider fails to read the message due to some internal error
MessageEOFException	if unexpected end of message stream has been reached
MessageFormatException	if this type conversion is invalid
MessageNotReadableException	if the message is in write-only mode

readLong

```
public long readLong()
```

Reads a 64-bit integer from the stream message.

RETURNS:

a 64-bit integer value from the stream message, interpreted as a `long`

THROWS:

JMSException	if the JMS provider fails to read the message due to some internal error
MessageEOFException	if unexpected end of message stream has been reached
MessageFormatException	if this type conversion is invalid
MessageNotReadableException	if the message is in write-only mode

readObject

```
public java.lang.Object readObject()
```

Reads an object from the stream message.

This method can be used to return, in objectified format, an object in the Java programming language ("Java object") that has been written to the stream with the equivalent writeObject method call, or its equivalent primitive writetype method.

Note that byte values are returned as byte[], not Byte[].

An attempt to call readObject to read a byte field value into a new byte[] object before the full value of the byte field has been read will throw a MessageFormatException.

RETURNS:
a Java object from the stream message, in objectified format (for example, if the object was written as an int, an Integer is returned)

THROWS:

JMSException	if the JMS provider fails to read the message due to some internal error
MessageEOFException	if unexpected end of message stream has been reached
MessageFormatException	if this type conversion is invalid
MessageNotReadableException	if the message is in write-only mode

readShort

```
public short readShort()
```

Reads a 16-bit integer from the stream message.

RETURNS:
a 16-bit integer from the stream message

THROWS:

JMSException	if the JMS provider fails to read the message due to some internal error
MessageEOFException	if unexpected end of message stream has been reached
MessageFormatException	if this type conversion is invalid
MessageNotReadableException	if the message is in write-only mode

readString

```
public java.lang.String readString()
```

Reads a `String` from the stream message.

RETURNS:
a Unicode string from the stream message

THROWS:

`JMSException`	if the JMS provider fails to read the message due to some internal error
`MessageEOFException`	if unexpected end of message stream has been reached
`MessageFormatException`	if this type conversion is invalid
`MessageNotReadableException`	if the message is in write-only mode

reset

```
public void reset()
```

Puts the message body in read-only mode and repositions the stream to the beginning.

THROWS:

`JMSException`	if the JMS provider fails to reset the message due to some internal error
`MessageFormatException`	if the message has an invalid format

writeBoolean

```
public void writeBoolean(boolean value)
```

Writes a `boolean` to the stream message. The value `true` is written as the value `(byte)1`; the value `false` is written as the value `(byte)0`.

PARAMETERS:

`value`	the `boolean` value to be written

THROWS:

`JMSException`	if the JMS provider fails to write the message due to some internal error
`MessageNotWriteableException`	if the message is in read-only mode

writeByte

```
public void writeByte(byte value)
```

Writes a byte to the stream message.

PARAMETERS:

value   the byte value to be written

THROWS:

JMSException   if the JMS provider fails to write the mes-
                                sage due to some internal error

MessageNotWriteableException if the message is in read-only mode

writeBytes(byte[])

```
public void writeBytes(byte[] value)
```

Writes a byte array field to the stream message.

The byte array value is written to the message as a byte array field. Consecutively written byte array fields are treated as two distinct fields when the
fields are read.

PARAMETERS:

value   the byte array value to be written

THROWS:

JMSException   if the JMS provider fails to write the mes-
                                sage due to some internal error

MessageNotWriteableException if the message is in read-only mode

writeBytes(byte[], int, int)

```
public void writeBytes(byte[] value, int offset, int length)
```

Writes a portion of a byte array as a byte array field to the stream
message.

The portion of the byte array value is written to the message as a byte
array field. Consecutively written byte array fields are treated as two distinct
fields when the fields are read.

PARAMETERS:

value	the byte array value to be written
offset	the initial offset within the byte array
length	the number of bytes to use

THROWS:

JMSException   if the JMS provider fails to write the message due to some internal error

MessageNotWriteableException if the message is in read-only mode

writeChar

```
public void writeChar(char value)
```

Writes a char to the stream message.

PARAMETERS:

value   the char value to be written

THROWS:

JMSException   if the JMS provider fails to write the message due to some internal error

MessageNotWriteableException if the message is in read-only mode

writeDouble

```
public void writeDouble(double value)
```

Writes a double to the stream message.

PARAMETERS:

value   the double value to be written

THROWS:

JMSException   if the JMS provider fails to write the message due to some internal error

MessageNotWriteableException if the message is in read-only mode

writeFloat

```
public void writeFloat(float value)
```

Writes a float to the stream message.

PARAMETERS:

value   the `float` value to be written

THROWS:

JMSException   if the JMS provider fails to write the mes-
                                   sage due to some internal error

MessageNotWriteableException if the message is in read-only mode

writeInt

```
public void writeInt(int value)
```

Writes an `int` to the stream message.

PARAMETERS:

value   the `int` value to be written

THROWS:

JMSException   if the JMS provider fails to write the mes-
                                   sage due to some internal error

MessageNotWriteableException if the message is in read-only mode

writeLong

```
public void writeLong(long value)
```

Writes a `long` to the stream message.

PARAMETERS:

value   the `long` value to be written

THROWS:

JMSException   if the JMS provider fails to write the mes-
                                   sage due to some internal error

MessageNotWriteableException if the message is in read-only mode

writeObject

```
public void writeObject(java.lang.Object value)
```

Writes an object to the stream message.

This method works only for the objectified primitive object types (`Integer`, `Double`, `Long` ...), `String` objects, and byte arrays.

PARAMETERS:

value   the Java object to be written

THROWS:

JMSException   if the JMS provider fails to write the mes-
                                       sage due to some internal error

MessageFormatException   if the object is invalid

MessageNotWriteableException if the message is in read-only mode

writeShort

```
public void writeShort(short value)
```

Writes a short to the stream message.

PARAMETERS:

value   the short value to be written

THROWS:

JMSException   if the JMS provider fails to write the mes-
                                       sage due to some internal error

MessageNotWriteableException if the message is in read-only mode

writeString

```
public void writeString(java.lang.String value)
```

Writes a String to the stream message.

PARAMETERS:

value   the String value to be written

THROWS:

JMSException   if the JMS provider fails to write the mes-
                                       sage due to some internal error

MessageNotWriteableException if the message is in read-only mode

CHAPTER 45

TemporaryQueue

45.1 Overview and Related Methods and Interfaces

A TemporaryQueue object is a unique Queue object created for the duration of a QueueConnection. It is a system-defined queue that can be consumed only by the QueueConnection that created it.

The related methods and interfaces are

- QueueSession.createTemporaryQueue
- Queue

45.2 Interface Definition

```
package javax.jms;
public interface TemporaryQueue extends Queue {
    void delete() throws JMSException;
}
```

45.3 Methods

The TemporaryQueue interface inherits the methods of the interface javax.jms.Queue. The following method is defined in the interface javax.jms.TemporaryQueue.

delete

```
public void delete()
```

Deletes this temporary queue. If there are existing receivers still using it, a JMSException will be thrown.

THROWS:

JMSException   if the JMS provider fails to delete the tempo-
                                       rary queue due to some internal error

CHAPTER 46

TemporaryTopic

46.1 Overview and Related Methods and Interfaces

A TemporaryTopic object is a unique Topic object created for the duration of a TopicConnection. It is a system-defined topic that can be consumed only by the TopicConnection that created it.

The related methods and interfaces are

* TopicSession.createTemporaryTopic

* Topic

46.2 Interface Definition

```
package javax.jms;
public interface TemporaryTopic extends Topic {
    void delete() throws JMSException;
}
```

46.3 Methods

The TemporaryTopic interface inherits the methods of the interface javax.jms.Topic. The following method is defined in the interface javax.jms.TemporaryTopic.

delete

```
public void delete()
```

Deletes this temporary topic. If there are existing subscribers still using it, a JMSException will be thrown.

THROWS:

JMSException   if the JMS provider fails to delete the tempo-
                                       rary topic due to some internal error

CHAPTER 47

TextMessage

47.1 Overview and Related Methods and Interfaces

A `TextMessage` object is used to send a message containing a `java.lang.String`. It inherits from the `Message` interface and adds a text message body.

The inclusion of this message type is based on the presumption that XML will likely become a popular mechanism for representing content of all kinds, including the content of JMS messages.

When a client receives a `TextMessage`, it is in read-only mode. If a client attempts to write to the message at this point, a `MessageNotWriteableException` is thrown. If `clearBody` is called, the message can now be both read from and written to.

The related methods and interfaces are

- `Session.createTextMessage()`
- `Session.createTextMessage(String)`
- `BytesMessage`
- `MapMessage`
- `Message`
- `ObjectMessage`
- `StreamMessage`

47.2   Interface Definition

```
package javax.jms;
public interface TextMessage extends Message {
    String getText() throws JMSException;
    void setText(String string) throws JMSException;
}
```

47.3   Methods

The TextMessage interface inherits the fields and the methods of the interface javax.jms.Message. The following methods are defined in the interface javax.jms.TextMessage.

getText

```
public java.lang.String getText()
```

Gets the string containing this message's data. The default value is null.

RETURNS:
the String containing the message's data

THROWS:
JMSException   if the JMS provider fails to get the text due to some internal error

setText

```
public void setText(java.lang.String string)
```

Sets the string containing this message's data.

PARAMETERS:
string   the String containing the message's data

THROWS:
JMSException   if the JMS provider fails to set the text due to some internal error
MessageNotWriteableExceptionif the message is in read-only mode

CHAPTER **48**

Topic

48.1 Overview and Related Methods and Interfaces

A `Topic` object encapsulates a provider-specific topic name. It is the way a client specifies the identity of a topic to JMS API methods.

Many publish/subscribe (pub/sub) providers group topics into hierarchies and provide various options for subscribing to parts of the hierarchy. The JMS API places no restriction on what a `Topic` object represents. It may be a leaf in a topic hierarchy, or it may be a larger part of the hierarchy.

The organization of topics and the granularity of subscriptions to them is an important part of a pub/sub application's architecture. The JMS API does not specify a policy for how this should be done. If an application takes advantage of a provider-specific topic-grouping mechanism, it should document this. If the application is installed using a different provider, it is the job of the administrator to construct an equivalent topic architecture and create equivalent `Topic` objects.

The related methods and interfaces are

* `TopicSession.createTopic`

* `Queue`

48.2 Interface Definition

```
package javax.jms;
public interface Topic extends Destination {
    String getTopicName() throws JMSException;
    String toString();
}
```

48.3   Methods

The Topic interface inherits from the interface javax.jms.Destination, which has no fields or methods. The following methods are defined in the interface javax.jms.Topic.

getTopicName

public java.lang.String **getTopicName**()

> Gets the name of this topic.
> Clients that depend upon the name are not portable.

RETURNS:
the topic name

THROWS:
JMSException

if the JMS provider implementation of Topic fails to return the topic name due to some internal error

toString

public java.lang.String **toString**()

> Returns a string representation of this object.

OVERRIDES:
toString() in class java.lang.Object

RETURNS:
the provider-specific identity values for this topic

CHAPTER 49

TopicConnection

49.1 Overview and Related Interfaces

A TopicConnection object is an active connection to a publish/subscribe JMS provider. A client uses a TopicConnection object to create one or more TopicSession objects for producing and consuming messages.

The related interfaces are

* Connection

* TopicConnectionFactory

49.2 Interface Definition

```
package javax.jms;
public interface TopicConnection extends Connection {
    TopicSession createTopicSession(boolean transacted,
                                    int acknowledgeMode)
                                               throws JMSException;
}
```

49.3 Methods

The TopicConnection interface inherits the fields and the methods of the interface javax.jms.Connection. The following method is defined in the interface javax.jms.TopicConnection.

createTopicSession

```
public TopicSession createTopicSession(boolean transacted,
                                          int acknowledgeMode)
```

Creates a TopicSession object.

The acknowledgeMode parameter is ignored if the session is transacted. Legal values are Session.AUTO_ACKNOWLEDGE, Session.CLIENT_ACKNOWLEDGE, and Session.DUPS_OK_ACKNOWLEDGE.

PARAMETERS:

transacted	indicates whether the session is transacted
acknowledgeMode	indicates whether the consumer or the client will acknowledge any messages it receives; ignored if the session is transacted. Legal values are: Session.AUTO_ACKNOWLEDGE Session.CLIENT_ACKNOWLEDGE Session.DUPS_OK_ACKNOWLEDGE

RETURNS:
a newly created topic session

THROWS:

JMSException	if the TopicConnection object fails to create a session due to some internal error or lack of support for the specific transaction and acknowledgement mode

SEE ALSO:
Session.AUTO_ACKNOWLEDGE
Session.CLIENT_ACKNOWLEDGE
Session.DUPS_OK_ACKNOWLEDGE

CHAPTER 50

TopicConnectionFactory

50.1 Overview and Related Interfaces

A client uses a `TopicConnectionFactory` object to create `TopicConnection` objects with a publish/subscribe JMS provider. The related interfaces are

- `Session`
- `MapMessage`
- `TextMessage`

50.2 Interface Definition

```
package javax.jms;
public interface TopicConnectionFactory extends ConnectionFactory {
    TopicConnection createTopicConnection() throws JMSException;
    TopicConnection createTopicConnection(String userName,
                                          String password)
                                                throws JMSException;
}
```

50.3 Methods

The `TopicConnectionFactory` interface inherits the fields and the methods of the interface `javax.jms.ConnectionFactory`. The following methods are defined in the interface `javax.jms.TopicConnectionFactory`.

createTopicConnection()

`public TopicConnection` **`createTopicConnection`**`()`

Creates a topic connection with the default user identity. The connection is created in stopped mode. No messages will be delivered until the `Connection.start` method is explicitly called.

RETURNS:
a newly created topic connection

THROWS:

`JMSException`	if the JMS provider fails to create a topic connection due to some internal error
`JMSSecurityException`	if client authentication fails due to an invalid user name or password

createTopicConnection(String, String)

`public TopicConnection` **`createTopicConnection`**`(java.lang.String userName,`
                                    `java.lang.String password)`

Creates a topic connection with the specified user identity. The connection is created in stopped mode. No messages will be delivered until the `Connection.start` method is explicitly called.

PARAMETERS:

userName	the caller's user name
password	the caller's password

RETURNS:
a newly created topic connection

THROWS:

`JMSException`	if the JMS provider fails to create a topic connection due to some internal error
`JMSSecurityException`	if client authentication fails due to an invalid user name or password

CHAPTER **51**

TopicPublisher

51.1 Overview and Related Method

A client uses a `TopicPublisher` object to publish messages on a topic. A `TopicPublisher` object is the publish/subscribe form of a message producer.

Normally, the `Topic` is specified when a `TopicPublisher` is created. In this case, an attempt to use the `publish` methods for an unidentified `TopicPublisher` will throw a `java.lang.UnsupportedOperationException`.

If the `TopicPublisher` is created with an unidentified `Topic`, an attempt to use the `publish` methods that assume that the `Topic` has been identified will throw a `java.lang.UnsupportedOperationException`.

During the execution of its `publish` method, a message must not be changed by other threads within the client. If the message is modified, the result of the `publish` is undefined.

After publishing a message, a client may retain and modify it without affecting the message that has been published. The same message object may be published multiple times.

The following message headers are set as part of publishing a message: `JMSDestination`, `JMSDeliveryMode`, `JMSExpiration`, `JMSPriority`, `JMSMessageID` and `JMSTimeStamp`. When the message is published, the values of these headers are ignored. After completion of the `publish`, the headers hold the values specified by the method publishing the message. It is possible for the `publish` method not to set `JMSMessageID` and `JMSTimeStamp` if the setting of these headers is explicitly disabled by the `MessageProducer.setDisableMessageID` or `MessageProducer.setDisableMessageTimestamp` method.

The related method is `TopicSession.createPublisher`.

51.2   Interface Definition

```
package javax.jms;
public interface TopicPublisher extends MessageProducer {
    Topic getTopic() throws JMSException;
    void publish(Message message) throws JMSException;
    void publish(Message message, int deliveryMode, int priority,
                                long timeToLive) throws JMSException;
    void publish(Topic topic, Message message) throws JMSException;
    void publish(Topic topic, Message message, int deliveryMode,
                                int priority, long timeToLive)
                                          throws JMSException;
}
```

51.3   Methods

The TopicPublisher interface inherits the fields and the methods of the interface javax.jms.MessageProducer. The following methods are defined in the interface javax.jms.TopicPublisher.

getTopic

```
public Topic getTopic()
```

Gets the topic associated with this TopicPublisher.

RETURNS:
this publisher's topic

THROWS:

JMSException   if the JMS provider fails to get the topic for this TopicPublisher due to some internal error

publish(Message)

```
public void publish(Message message)
```

Publishes a message to the topic. Uses the TopicPublisher's default delivery mode, priority, and time to live.

PARAMETERS:

`message`	the message to publish

THROWS:

`JMSException`	if the JMS provider fails to publish the message due to some internal error
`MessageFormatException`	if an invalid message is specified
`InvalidDestinationException`	if a client uses this method with a `Topic-Publisher` with an invalid topic
`java.lang.UnsupportedOperationException`	
	if a client uses this method with a `Topic-Publisher` that did not specify a topic at creation time

SEE ALSO:

`MessageProducer.getDeliveryMode`
`MessageProducer.getTimeToLive`
`MessageProducer.getPriority`

publish(Message, int, int, long)

```
public void publish(Message message, int deliveryMode, int priority,
                                                    long timeToLive)
```

Publishes a message to the topic, specifying delivery mode, priority, and time to live.

PARAMETERS:

`message`	the message to publish
`deliveryMode`	the delivery mode to use
`priority`	the priority for this message
`timeToLive`	the message's lifetime (in milliseconds)

THROWS:

`JMSException`	if the JMS provider fails to publish the message due to some internal error
`MessageFormatException`	if an invalid message is specified
`InvalidDestinationException`	if a client uses this method with a `Topic-Publisher` with an invalid topic
`java.lang.UnsupportedOperationException`	
	if a client uses this method with a `Topic-Publisher` that did not specify a topic at creation time

publish(Topic, Message)

```
public void publish(Topic topic, Message message)
```

Publishes a message to a topic for an unidentified message producer. Uses the `TopicPublisher`'s default delivery mode, priority, and time to live.

Typically, a message producer is assigned a topic at creation time; however, the JMS API also supports unidentified message producers, which require that the topic be supplied every time a message is published.

PARAMETERS:

`topic`	the topic to publish this message to
`message`	the message to publish

THROWS:

`JMSException`	if the JMS provider fails to publish the message due to some internal error
`MessageFormatException`	if an invalid message is specified
`InvalidDestinationException`	if a client uses this method with an invalid topic

SEE ALSO:

```
MessageProducer.setDeliveryMode
MessageProducer.setTimeToLive
MessageProducer.setPriority
```

publish(Topic, Message, int, int, long)

```
public void publish(Topic topic, Message message, int deliveryMode,
                                    int priority, long timeToLive)
```

Publishes a message to a topic for an unidentified message producer, specifying delivery mode, priority and time to live.

Typically, a message producer is assigned a topic at creation time; however, the JMS API also supports unidentified message producers, which require that the topic be supplied every time a message is published.

PARAMETERS:

`topic`	the topic to publish this message to
`message`	the message to publish
`deliveryMode`	the delivery mode to use
`priority`	the priority for this message
`timeToLive`	the message's lifetime (in milliseconds)

THROWS:

JMSException	if the JMS provider fails to publish the message due to some internal error
MessageFormatException	if an invalid message is specified
InvalidDestinationException	if a client uses this method with an invalid topic

CHAPTER 52

TopicRequestor

52.1 Overview and Related Interface

The TopicRequestor helper class simplifies making service requests.

The TopicRequestor constructor is given a non-transacted TopicSession and a destination Topic. It creates a TemporaryTopic for the responses and provides a request method that sends the request message and waits for its reply.

This is a basic request/reply abstraction that should be sufficient for most uses. JMS providers and clients are free to create more sophisticated versions.

The related interface is QueueRequestor.

52.2 Class Definition

```
package javax.jms;
public interface TopicRequestor extends java.lang.Object {
    public TopicRequestor(TopicSession session, Topic topic)
                                              throws JMSException;
    public void close() throws JMSException;
    public Message request(Message message) throws JMSException;
}
```

52.3   Constructor

The following constructor is defined by the class `javax.jms.TopicRequestor`.

TopicRequestor

`public **TopicRequestor**(TopicSession *session*, Topic *topic*)`

Constructor for the `TopicRequestor` class.

This implementation assumes the session parameter to be non-transacted, with a delivery mode of either `AUTO_ACKNOWLEDGE` or `DUPS_OK_ACKNOWLEDGE`.

PARAMETERS:

session	the `TopicSession` the topic belongs to
topic	the topic to perform the request/reply call on

THROWS:

`JMSException`	if the JMS provider fails to create the `TopicRequestor` due to some internal error
`InvalidDestinationException`	if an invalid topic is specified

52.4   Methods

The `TopicRequestor` interface inherits the methods of the class `java.lang.Object`. The following methods are defined in the interface `javax.jms.TopicRequestor`.

close

`public void **close**()`

Closes the `TopicRequestor` and its session.

Since a provider may allocate some resources on behalf of a `TopicRequestor` outside the Java virtual machine, clients should close them when they are not needed. Relying on garbage collection to eventually reclaim these resources may not be timely enough.

Note that this method closes the `TopicSession` object passed to the `TopicRequestor` constructor.

THROWS:

JMSException   if the JMS provider fails to close the `Topic-Requestor` due to some internal error

request

```
public Message request(Message message)
```

Sends a request and waits for a reply. The temporary topic is used for the JMSReplyTo destination; the first reply is returned, and any following replies are discarded.

PARAMETERS:

message   the message to send

RETURNS:

the reply message

THROWS:

JMSException   if the JMS provider fails to complete the request due to some internal error

CHAPTER 53

TopicSession

53.1 Overview and Related Methods and Interfaces

A `TopicSession` object provides methods for creating `TopicPublisher`, `Topic-Subscriber`, and `TemporaryTopic` objects. It also provides a method for deleting its client's durable subscribers.

The related methods and interfaces are

- `TopicConnection.createTopicSession`

- `Session`

53.2 Interface Definition

```
package javax.jms;
public interface TopicSession extends Session {
    TopicSubscriber createDurableSubscriber(Topic topic, String name)
                                            throws JMSException;
    TopicSubscriber createDurableSubscriber(Topic topic, String name,
                            String messageSelector,
                            boolean noLocal) throws JMSException;
    TopicPublisher createPublisher(Topic topic) throws JMSException;
    TopicSubscriber createSubscriber(Topic topic) throws JMSException;
    TopicSubscriber createSubscriber(Topic topic,
                            String messageSelector,
                            boolean noLocal) throws JMSException;
    TemporaryTopic createTemporaryTopic() throws JMSException;
```

```
    Topic createTopic(String topicName) throws JMSException;
    void unsubscribe(String name) throws JMSException;
}
```

53.3 Methods

The `TopicSession` interface inherits the fields and the methods of the interface `javax.jms.Session`. The following methods are defined in the interface `javax.jms.TopicSession`.

createDurableSubscriber(Topic, String)

```
public TopicSubscriber createDurableSubscriber(Topic topic,
                                        java.lang.String name)
```

Creates a durable subscriber to the specified topic.

If a client needs to receive all the messages published on a topic, including the ones published while the subscriber is inactive, it uses a durable `TopicSubscriber`. The JMS provider retains a record of this durable subscription and insures that all messages from the topic's publishers are retained until they are acknowledged by this durable subscriber or they have expired.

Sessions with durable subscribers must always provide the same client identifier. In addition, each client must specify a name that uniquely identifies (within client identifier) each durable subscription it creates. Only one session at a time can have a `TopicSubscriber` for a particular durable subscription.

A client can change an existing durable subscription by creating a durable `TopicSubscriber` with the same name and a new topic and/or message selector. Changing a durable subscriber is equivalent to unsubscribing (deleting) the old one and creating a new one.

In some cases, a connection may both publish and subscribe to a topic. The subscriber `NoLocal` attribute allows a subscriber to inhibit the delivery of messages published by its own connection. The default value for this attribute is false.

PARAMETERS:

topic	the non-temporary `Topic` to subscribe to
name	the name used to identify this subscription

THROWS:

JMSException	if the session fails to create a subscriber due to some internal error
InvalidDestinationException	if an invalid topic is specified

createDurableSubscriber(Topic, String, String, boolean)

```
public TopicSubscriber createDurableSubscriber(Topic topic,
                        java.lang.String name,
                        java.lang.String messageSelector,
                        boolean noLocal)
```

Creates a durable subscriber to the specified topic, using a message selector or specifying whether messages published by its own connection should be delivered to it.

If a client needs to receive all the messages published on a topic, including the ones published while the subscriber is inactive, it uses a durable TopicSubscriber. The JMS provider retains a record of this durable subscription and insures that all messages from the topic's publishers are retained until they are acknowledged by this durable subscriber or they have expired.

Sessions with durable subscribers must always provide the same client identifier. In addition, each client must specify a name which uniquely identifies (within client identifier) each durable subscription it creates. Only one session at a time can have a TopicSubscriber for a particular durable subscription. An inactive durable subscriber is one that exists but does not currently have a message consumer associated with it.

A client can change an existing durable subscription by creating a durable TopicSubscriber with the same name and a new topic and/or message selector. Changing a durable subscriber is equivalent to unsubscribing (deleting) the old one and creating a new one.

PARAMETERS:

topic	the non-temporary Topic to subscribe to
name	the name used to identify this subscription
messageSelector	only messages with properties matching the message selector expression are delivered; a value of null or an empty string indicates that there is no message selector for the message consumer
noLocal	if set, inhibits the delivery of messages published by its own connection

THROWS:

JMSException	if the session fails to create a subscriber due to some internal error
InvalidDestinationException	if an invalid topic is specified
InvalidSelectorException	if the message selector is invalid

createPublisher

```
public TopicPublisher createPublisher(Topic topic)
```

Creates a publisher for the specified topic.

A client uses a TopicPublisher object to publish messages on a topic. Each time a client creates a TopicPublisher on a topic, it defines a new sequence of messages that have no ordering relationship with the messages it has previously sent.

PARAMETERS:

topic	the Topic to publish to, or null if this is an unidentified producer

THROWS:

JMSException	if the session fails to create a publisher due to some internal error
InvalidDestinationException	if an invalid topic is specified

createSubscriber(Topic)

```
public TopicSubscriber createSubscriber(Topic topic)
```

Creates a nondurable subscriber to the specified topic.

A client uses a TopicSubscriber object to receive messages that have been published to a topic.

Regular TopicSubscriber objects are not durable. They receive only messages that are published while they are active.

In some cases, a connection may both publish and subscribe to a topic. The subscriber NoLocal attribute allows a subscriber to inhibit the delivery of messages published by its own connection. The default value for this attribute is false.

PARAMETERS:

topic	the Topic to subscribe to

THROWS:

JMSException	if the session fails to create a subscriber due to some internal error
InvalidDestinationException	if an invalid topic is specified

createSubscriber(Topic, String, boolean)

```
public TopicSubscriber createSubscriber(Topic topic,
                                        java.lang.String messageSelector,
                                        boolean noLocal)
```

Creates a nondurable subscriber to the specified topic, using a message selector or specifying whether messages published by its own connection should be delivered to it.

A client uses a TopicSubscriber object to receive messages that have been published to a topic.

Regular TopicSubscriber objects are not durable. They receive only messages that are published while they are active.

Messages filtered out by a subscriber's message selector will never be delivered to the subscriber. From the subscriber's perspective, they do not exist.

In some cases, a connection may both publish and subscribe to a topic. The subscriber NoLocal attribute allows a subscriber to inhibit the delivery of messages published by its own connection. The default value for this attribute is false.

PARAMETERS:

topic	the Topic to subscribe to
messageSelector	only messages with properties matching the message selector expression are delivered; a value of null or an empty string indicates that there is no message selector for the message consumer
noLocal	if set, inhibits the delivery of messages published by its own connection

THROWS:

JMSException	if the session fails to create a subscriber due to some internal error
InvalidDestinationException	if an invalid topic is specified
InvalidSelectorException	if the message selector is invalid

createTemporaryTopic

`public TemporaryTopic` **`createTemporaryTopic`**`()`

Creates a `TemporaryTopic` object. Its lifetime will be that of the `Topic-Connection` unless it is deleted earlier.

RETURNS:
a temporary topic identity

THROWS:

JMSException	if the session fails to create a temporary topic due to some internal error

createTopic

`public Topic` **`createTopic`**`(java.lang.String topicName)`

Creates a topic identity given a `Topic` name.

This facility is provided for the rare cases where clients need to dynamically manipulate topic identity. This allows the creation of a topic identity with a provider-specific name. Clients that depend on this ability are not portable.

Note that this method is not for creating the physical topic. The physical creation of topics is an administrative task and is not to be initiated by the JMS API. The one exception is the creation of temporary topics, which is accomplished with the `createTemporaryTopic` method.

PARAMETERS:

topicName	the name of this `Topic`

RETURNS:
a `Topic` with the given name

THROWS:

JMSException	if the session fails to create a topic due to some internal error

unsubscribe

`public void` **`unsubscribe`**`(java.lang.String name)`

Unsubscribes a durable subscription that has been created by a client.

This method deletes the state being maintained on behalf of the subscriber by its provider.

It is erroneous for a client to delete a durable subscription while there is an active `TopicSubscriber` for the subscription, or while a consumed message is part of a pending transaction or has not been acknowledged in the session.

PARAMETERS:

name   the name used to identify this subscription

THROWS:

`JMSException`   if the session fails to unsubscribe to the durable subscription due to some internal error

`InvalidDestinationException` if an invalid subscription name is specified

TopicSubscriber

54.1 Overview and Related Methods and Interfaces

A client uses a TopicSubscriber object to receive messages that have been published to a topic. A TopicSubscriber object is the publish/subscribe form of a
message consumer.

A TopicSession allows the creation of multiple TopicSubscriber objects per
topic. It will deliver each message for a topic to each subscriber eligible to receive
it. Each copy of the message is treated as a completely separate message. Work
done on one copy has no effect on the others; acknowledging one does not
acknowledge the others; one message may be delivered immediately, while
another waits for its subscriber to process messages ahead of it.

Regular TopicSubscriber objects are not durable. They receive only messages that are published while they are active.

Messages filtered out by a subscriber's message selector will never be delivered to the subscriber. From the subscriber's perspective, they do not exist.

In some cases, a connection may both publish and subscribe to a topic. The
subscriber NoLocal attribute allows a subscriber to inhibit the delivery of messages published by its own connection.

If a client needs to receive all the messages published on a topic, including the
ones published while the subscriber is inactive, it uses a durable TopicSubscriber.
The JMS provider retains a record of this durable subscription and insures that all
messages from the topic's publishers are retained until they are acknowledged by
this durable subscriber or they have expired.

Sessions with durable subscribers must always provide the same client identifier. In addition, each client must specify a name that uniquely identifies (within

client identifier) each durable subscription it creates. Only one session at a time can have a TopicSubscriber for a particular durable subscription.

A client can change an existing durable subscription by creating a durable TopicSubscriber with the same name and a new topic and/or message selector. Changing a durable subscription is equivalent to unsubscribing (deleting) the old one and creating a new one.

TopicSessions provide the unsubscribe method for deleting a durable subscription created by their client. This method deletes the state being maintained on behalf of the subscriber by its provider.

The related methods and interfaces are

- TopicSession.createSubscriber(Topic)

- TopicSession.createSubscriber(Topic, String, boolean)

- TopicSession.createDurableSubscriber(Topic, String)

- TopicSession.createDurableSubscriber(Topic, String, String, boolean)

- MessageConsumer

54.2   Interface Definition

```
package javax.jms;
public interface TopicSubscriber extends MessageConsumer {
    boolean getNoLocal() throws JMSException;
    Topic getTopic() throws JMSException;
}
```

54.3   Methods

The TopicSubscriber interface inherits the methods of the interface javax.jms.MessageConsumer. The following methods are defined in the interface javax.jms.TopicSubscriber.

getNoLocal

```
public boolean getNoLocal()
```

Gets the `NoLocal` attribute for this subscriber. The default value for this attribute is false.

RETURNS:
true if locally published messages are being inhibited

THROWS:

JMSException   if the JMS provider fails to get the `NoLocal` attribute for this topic subscriber due to some internal error

getTopic

```
public Topic getTopic()
```

Gets the `Topic` associated with this subscriber.

RETURNS:
this subscriber's `Topic`

THROWS:

JMSException   if the JMS provider fails to get the topic for this topic subscriber due to some internal error

CHAPTER 55

TransactionInProgress-Exception

55.1 Overview

This exception is thrown when an operation is invalid because a transaction is in progress. For instance, an attempt to call Session.commit when a session is part of a distributed transaction should throw a TransactionInProgressException.

The TransactionInProgressException class inherits the methods of the class javax.jms.JMSException.

55.2 Class Definition

```
package javax.jms;
public class TransactionInProgressException extends JMSException {
    public TransactionInProgressException(String reason);
    public TransactionInProgressException(String reason,
                                                String errorCode);
}
```

55.3   Constructors

The following constructors are defined by the class `javax.jms.TransactionIn-ProgressException`.

TransactionInProgressException(String)

public **TransactionInProgressException**(java.lang.String *reason*)

Constructs a `TransactionInProgressException` with the specified reason. The error code defaults to null.

PARAMETERS:

reason   a description of the exception

TransactionInProgressException(String, String)

public **TransactionInProgressException**(java.lang.String *reason*,
                                          java.lang.String *errorCode*)

Constructs a `TransactionInProgressException` with the specified reason and error code.

PARAMETERS:

reason   a description of the exception

errorCode   a string specifying the vendor-specific error
                              code

CHAPTER 56

TransactionRolledBack-Exception

56.1 Overview

This exception must be thrown when a call to `Session.commit` results in a rollback of the current transaction.

The `TransactionRolledBackException` class inherits the methods of the class `javax.jms.JMSException`.

56.2 Class Definition

```
package javax.jms;
public class TransactionRolledBackException extends JMSException {
    public TransactionRolledBackException(String reason);
    public TransactionRolledBackException(String reason,
                                                String errorCode);
}
```

56.3   Constructors

The following constructors are defined by the class `javax.jms.Transaction-RolledBackException`.

TransactionRolledBackException(String)

public **TransactionRolledBackException**(java.lang.String *reason*)

Constructs a `TransactionRolledBackException` with the specified reason. The error code defaults to null.

PARAMETERS:

reason   a description of the exception

TransactionRolledBackException(String, String)

public **TransactionRolledBackException**(java.lang.String *reason*,
                                        java.lang.String *errorCode*)

Constructs a `TransactionRolledBackException` with the specified reason and error code.

PARAMETERS:

reason   a description of the exception

errorCode   a string specifying the vendor-specific error
                                 code

JMS Client Examples

THIS appendix contains a number of sample programs that illustrate JMS API concepts and features. The samples are as follows:

- DurableSubscriberExample.java, a program that illustrates the use of durable subscriptions

- TransactedExample.java, a program that shows how to use transactions in standalone applications

- AckEquivExample.java, a program that illustrates acknowledgment modes

- SampleUtilities.java, a utility class containing methods called by the other sample programs

The programs are all self-contained threaded applications. The programs include producer and consumer classes that send and receive messages. If you downloaded the tutorial examples as described in the preface, you will find the examples for this chapter in the directory jms_tutorial/examples/appendix (on UNIX systems) or jms_tutorial\examples\appendix (on Microsoft Windows systems). You can compile and run the examples using the instructions in Chapter 4.

A.1 Durable Subscriptions

The DurableSubscriberExample.java program shows how durable subscriptions work. It demonstrates that a durable subscription is active even when the subscriber is not active. The program contains a DurableSubscriber class, a

MultiplePublisher class, a main method, and a method that instantiates the classes and calls their methods in sequence.

The program begins like any publish/subscribe program: The subscriber starts, the publisher publishes some messages, and the subscriber receives them. At this point, the subscriber closes itself. The publisher then publishes some messages while the subscriber is not active. The subscriber then restarts and receives the messages.

Before you run this program, create a connection factory with a client ID. You can use the command shown in Section 8.2.3 on page 110. Then specify the connection factory name and the topic name on the command line when you run the program, as in the following sample command, which should all be on one line, for a Microsoft Windows system:

```
java -Djms.properties=%J2EE_HOME%\config\jms_client.properties
DurableSubscriberExample DurableTopicCF jms/Topic
```

The output looks something like this:

```
Connection factory name is DurableTopicCF
Topic name is jms/Topic
Java(TM) Message Service 1.0.2 Reference Implementation (build b14)
Starting subscriber
PUBLISHER: Publishing message: Here is a message 1
PUBLISHER: Publishing message: Here is a message 2
PUBLISHER: Publishing message: Here is a message 3
SUBSCRIBER: Reading message: Here is a message 1
SUBSCRIBER: Reading message: Here is a message 2
SUBSCRIBER: Reading message: Here is a message 3
Closing subscriber
PUBLISHER: Publishing message: Here is a message 4
PUBLISHER: Publishing message: Here is a message 5
PUBLISHER: Publishing message: Here is a message 6
Starting subscriber
SUBSCRIBER: Reading message: Here is a message 4
SUBSCRIBER: Reading message: Here is a message 5
SUBSCRIBER: Reading message: Here is a message 6
Closing subscriber
Unsubscribing from durable subscription
```

```
import javax.naming.*;
import javax.jms.*;

public class DurableSubscriberExample {
    String      conFacName = null;
    String      topicName = null;
    static int  startindex = 0;

    /**
     * The DurableSubscriber class contains a constructor, a
     * startSubscriber method, a closeSubscriber method, and a
     * finish method.
     *
     * The class fetches messages asynchronously, using a message
     * listener, TextListener.
     */
    public class DurableSubscriber {
        Context                   jndiContext = null;
        TopicConnectionFactory    topicConnectionFactory = null;
        TopicConnection           topicConnection = null;
        TopicSession              topicSession = null;
        Topic                     topic = null;
        TopicSubscriber           topicSubscriber = null;
        TextListener              topicListener = null;

        /**
         * The TextListener class implements the MessageListener
         * interface by defining an onMessage method for the
         * DurableSubscriber class.
         */
        private class TextListener implements MessageListener {
            final SampleUtilities.DoneLatch  monitor =
                new SampleUtilities.DoneLatch();

            /**
             * Casts the message to a TextMessage and displays
             * its text. A non-text message is interpreted as the
```

```
         * end of the message stream, and the message
         * listener sets its monitor state to all done
         * processing messages.
         *
         * @param message      the incoming message
         */
        public void onMessage(Message message) {
            if (message instanceof TextMessage) {
                TextMessage  msg = (TextMessage) message;

                try {
                    System.out.println("SUBSCRIBER: " +
                        "Reading message: " + msg.getText());
                } catch (JMSException e) {
                    System.err.println("Exception in " +
                        "onMessage(): " + e.toString());
                }
            } else {
                monitor.allDone();
            }
        }
    }


    /**
     * Constructor: looks up a connection factory and topic
     * and creates a connection and session.
     */
    public DurableSubscriber() {

        /*
         * Create a JNDI API InitialContext object if none
         * exists yet.
         */
        try {
            jndiContext = new InitialContext();

        } catch (NamingException e) {
            System.err.println("Could not create JNDI API " +
                "context: " + e.toString());
```

```
            System.exit(1);
        }

        /*
         * Look up connection factory and topic.  If either
         * does not exist, exit.
         */
        try {
            topicConnectionFactory = (TopicConnectionFactory)
                jndiContext.lookup(conFacName);
        } catch (NamingException e) {
            System.err.println("JNDI API lookup failed: " +
                e.toString());
            System.exit(1);
        }

        try {
            topicConnection =
              topicConnectionFactory.createTopicConnection();
            topicSession =
                topicConnection.createTopicSession(false,
                    Session.AUTO_ACKNOWLEDGE);
            topic = SampleUtilities.getTopic(topicName,
                topicSession);
        } catch (Exception e) {
            System.err.println("Connection problem: " +
                e.toString());
            if (topicConnection != null) {
                try {
                    topicConnection.close();
                } catch (JMSException ee) {}
            }
        System.exit(1);
        }
    }

    /**
     * Stops connection, then creates durable subscriber,
     * registers message listener (TextListener), and starts
```

```
 * message delivery; listener displays the messages
 * obtained.
 */
public void startSubscriber() {
    try {
        System.out.println("Starting subscriber");
        topicConnection.stop();
        topicSubscriber =
            topicSession.createDurableSubscriber(topic,
                "MakeItLast");
        topicListener = new TextListener();
      topicSubscriber.setMessageListener(topicListener);
        topicConnection.start();
    } catch (JMSException e) {
        System.err.println("Exception occurred: " +
            e.toString());
    }
}


/**
 * Blocks until publisher issues a control message
 * indicating end of publish stream, then closes
 * subscriber.
 */
public void closeSubscriber() {
    try {
        topicListener.monitor.waitTillDone();
        System.out.println("Closing subscriber");
        topicSubscriber.close();
    } catch (JMSException e) {
        System.err.println("Exception occurred: " +
            e.toString());
    }
}


/**
 * Closes the connection.
 */
```

```java
    public void finish() {
        if (topicConnection != null) {
            try {
                System.out.println("Unsubscribing from " +
                    "durable subscription");
                topicSession.unsubscribe("MakeItLast");
                topicConnection.close();
            } catch (JMSException e) {}
        }
    }
}


/**
 * The MultiplePublisher class publishes several messages to
 * a topic. It contains a constructor, a publishMessages
 * method, and a finish method.
 */
public class MultiplePublisher {
    TopicConnection  topicConnection = null;
    TopicSession     topicSession = null;
    Topic            topic = null;
    TopicPublisher   topicPublisher = null;

    /**
     * Constructor: looks up a connection factory and topic
     * and creates a connection, session, and publisher.
     */
    public MultiplePublisher() {
        TopicConnectionFactory topicConnectionFactory = null;

        try {
            topicConnectionFactory =
                SampleUtilities.getTopicConnectionFactory();
            topicConnection =
              topicConnectionFactory.createTopicConnection();

            topicSession =
                topicConnection.createTopicSession(false,
                    Session.AUTO_ACKNOWLEDGE);
```

```
                topic =
                    SampleUtilities.getTopic(topicName,
                        topicSession);
                topicPublisher =
                    topicSession.createPublisher(topic);
            } catch (Exception e) {
                System.err.println("Connection problem: " +
                    e.toString());
                if (topicConnection != null) {
                    try {
                        topicConnection.close();
                    } catch (JMSException ee) {}
                }
        System.exit(1);
            }
        }


    /**
     * Creates text message.
     * Sends some messages, varying text slightly.
     * Messages must be persistent.
     */
    public void publishMessages() {
        TextMessage   message = null;
        int           i;
        final int     NUMMSGS = 3;
        final String MSG_TEXT =
                        new String("Here is a message");

        try {
            message = topicSession.createTextMessage();
            for (i = startindex;
                    i < startindex + NUMMSGS; i++) {
                message.setText(MSG_TEXT + " " + (i + 1));
                System.out.println("PUBLISHER: Publishing " +
                    "message: " + message.getText());
                topicPublisher.publish(message);
            }
```

```
            /*
             * Send a non-text control message indicating end
             * of messages.
             */
        topicPublisher.publish(topicSession.createMessage());
            startindex = i;
        } catch (JMSException e) {
            System.err.println("Exception occurred: " +
                e.toString());
        }
    }


    /**
     * Closes the connection.
     */
    public void finish() {
        if (topicConnection != null) {
            try {
                topicConnection.close();
            } catch (JMSException e) {}
        }
    }
}


/**
 * Instantiates the subscriber and publisher classes.
 * Starts the subscriber; the publisher publishes some
 *   messages.
 * Closes the subscriber; while it is closed, the publisher
 *   publishes some more messages.
 * Restarts the subscriber and fetches the messages.
 * Finally, closes the connections.
 */
public void run_program() {
    DurableSubscriber  durableSubscriber =
                                new DurableSubscriber();
    MultiplePublisher  multiplePublisher =
                                new MultiplePublisher();
```

```java
            durableSubscriber.startSubscriber();
            multiplePublisher.publishMessages();
            durableSubscriber.closeSubscriber();
            multiplePublisher.publishMessages();
            durableSubscriber.startSubscriber();
            durableSubscriber.closeSubscriber();
            multiplePublisher.finish();
            durableSubscriber.finish();
        }


        /**
         * Reads the topic name from the command line, then calls the
         * run_program method.
         *
         * @param args      the topic used by the example
         */
        public static void main(String[] args) {
            DurableSubscriberExample  dse =
                                    new DurableSubscriberExample();

            if (args.length != 2) {
            System.out.println("Usage: java " +
                "DurableSubscriberExample " +
                "<connection_factory_name> <topic_name>");
            System.exit(1);
        }
        dse.conFacName = new String(args[0]);
            System.out.println("Connection factory name is " +
                dse.conFacName);
            dse.topicName = new String(args[1]);
            System.out.println("Topic name is " + dse.topicName);

        dse.run_program();
        }
    }
```

Code Example A.1 `DurableSubscriberExample.java`

A.2 Transactions

The `TransactedExample.java` program demonstrates the use of transactions in a JMS client application. The program represents a highly simplified e-Commerce application, in which the following things happen.

1. A retailer sends a message to the vendor order queue, ordering a quantity of computers, and waits for the vendor's reply.

2. The vendor receives the retailer's order message and places an order message into each of its suppliers' order queues, all in one transaction. This JMS transaction combines one synchronous receive with multiple sends.

3. One supplier receives the order from its order queue, checks its inventory, and sends the items ordered to the destination named in the order message's `JMSReplyTo` field. If it does not have enough in stock, the supplier sends what it has. The synchronous receive and the send take place in one JMS transaction.

4. The other supplier receives the order from its order queue, checks its inventory, and sends the items ordered to the destination named in the order message's `JMSReplyTo` field. If it does not have enough in stock, the supplier sends what it has. The synchronous receive and the send take place in one JMS transaction.

5. The vendor receives the replies from the suppliers from its confirmation queue and updates the state of the order. Messages are processed by an asynchronous message listener; this step illustrates using JMS transactions with a message listener.

6. When all outstanding replies are processed for a given order, the vendor sends a message notifying the retailer whether it can fulfill the order.

7. The retailer receives the message from the vendor.

Figure A.1 illustrates these steps.

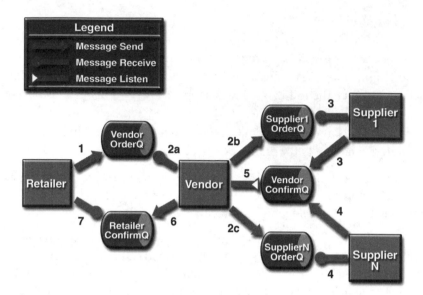

Figure A.1   Transactions: JMS Client Example

The program contains five classes: `Retailer`, `Vendor`, `GenericSupplier`, `VendorMessageListener`, and `Order`. The program also contains a main method and a method that runs the threads of the `Retail`, `Vendor`, and two supplier classes.

All the messages use the `MapMessage` message type. Synchronous receives are used for all message reception except for the case of the vendor processing the replies of the suppliers. These replies are processed asynchronously and demonstrate how to use transactions within a message listener.

At random intervals, the `Vendor` class throws an exception to simulate a database problem and cause a rollback.

All classes except `Retailer` use transacted sessions.

The program uses five queues. Before you run the program, create the queues and name them `A`, `B`, `C`, `D` and `E`.

When you run the program, specify on the command line the number of computers to be ordered. For example, on a Microsoft Windows system:

```
java -Djms.properties=%J2EE_HOME%\config\jms_client.properties
TransactedExample 3
```

The output looks something like this:

```
Quantity to be ordered is 3
Java(TM) Message Service 1.0.2 Reference Implementation (build b14)
Java(TM) Message Service 1.0.2 Reference Implementation (build b14)
Java(TM) Message Service 1.0.2 Reference Implementation (build b14)
Java(TM) Message Service 1.0.2 Reference Implementation (build b14)
Retailer: ordered 3 computer(s)
Vendor: JMSException occurred: javax.jms.JMSException: Simulated
database concurrent access exception
javax.jms.JMSException: Simulated database concurrent access excep-
tion at TransactedExample$Vendor.run(TransactedExample.java:300)
  Vendor: rolled back transaction 1
Vendor: Retailer ordered 3 Computer(s)
Vendor: ordered 3 Monitor(s)
Vendor: ordered 3 Hard Drive(s)
Hard Drive Supplier: Vendor ordered 3 Hard Drive(s)
Hard Drive Supplier: sent 3 Hard Drive(s)
  Vendor: committed transaction 1
Monitor Supplier: Vendor ordered 3 Monitor(s)
Monitor Supplier: sent 3 Monitor(s)
  Hard Drive Supplier: committed transaction
  Monitor Supplier: committed transaction
Vendor: Completed processing for order 1
Vendor: sent 3 computer(s)
  Vendor: committed transaction 2
Retailer: Order filled
Retailer: placing another order
Retailer: ordered 6 computer(s)
Vendor: Retailer ordered 6 Computer(s)
Vendor: ordered 6 Monitor(s)
Vendor: ordered 6 Hard Drive(s)
  Vendor: committed transaction 1
Monitor Supplier: Vendor ordered 6 Monitor(s)
Hard Drive Supplier: Vendor ordered 6 Hard Drive(s)
Hard Drive Supplier: sent 6 Hard Drive(s)
Monitor Supplier: sent 0 Monitor(s)
  Monitor Supplier: committed transaction
  Hard Drive Supplier: committed transaction
```

```
Vendor: Completed processing for order 2
Vendor: unable to send 6 computer(s)
  Vendor: committed transaction 2
Retailer: Order not filled
```

```java
import java.util.*;
import javax.jms.*;

public class TransactedExample {
    public static String  vendorOrderQueueName = null;
    public static String  retailerConfirmQueueName = null;
    public static String  monitorOrderQueueName = null;
    public static String  storageOrderQueueName = null;
    public static String  vendorConfirmQueueName = null;

    /**
     * The Retailer class orders a number of computers by sending
     * a message to a vendor.  It then waits for the order to be
     * confirmed.
     *
     * In this example, the Retailer places two orders, one for
     * the quantity specified on the command line and one for
     * twice that number.
     *
     * This class does not use transactions.
     */
    public static class Retailer extends Thread {
        int  quantity = 0;

        /**
         * Constructor.  Instantiates the retailer with the
         * quantity of computers being ordered.
         *
         * @param q     the quantity specified in the program
         *              arguments
         */
```

```java
public Retailer(int q) {
    quantity = q;
}

/**
 * Runs the thread.
 */
public void run() {
    QueueConnectionFactory queueConnectionFactory = null;
    QueueConnection         queueConnection = null;
    QueueSession            queueSession = null;
    Queue                   vendorOrderQueue = null;
    Queue                   retailerConfirmQueue = null;
    QueueSender             queueSender = null;
    MapMessage              outMessage = null;
    QueueReceiver           orderConfirmReceiver = null;
    MapMessage              inMessage = null;

    try {
        queueConnectionFactory =
            SampleUtilities.getQueueConnectionFactory();
        queueConnection =
          queueConnectionFactory.createQueueConnection();
        queueSession =
            queueConnection.createQueueSession(false,
                Session.AUTO_ACKNOWLEDGE);
        vendorOrderQueue =
            SampleUtilities.getQueue(vendorOrderQueueName,
                queueSession);
        retailerConfirmQueue =
        SampleUtilities.getQueue(retailerConfirmQueueName,
            queueSession);
    } catch (Exception e) {
        System.err.println("Connection problem: " +
            e.toString());
        System.err.println("Program assumes five " +
            "queues named A B C D E");
```

```
        if (queueConnection != null) {
            try {
                queueConnection.close();
            } catch (JMSException ee) {}
        }
        System.exit(1);
    }

    /*
     * Create non-transacted session and sender for
     * vendor order queue.
     * Create message to vendor, setting item and
     * quantity values.
     * Send message.
     * Create receiver for retailer confirmation queue.
     * Get message and report result.
     * Send an end-of-message-stream message so vendor
     * will stop processing orders.
     */
    try {
        queueSender =
            queueSession.createSender(vendorOrderQueue);
        outMessage = queueSession.createMapMessage();
        outMessage.setString("Item", "Computer(s)");
        outMessage.setInt("Quantity", quantity);
        outMessage.setJMSReplyTo(retailerConfirmQueue);
        queueSender.send(outMessage);
        System.out.println("Retailer: ordered " +
            quantity + " computer(s)");

        orderConfirmReceiver =
        queueSession.createReceiver(retailerConfirmQueue);
        queueConnection.start();
        inMessage =
            (MapMessage) orderConfirmReceiver.receive();
        if (inMessage.getBoolean("OrderAccepted")
                == true) {
            System.out.println("Retailer: Order filled");
        } else {
```

```java
            System.out.println("Retailer: Order not " +
                "filled");
        }

        System.out.println("Retailer: placing another " +
            "order");
        outMessage.setInt("Quantity", quantity * 2);
        queueSender.send(outMessage);
        System.out.println("Retailer: ordered " +
            outMessage.getInt("Quantity") +
            " computer(s)");
        inMessage =
            (MapMessage) orderConfirmReceiver.receive();
        if (inMessage.getBoolean("OrderAccepted")
                == true) {
            System.out.println("Retailer: Order filled");
        } else {
            System.out.println("Retailer: Order not " +
                "filled");
        }

        /*
         * Send a non-text control message indicating end
         * of messages.
         */
        queueSender.send(queueSession.createMessage());
    } catch (Exception e) {
        System.err.println("Retailer: Exception " +
            "occurred: " + e.toString());
        e.printStackTrace();
    } finally {
        if (queueConnection != null) {
            try {
                queueConnection.close();
            } catch (JMSException e) {}
        }
    }
}
}
```

```
/**
 * The Vendor class uses one transaction to receive the
 * computer order from the retailer and order the needed
 * number of monitors and disk drives from its suppliers.
 * At random intervals, it throws an exception to simulate a
 * database problem and cause a rollback.
 *
 * The class uses an asynchronous message listener to process
 * replies from suppliers. When all outstanding supplier
 * inquiries complete, it sends a message to the Retailer
 * accepting or refusing the order.
 */
public static class Vendor extends Thread {
    Random   rgen = new Random();
    int      throwException = 1;

    /**
     * Runs the thread.
     */
    public void run() {
        QueueConnectionFactory queueConnectionFactory = null;
        QueueConnection        queueConnection = null;
        QueueSession           queueSession = null;
        QueueSession           asyncQueueSession = null;
        Queue                  vendorOrderQueue = null;
        Queue                  monitorOrderQueue = null;
        Queue                  storageOrderQueue = null;
        Queue                  vendorConfirmQueue = null;
        QueueReceiver          vendorOrderQueueReceiver = null;
        QueueSender            monitorOrderQueueSender = null;
        QueueSender            storageOrderQueueSender = null;
        MapMessage             orderMessage = null;
        QueueReceiver          vendorConfirmQueueReceiver = null;
        VendorMessageListener  listener = null;
        Message                inMessage = null;
        MapMessage             vendorOrderMessage = null;
        Message                endOfMessageStream = null;
        Order                  order = null;
        int                    quantity = 0;
```

```
try {
    queueConnectionFactory =
        SampleUtilities.getQueueConnectionFactory();
    queueConnection =
      queueConnectionFactory.createQueueConnection();
    queueSession =
        queueConnection.createQueueSession(true, 0);
    asyncQueueSession =
        queueConnection.createQueueSession(true, 0);
    vendorOrderQueue =
        SampleUtilities.getQueue(vendorOrderQueueName,
            queueSession);
    monitorOrderQueue =
      SampleUtilities.getQueue(monitorOrderQueueName,
            queueSession);
    storageOrderQueue =
      SampleUtilities.getQueue(storageOrderQueueName,
            queueSession);
    vendorConfirmQueue =
      SampleUtilities.getQueue(vendorConfirmQueueName,
            queueSession);
} catch (Exception e) {
    System.err.println("Connection problem: " +
        e.toString());
    System.err.println("Program assumes five " +
        "queues named A B C D E");
    if (queueConnection != null) {
        try {
            queueConnection.close();
        } catch (JMSException ee) {}
    }
    System.exit(1);
}

try {
    /*
     * Create receiver for vendor order queue, sender
     * for supplier order queues, and message to send
     * to suppliers.
```

```
      */
     vendorOrderQueueReceiver =
        queueSession.createReceiver(vendorOrderQueue);
     monitorOrderQueueSender =
        queueSession.createSender(monitorOrderQueue);
     storageOrderQueueSender =
        queueSession.createSender(storageOrderQueue);
     orderMessage = queueSession.createMapMessage();

     /*
      * Configure an asynchronous message listener to
      * process supplier replies to inquiries for
      * parts to fill order.  Start delivery.
      */
     vendorConfirmQueueReceiver =
   asyncQueueSession.createReceiver(vendorConfirmQueue);
     listener =
        new VendorMessageListener(asyncQueueSession,
           2);
   vendorConfirmQueueReceiver.setMessageListener(listener);
     queueConnection.start();

     /*
      * Process orders in vendor order queue.
      * Use one transaction to receive order from
      * order queue and send messages to suppliers'
      * order queues to order components to fulfill
      * the order placed with the vendor.
      */
     while (true) {
        try {

           // Receive an order from a retailer.
           inMessage =
              vendorOrderQueueReceiver.receive();
           if (inMessage instanceof MapMessage) {
              vendorOrderMessage =
                 (MapMessage) inMessage;
           } else {
```

```
                    /*
                     * Message is an end-of-message-
                     * stream message from retailer.
                     * Send similar messages to
                     * suppliers, then break out of
                     * processing loop.
                     */
                    endOfMessageStream =
                        queueSession.createMessage();
endOfMessageStream.setJMSReplyTo(vendorConfirmQueue);
    monitorOrderQueueSender.send(endOfMessageStream);
    storageOrderQueueSender.send(endOfMessageStream);
                    queueSession.commit();
                    break;
                }

                /*
                 * A real application would check an
                 * inventory database and order only the
                 * quantities needed.  Throw an exception
                 * every few times to simulate a database
                 * concurrent-access exception and cause
                 * a rollback.
                 */
                if (rgen.nextInt(3) == throwException) {
                    throw new JMSException("Simulated " +
                    "database concurrent access " +
                    "exception");
                }

                /*
                 * Record retailer order as a pending
                 * order.
                 */
                order = new Order(vendorOrderMessage);

                /*
                 * Set order number and reply queue for
                 * outgoing message.
```

```
                             */
            orderMessage.setInt("VendorOrderNumber",
                order.orderNumber);
        orderMessage.setJMSReplyTo(vendorConfirmQueue);
    quantity = vendorOrderMessage.getInt("Quantity");
            System.out.println("Vendor: Retailer " +
                "ordered " + quantity + " " +
                vendorOrderMessage.getString("Item"));

            // Send message to monitor supplier.
            orderMessage.setString("Item",
                "Monitor");
            orderMessage.setInt("Quantity",
                quantity);
        monitorOrderQueueSender.send(orderMessage);
            System.out.println("Vendor: ordered " +
                quantity + " " +
                orderMessage.getString("Item") +
                "(s)");

            /*
             * Reuse message to send to storage
             * supplier, changing only item name.
             */
            orderMessage.setString("Item",
                "Hard Drive");
        storageOrderQueueSender.send(orderMessage);
            System.out.println("Vendor: ordered " +
                quantity + " " +
                orderMessage.getString("Item") +
                "(s)");

            // Commit session.
            queueSession.commit();
            System.out.println("  Vendor: " +
                "committed transaction 1");
        } catch(JMSException e) {
            System.err.println("Vendor: " +
                "JMSException occurred: " +
```

```
                        e.toString());
                    e.printStackTrace();
                    queueSession.rollback();
                    System.err.println(" Vendor: rolled " +
                        "back transaction 1");
                }
            }

            // Wait till suppliers get back with answers.
            listener.monitor.waitTillDone();
        } catch (JMSException e) {
            System.err.println("Vendor: Exception " +
                "occurred: " + e.toString());
            e.printStackTrace();
        } finally {
            if (queueConnection != null) {
                try {
                    queueConnection.close();
                } catch (JMSException e) {}
            }
        }
    }
}


/**
 * The Order class represents a Retailer order placed with a
 * Vendor. It maintains a table of pending orders.
 */
public static class Order {
    private static Hashtable pendingOrders = new Hashtable();
    private static int       nextOrderNumber = 1;
    private static final int  PENDING_STATUS   = 1;
    private static final int  CANCELLED_STATUS = 2;
    private static final int  FULFILLED_STATUS = 3;
    int                      status;
    public final int         orderNumber;
    public int               quantity;

    // Original order from retailer
```

```java
public final MapMessage   order;
// Reply from supplier
public MapMessage          monitor = null;
// Reply from supplier
public MapMessage          storage = null;

/**
 * Returns the next order number and increments the
 * static variable that holds this value.
 *
 * @return     the next order number
 */
private static int getNextOrderNumber() {
    int   result = nextOrderNumber;
    nextOrderNumber++;
    return result;
}


/**
 * Constructor.  Sets order number; sets order and
 * quantity from incoming message. Sets status to
 * pending, and adds order to hash table of pending
 * orders.
 *
 * @param order     the message containing the order
 */
public Order(MapMessage order) {
    this.orderNumber = getNextOrderNumber();
    this.order = order;
    try {
        this.quantity = order.getInt("Quantity");
    } catch (JMSException je) {
        System.err.println("Unexpected error. Message " +
            "missing Quantity");
        this.quantity = 0;
    }
    status = PENDING_STATUS;
    pendingOrders.put(new Integer(orderNumber), this);
}
```

```java
/**
 * Returns the number of orders in the hash table.
 *
 * @return     the number of pending orders
 */
public static int outstandingOrders() {
    return pendingOrders.size();
}


/**
 * Returns the order corresponding to a given order
 * number.
 *
 * @param orderNumber    the number of the requested order
 * @return               the requested order
 */
public static Order getOrder(int orderNumber) {
    return (Order)
        pendingOrders.get(new Integer(orderNumber));
}


/**
 * Called by the onMessage method of the
 * VendorMessageListener class to process a reply from
 * a supplier to the Vendor.
 *
 * @param component    the message from the supplier
 * @return             the order with updated status
 *                     information
 */
public Order processSubOrder(MapMessage component) {
    String  itemName = null;

    // Determine which subcomponent this is.
    try {
        itemName = component.getString("Item");
    } catch (JMSException je) {
        System.err.println("Unexpected exception. " +
            "Message missing Item");
```

```
            }
            if (itemName.compareTo("Monitor") == 0) {
                monitor = component;
            } else if (itemName.compareTo("Hard Drive") == 0 ) {
                storage = component;
            }

            /*
             * If notification for all subcomponents has been
             * received, verify the quantities to compute if able
             * to fulfill order.
             */
            if ( (monitor != null) && (storage != null) ) {
                try {
                    if (quantity > monitor.getInt("Quantity")) {
                        status = CANCELLED_STATUS;
                  } else if (quantity >
                                    storage.getInt("Quantity")) {
                        status = CANCELLED_STATUS;
                    } else {
                        status = FULFILLED_STATUS;
                    }
                } catch (JMSException je) {
                    System.err.println("Unexpected exception: " +
                        je.toString());
                    status = CANCELLED_STATUS;
                }

                /*
                 * Processing of order is complete, so remove it
                 * from pending-order list.
                 */
                pendingOrders.remove(new Integer(orderNumber));
            }
            return this;
        }

    /**
     * Determines if order status is pending.
```

```
 *
 * @return    true if order is pending, false if not
 */
public boolean isPending() {
    return status == PENDING_STATUS;
}

/**
 * Determines if order status is cancelled.
 *
 * @return    true if order is cancelled, false if not
 */
public boolean isCancelled() {
    return status == CANCELLED_STATUS;
}

/**
 * Determines if order status is fulfilled.
 *
 * @return    true if order is fulfilled, false if not
 */
public boolean isFulfilled() {
    return status == FULFILLED_STATUS;
}
}


/**
 * The VendorMessageListener class processes an order
 * confirmation message from a supplier to the vendor.
 *
 * It demonstrates the use of transactions within message
 * listeners.
 */
public static class VendorMessageListener
        implements MessageListener {
    final SampleUtilities.DoneLatch  monitor =
                            new SampleUtilities.DoneLatch();
    private final              QueueSession session;
    int                        numSuppliers;
```

```
/**
 * Constructor.  Instantiates the message listener with
 * the session of the consuming class (the vendor).
 *
 * @param qs              the session of the consumer
 * @param numSuppliers    the number of suppliers
 */
public VendorMessageListener(QueueSession qs,
                                   int numSuppliers) {
    this.session = qs;
    this.numSuppliers = numSuppliers;
}


/**
 * Casts the message to a MapMessage and processes the
 * order. A message that is not a MapMessage is
 * interpreted as the end of the message stream, and the
 * message listener sets its monitor state to all done
 * processing messages.
 *
 * Each message received represents a fulfillment message
 * from a supplier.
 *
 * @param message     the incoming message
 */
public void onMessage(Message message) {

    /*
     * If message is an end-of-message-stream message and
     * this is the last such message, set monitor status
     * to all done processing messages and commit
     * transaction.
     */
    if (! (message instanceof MapMessage)) {
        if (Order.outstandingOrders() == 0) {
            numSuppliers--;
            if (numSuppliers == 0) {
        monitor.allDone();
    }
```

```
        }
        try {
            session.commit();
        } catch (JMSException je) {}
        return;
    }

    /*
     * Message is an order confirmation message from a
     * supplier.
     */
    int orderNumber = -1;
    try {
        MapMessage component = (MapMessage) message;

        /*
         * Process the order confirmation message and
         * commit the transaction.
         */
        orderNumber =
            component.getInt("VendorOrderNumber");
        Order order =
Order.getOrder(orderNumber).processSubOrder(component);
        session.commit();

        /*
         * If this message is the last supplier message,
         * send message to Retailer and commit
         * transaction.
         */
        if (! order.isPending()) {
            System.out.println("Vendor: Completed " +
                "processing for order " +
                order.orderNumber);
            Queue replyQueue =
                (Queue) order.order.getJMSReplyTo();
            QueueSender qs =
                session.createSender(replyQueue);
```

```
                    MapMessage retailerConfirmMessage =
                        session.createMapMessage();
                    if (order.isFulfilled()) {
                retailerConfirmMessage.setBoolean("OrderAccepted",
                            true);
                        System.out.println("Vendor: sent " +
                            order.quantity + " computer(s)");
                    } else if (order.isCancelled()) {
                retailerConfirmMessage.setBoolean("OrderAccepted",
                            false);
                        System.out.println("Vendor: unable to " +
                            "send " + order.quantity +
                            " computer(s)");
                    }
                    qs.send(retailerConfirmMessage);
                    session.commit();
                    System.out.println("  Vendor: committed " +
                        "transaction 2");
                }
            } catch (JMSException je) {
                je.printStackTrace();
                try {
                    session.rollback();
                } catch (JMSException je2) {}
            } catch (Exception e) {
                e.printStackTrace();
                try {
                    session.rollback();
                } catch (JMSException je2) {}
            }
        }
    }

    /**
     * The GenericSupplier class receives an item order from the
     * vendor and sends a message accepting or refusing it.
     */
    public static class GenericSupplier extends Thread {
        final String  PRODUCT_NAME;
```

```java
final String  IN_ORDER_QUEUE;
int           quantity = 0;

/**
 * Constructor.  Instantiates the supplier as the
 * supplier for the kind of item being ordered.
 *
 * @param itemName    the name of the item being ordered
 * @param inQueue     the queue from which the order is
 *                    obtained
 */
public GenericSupplier(String itemName, String inQueue) {
    PRODUCT_NAME = itemName;
    IN_ORDER_QUEUE = inQueue;
}


/**
 * Checks to see if there are enough items in inventory.
 * Rather than go to a database, it generates a random
 * number related to the order quantity, so that some of
 * the time there won't be enough in stock.
 *
 * @return    the number of items in inventory
 */
public int checkInventory() {
    Random  rgen = new Random();

    return (rgen.nextInt(quantity * 5));
}


/**
 * Runs the thread.
 */
public void run() {
    QueueConnectionFactory queueConnectionFactory = null;
    QueueConnection        queueConnection = null;
    QueueSession           queueSession = null;
    Queue                  orderQueue = null;
    QueueReceiver          queueReceiver = null;
```

```
Message              inMessage = null;
MapMessage           orderMessage = null;
MapMessage           outMessage = null;

try {
    queueConnectionFactory =
        SampleUtilities.getQueueConnectionFactory();
    queueConnection =
      queueConnectionFactory.createQueueConnection();
    queueSession =
        queueConnection.createQueueSession(true, 0);
    orderQueue =
        SampleUtilities.getQueue(IN_ORDER_QUEUE,
            queueSession);
} catch (Exception e) {
    System.err.println("Connection problem: " +
        e.toString());
    System.err.println("Program assumes five " +
        "queues named A B C D E");
    if (queueConnection != null) {
        try {
            queueConnection.close();
        } catch (JMSException ee) {}
    }
    System.exit(1);
}


/*
 * Create receiver for order queue and start message
 * delivery.
 */
try {
    queueReceiver =
        queueSession.createReceiver(orderQueue);
    queueConnection.start();
} catch (JMSException je) {}

/*
 * Keep checking supplier order queue for order
```

```
         * request until end-of-message-stream message is
         * received. Receive order and send an order
         * confirmation as one transaction.
         */
while (true) {
    try {
        inMessage = queueReceiver.receive();
        if (inMessage instanceof MapMessage) {
            orderMessage = (MapMessage) inMessage;
        } else {
            /*
             * Message is an end-of-message-stream
             * message. Send a similar message to
             * reply queue, commit transaction, then
             * stop processing orders by breaking out
             * of loop.
             */
            QueueSender queueSender =
                queueSession.createSender((Queue)
                    inMessage.getJMSReplyTo());
    queueSender.send(queueSession.createMessage());
            queueSession.commit();
            break;
        }

        /*
         * Extract quantity ordered from order
         * message.
         */
        quantity = orderMessage.getInt("Quantity");
        System.out.println(PRODUCT_NAME +
            " Supplier: Vendor ordered " + quantity +
            " " + orderMessage.getString("Item") +
            "(s)");

        /*
         * Create sender and message for reply queue.
         * Set order number and item; check inventory
         * and set quantity available.
```

```
                         * Send message to vendor and commit
                         * transaction.
                         */
                        QueueSender queueSender =
                            queueSession.createSender((Queue)
                                orderMessage.getJMSReplyTo());
                        outMessage = queueSession.createMapMessage();
                        outMessage.setInt("VendorOrderNumber",
                            orderMessage.getInt("VendorOrderNumber"));
                        outMessage.setString("Item", PRODUCT_NAME);
                        int numAvailable = checkInventory();
                        if (numAvailable >= quantity) {
                            outMessage.setInt("Quantity", quantity);
                        } else {
                            outMessage.setInt("Quantity",
                                numAvailable);
                        }
                        queueSender.send(outMessage);
                        System.out.println(PRODUCT_NAME +
                            " Supplier: sent " +
                            outMessage.getInt("Quantity") + " " +
                            outMessage.getString("Item") + "(s)");
                        queueSession.commit();
                        System.out.println("  " + PRODUCT_NAME +
                            " Supplier: committed transaction");
                    } catch (Exception e) {
                        System.err.println(PRODUCT_NAME +
                            " Supplier: Exception occurred: " +
                            e.toString());
                        e.printStackTrace();
                    }
                }
                if (queueConnection != null) {
                    try {
                        queueConnection.close();
                    } catch (JMSException e) {}
                }
            }
        }
```

```java
/**
 * Creates the Retailer and Vendor classes and the two
 * supplier classes, then starts the threads.
 *
 * @param quantity    the quantity specified on the command
 *                    line
 */
public static void run_threads(int quantity) {
    Retailer        r = new Retailer(quantity);
    Vendor          v = new Vendor();
    GenericSupplier ms = new GenericSupplier("Monitor",
                            monitorOrderQueueName);
    GenericSupplier ss = new GenericSupplier("Hard Drive",
                            storageOrderQueueName);

    r.start();
    v.start();
    ms.start();
    ss.start();
    try {
        r.join();
        v.join();
        ms.join();
        ss.join();
    } catch (InterruptedException e) {}
}


/**
 * Reads the order quantity from the command line, then
 * calls the run_threads method to execute the program
 * threads.
 *
 * @param args    the quantity of computers being ordered
 */
public static void main(String[] args) {
    TransactedExample te = new TransactedExample();
    int               quantity = 0;

    if (args.length != 1) {
```

```
        System.out.println("Usage: java TransactedExample " +
            "<integer>");
        System.out.println("Program assumes five queues " +
            "named A B C D E");
        System.exit(1);
    }
    te.vendorOrderQueueName = new String("A");
    te.retailerConfirmQueueName = new String("B");
    te.monitorOrderQueueName = new String("C");
    te.storageOrderQueueName = new String("D");
    te.vendorConfirmQueueName = new String("E");
    quantity = (new Integer(args[0])).intValue();
    System.out.println("Quantity to be ordered is " +
        quantity);
    if (quantity > 0) {
        te.run_threads(quantity);
    } else {
        System.out.println("Quantity must be positive and " +
            "nonzero");
    }
    }
  }
}
```

Code Example A.2 `TransactedExample.java`

A.3   Acknowledgment Modes

The `AckEquivExample.java` program shows how the following two scenarios both ensure that a message will not be acknowledged until processing of it is complete:

- Using an asynchronous receiver—a message listener—in an `AUTO_ACKNOWLEDGE` session

- Using a synchronous receiver in a `CLIENT_ACKNOWLEDGE` session

With a message listener, the automatic acknowledgment happens when the `onMessage` method returns—that is, after message processing has finished. With a synchronous receiver, the client acknowledges the message after processing is complete. (If you use AUTO_ACKNOWLEDGE with a synchronous receive, the acknowledgment happens immediately after the receive call; if any subsequent processing steps fail, the message cannot be redelivered.)

The program contains a SynchSender class, a SynchReceiver class, an AsynchSubscriber class with a TextListener class, a MultiplePublisher class, a main method, and a method that runs the other classes' threads.

The program needs two queues, a topic, and a connection factory with a client ID, similar to the one in the example in Section A.1 on page 429. You can use existing administered objects or create new ones. Edit the names at the beginning of the source file before compiling if you do not use the objects already specified. You can run the program with a command on one line similar to the following example for UNIX systems:

```
java -Djms.properties=$J2EE_HOME/config/jms_client.properties
AckEquivExample
```

The output looks like this:

```
java -Djms.properties=$J2EE_HOME/config/jms_client.properties
AckEquivExample
Queue name is controlQueue
Queue name is jms/Queue
Topic name is jms/Topic
Connection factory name is DurableTopicCF
Java(TM) Message Service 1.0.2 Reference Implementation (build b14)
Java(TM) Message Service 1.0.2 Reference Implementation (build b14)
  SENDER: Created client-acknowledge session
  RECEIVER: Created client-acknowledge session
  SENDER: Sending message: Here is a client-acknowledge message
  RECEIVER: Processing message: Here is a client-acknowledge message
  RECEIVER: Now I'll acknowledge the message
SUBSCRIBER: Created auto-acknowledge session
PUBLISHER: Created auto-acknowledge session
PUBLISHER: Receiving synchronize messages from controlQueue; count
= 1
SUBSCRIBER: Sending synchronize message to controlQueue
PUBLISHER: Received synchronize message;  expect 0 more
PUBLISHER: Publishing message: Here is an auto-acknowledge message 1
```

```
PUBLISHER: Publishing message: Here is an auto-acknowledge message 2
PUBLISHER: Publishing message: Here is an auto-acknowledge message 3
SUBSCRIBER: Processing message: Here is an auto-acknowledge message
1
SUBSCRIBER: Processing message: Here is an auto-acknowledge message
2
SUBSCRIBER: Processing message: Here is an auto-acknowledge message
3
```

```java
import javax.jms.*;
import javax.naming.*;

public class AckEquivExample {
    final String   CONTROL_QUEUE = "controlQueue";
    final String   queueName = "jms/Queue";
    final String   topicName = "jms/Topic";
    final String   conFacName = "DurableTopicCF";

    /**
     * The SynchSender class creates a session in
     * CLIENT_ACKNOWLEDGE mode and sends a message.
     */
    public class SynchSender extends Thread {

        /**
         * Runs the thread.
         */
        public void run() {
            QueueConnectionFactory queueConnectionFactory = null;
            QueueConnection        queueConnection = null;
            QueueSession           queueSession = null;
            Queue                  queue = null;
            QueueSender            queueSender = null;
            final String           MSG_TEXT =
                new String("Here is a client-acknowledge message");
            TextMessage             message = null;
```

```
try {
    queueConnectionFactory =
        SampleUtilities.getQueueConnectionFactory();
    queueConnection =
      queueConnectionFactory.createQueueConnection();
    queueSession =
        queueConnection.createQueueSession(false,
            Session.CLIENT_ACKNOWLEDGE);
    queue = SampleUtilities.getQueue(queueName,
        queueSession);
} catch (Exception e) {
    System.err.println("Connection problem: " +
        e.toString());
    if (queueConnection != null) {
        try {
            queueConnection.close();
        } catch (JMSException ee) {}
    }
    System.exit(1);
}


/*
 * Create client-acknowledge sender.
 * Create and send message.
 */

try {
    System.out.println("  SENDER: Created " +
        "client-acknowledge session");
    queueSender = queueSession.createSender(queue);
    message = queueSession.createTextMessage();
    message.setText(MSG_TEXT);
    System.out.println("  SENDER: Sending " +
        "message: " + message.getText());
    queueSender.send(message);
} catch (JMSException e) {
    System.err.println("Exception occurred: " +
        e.toString());
} finally {
```

```java
                    if (queueConnection != null) {
                        try {
                            queueConnection.close();
                        } catch (JMSException e) {}
                    }
                }
            }
        }


    /**
     * The SynchReceiver class creates a session in
     * CLIENT_ACKNOWLEDGE mode and receives the message sent by
     * the SynchSender class.
     */
    public class SynchReceiver extends Thread {

        /**
         * Runs the thread.
         */
        public void run() {
            QueueConnectionFactory queueConnectionFactory = null;
            QueueConnection        queueConnection = null;
            QueueSession           queueSession = null;
            Queue                  queue = null;
            QueueReceiver          queueReceiver = null;
            TextMessage            message = null;
            try {
                queueConnectionFactory =
                    SampleUtilities.getQueueConnectionFactory();
                queueConnection =
                  queueConnectionFactory.createQueueConnection();
                queueSession =
                    queueConnection.createQueueSession(false,
                        Session.CLIENT_ACKNOWLEDGE);
                queue =
                    SampleUtilities.getQueue(queueName,
                        queueSession);
            } catch (Exception e) {
                System.err.println("Connection problem: " +
```

```
                e.toString());
        if (queueConnection != null) {
            try {
                queueConnection.close();
            } catch (JMSException ee) {}
        }
        System.exit(1);
    }

    /*
     * Create client-acknowledge receiver.
     * Receive message and process it.
     * Acknowledge message.
     */
    try {
        System.out.println("  RECEIVER: Created " +
            "client-acknowledge session");
        queueReceiver =
            queueSession.createReceiver(queue);
        queueConnection.start();
        message = (TextMessage) queueReceiver.receive();
        System.out.println("  RECEIVER: Processing " +
            "message: " + message.getText());
        System.out.println("  RECEIVER: Now I'll " +
            "acknowledge the message");
        message.acknowledge();
    } catch (JMSException e) {
        System.err.println("Exception occurred: " +
            e.toString());
    } finally {
        if (queueConnection != null) {
            try {
                queueConnection.close();
            } catch (JMSException e) {}
        }
    }
    }
}
```

```
/**
 * The AsynchSubscriber class creates a session in
 * AUTO_ACKNOWLEDGE mode and fetches several messages from a
 * topic asynchronously, using a message listener,
 * TextListener.
 *
 * Each message is acknowledged after the onMessage method
 * completes.
 */
public class AsynchSubscriber extends Thread {

    /**
     * The TextListener class implements the MessageListener
     * interface by defining an onMessage method for the
     * AsynchSubscriber class.
     */
    private class TextListener implements MessageListener {
        final SampleUtilities.DoneLatch  monitor =
            new SampleUtilities.DoneLatch();

        /**
         * Casts the message to a TextMessage and displays
         * its text. A non-text message is interpreted as the
         * end of the message stream, and the message
         * listener sets its monitor state to all done
         * processing messages.
         *
         * @param message     the incoming message
         */
        public void onMessage(Message message) {
            if (message instanceof TextMessage) {
                TextMessage  msg = (TextMessage) message;

                try {
                    System.out.println("SUBSCRIBER: " +
                        "Processing message: " +
                        msg.getText());
                } catch (JMSException e) {
```

```
                    System.err.println("Exception in " +
                        "onMessage(): " + e.toString());
                }
            } else {
                monitor.allDone();
            }
        }
    }

    /**
     * Runs the thread.
     */
    public void run() {
        Context                jndiContext = null;
        TopicConnectionFactory topicConnectionFactory = null;
        TopicConnection        topicConnection = null;
        TopicSession           topicSession = null;
        Topic                  topic = null;
        TopicSubscriber        topicSubscriber = null;
        TextListener           topicListener = null;

        /*
         * Create a JNDI API InitialContext object if none
         * exists yet.
         */
        try {
            jndiContext = new InitialContext();
        } catch (NamingException e) {
            System.err.println("Could not create JNDI API " +
                "context: " + e.toString());
            System.exit(1);
        }

        /*
         * Look up connection factory and topic.  If either
         * does not exist, exit.
         */
```

```
        try {
            topicConnectionFactory = (TopicConnectionFactory)
                jndiContext.lookup(conFacName);
            topicConnection =
              topicConnectionFactory.createTopicConnection();
            topicSession =
                topicConnection.createTopicSession(false,
                    Session.AUTO_ACKNOWLEDGE);
            System.out.println("SUBSCRIBER: Created " +
                "auto-acknowledge session");
            topic = SampleUtilities.getTopic(topicName,
                topicSession);
        } catch (Exception e) {
            System.err.println("Connection problem: " +
                e.toString());
            if (topicConnection != null) {
                try {
                    topicConnection.close();
                } catch (JMSException ee) {}
            }
            System.exit(1);
        }


        /*
         * Create auto-acknowledge subscriber.
         * Register message listener (TextListener).
         * Start message delivery.
         * Send synchronize message to publisher, then wait
         *   till all messages have arrived.
         * Listener displays the messages obtained.
         */
        try {
            topicSubscriber =
                topicSession.createDurableSubscriber(topic,
                    "AckSub");
            topicListener = new TextListener();
          topicSubscriber.setMessageListener(topicListener);
            topicConnection.start();
```

```
                    // Let publisher know that subscriber is ready.
                    try {
                SampleUtilities.sendSynchronizeMessage("SUBSCRIBER: ",
                        CONTROL_QUEUE);
                } catch (Exception e) {
                    System.err.println("Queue probably " +
                        "missing: " + e.toString());
                    if (topicConnection != null) {
                        try {
                            topicConnection.close();
                        } catch (JMSException ee) {}
                    }
                    System.exit(1);
                }

                /*
                 * Asynchronously process messages.
                 * Block until publisher issues a control message
                 * indicating end of publish stream.
                 */
                topicListener.monitor.waitTillDone();
                topicSubscriber.close();
                topicSession.unsubscribe("AckSub");
            } catch (JMSException e) {
                System.err.println("Exception occurred: " +
                    e.toString());
            } finally {
                if (topicConnection != null) {
                    try {
                        topicConnection.close();
                    } catch (JMSException e) {}
                }
            }
        }
    }
}

/**
 * The MultiplePublisher class creates a session in
 * AUTO_ACKNOWLEDGE mode and publishes three messages
```

```
 * to a topic.
 */
public class MultiplePublisher extends Thread {

    /**
     * Runs the thread.
     */
    public void run() {
        TopicConnectionFactory topicConnectionFactory = null;
        TopicConnection        topicConnection = null;
        TopicSession           topicSession = null;
        Topic                  topic = null;
        TopicPublisher         topicPublisher = null;
        TextMessage            message = null;
        final int              NUMMSGS = 3;
        final String           MSG_TEXT =
            new String("Here is an auto-acknowledge message");

        try {
            topicConnectionFactory =
                SampleUtilities.getTopicConnectionFactory();
            topicConnection =
              topicConnectionFactory.createTopicConnection();
            topicSession =
                topicConnection.createTopicSession(false,
                    Session.AUTO_ACKNOWLEDGE);
            System.out.println("PUBLISHER: Created " +
                "auto-acknowledge session");
            topic =
                SampleUtilities.getTopic(topicName,
                    topicSession);
        } catch (Exception e) {
            System.err.println("Connection problem: " +
                e.toString());
            if (topicConnection != null) {
                try {
                    topicConnection.close();
                } catch (JMSException ee) {}
            }
```

```
            System.exit(1);
        }

        /*
         * After synchronizing with subscriber, create
         *   publisher.
         * Send 3 messages, varying text slightly.
         * Send end-of-messages message.
         */
        try {
            /*
             * Synchronize with subscriber.  Wait for message
             * indicating that subscriber is ready to receive
             * messages.
             */
            try {
SampleUtilities.receiveSynchronizeMessages("PUBLISHER: ",
                CONTROL_QUEUE, 1);
            } catch (Exception e) {
                System.err.println("Queue probably " +
                    "missing: " + e.toString());
                if (topicConnection != null) {
                    try {
                        topicConnection.close();
                    } catch (JMSException ee) {}
                }
                System.exit(1);
            }

            topicPublisher =
                topicSession.createPublisher(topic);
            message = topicSession.createTextMessage();
            for (int i = 0; i < NUMMSGS; i++) {
                message.setText(MSG_TEXT + " " + (i + 1));
                System.out.println("PUBLISHER: Publishing " +
                    "message: " + message.getText());
                topicPublisher.publish(message);
            }
```

```
                    /*
                     * Send a non-text control message indicating
                     * end of messages.
                     */
                topicPublisher.publish(topicSession.createMessage());
                } catch (JMSException e) {
                    System.err.println("Exception occurred: " +
                        e.toString());
                } finally {
                    if (topicConnection != null) {
                        try {
                            topicConnection.close();
                        } catch (JMSException e) {}
                    }
                }
            }
        }


    /**
     * Instantiates the sender, receiver, subscriber, and
     * publisher classes and starts their threads.
     * Calls the join method to wait for the threads to die.
     */
    public void run_threads() {
        SynchSender        synchSender = new SynchSender();
        SynchReceiver      synchReceiver = new SynchReceiver();
        AsynchSubscriber   asynchSubscriber =
                                        new AsynchSubscriber();
        MultiplePublisher  multiplePublisher =
                                        new MultiplePublisher();

        synchSender.start();
        synchReceiver.start();
        try {
            synchSender.join();
            synchReceiver.join();
        } catch (InterruptedException e) {}

        asynchSubscriber.start();
```

```
        multiplePublisher.start();
        try {
            asynchSubscriber.join();
            multiplePublisher.join();
        } catch (InterruptedException e) {}
    }

    /**
     * Reads the queue and topic names from the command line,
     * then calls the run_threads method to execute the program
     * threads.
     *
     * @param args     the topic used by the example
     */
    public static void main(String[] args) {
        AckEquivExample  aee = new AckEquivExample();

        if (args.length != 0) {
            System.out.println("Usage: java AckEquivExample");
            System.exit(1);
        }
        System.out.println("Queue name is " + aee.queueName);
        System.out.println("Topic name is " + aee.topicName);
        System.out.println("Connection factory name is " +
            aee.conFacName);

        aee.run_threads();
    }
}
```

Code Example A.3 `AckEquivExample.java`

A.4   Utility Class

The SampleUtilities class, in SampleUtilities.java, is a utility class for the other sample programs. It contains the following methods:

- getQueueConnectionFactory

- getTopicConnectionFactory

- getQueue

- getTopic

- jndiLookup

- receiveSynchronizeMessages

- sendSynchronizeMessages

It also contains the class DoneLatch, which has the following methods:

- waitTillDone

- allDone

```java
import javax.naming.*;
import javax.jms.*;

public class SampleUtilities {
    public static final String  QUEUECONFAC =
                                    "QueueConnectionFactory";
    public static final String  TOPICCONFAC =
                                    "TopicConnectionFactory";
    private static Context      jndiContext = null;

    /**
     * Returns a QueueConnectionFactory object.
     *
     * @return    a QueueConnectionFactory object
     * @throws    javax.naming.NamingException (or other
     *            exception) if name cannot be found
```

```
     */
    public static QueueConnectionFactory
            getQueueConnectionFactory() throws Exception {
        return (QueueConnectionFactory) jndiLookup(QUEUECONFAC);
    }

    /**
     * Returns a TopicConnectionFactory object.
     *
     * @return     a TopicConnectionFactory object
     * @throws     javax.naming.NamingException (or other
     *             exception) if name cannot be found
     */
    public static TopicConnectionFactory
            getTopicConnectionFactory() throws Exception {
        return (TopicConnectionFactory) jndiLookup(TOPICCONFAC);
    }

    /**
     * Returns a Queue object.
     *
     * @param name       String specifying queue name
     * @param session    a QueueSession object
     *
     * @return           a Queue object
     * @throws           javax.naming.NamingException (or other
     *                   exception) if name cannot be found
     */
    public static Queue getQueue(String name,
            QueueSession session) throws Exception {
        return (Queue) jndiLookup(name);
    }

    /**
     * Returns a Topic object.
     *
     * @param name       String specifying topic name
     * @param session    a TopicSession object
     *
```

```
    * @return        a Topic object
    * @throws        javax.naming.NamingException (or other
    *                exception) if name cannot be found
    */
   public static Topic getTopic(String name,
           TopicSession session) throws Exception {
      return (Topic) jndiLookup(name);
   }

   /**
    * Creates a JNDI API InitialContext object if none exists
    * yet. Then looks up the string argument and returns the
    * associated object.
    *
    * @param name     the name of the object to be looked up
    *
    * @return         the object bound to name
    * @throws         javax.naming.NamingException (or other
    *                 exception) if name cannot be found
    */
   public static Object jndiLookup(String name)
       throws NamingException {
      Object    obj = null;

      if (jndiContext == null) {
          try {
              jndiContext = new InitialContext();
          } catch (NamingException e) {
              System.err.println("Could not create JNDI API " +
                  "context: " + e.toString());
              throw e;
          }
      }
      try {
         obj = jndiContext.lookup(name);
      } catch (NamingException e) {
         System.err.println("JNDI API lookup failed: " +
             e.toString());
         throw e;
```

```
        }
        return obj;
    }

    /**
     * Waits for 'count' messages on controlQueue before
     * continuing.  Called by a publisher to make sure that
     * subscribers have started before it begins publishing
     * messages.
     *
     * If controlQueue does not exist, the method throws an
     * exception.
     *
     * @param prefix      prefix (publisher or subscriber) to be
     *                    displayed
     * @param controlQueueName  name of control queue
     * @param count       number of messages to receive
     */
    public static void receiveSynchronizeMessages(String prefix,
            String controlQueueName, int count)
            throws Exception {
        QueueConnectionFactory  queueConnectionFactory = null;
        QueueConnection         queueConnection = null;
        QueueSession            queueSession = null;
        Queue                   controlQueue = null;
        QueueReceiver           queueReceiver = null;

        try {
            queueConnectionFactory =
                SampleUtilities.getQueueConnectionFactory();
            queueConnection =
                queueConnectionFactory.createQueueConnection();
            queueSession =
                queueConnection.createQueueSession(false,
                    Session.AUTO_ACKNOWLEDGE);
            controlQueue = getQueue(controlQueueName,
                queueSession);
            queueConnection.start();
        } catch (Exception e) {
```

```
            System.err.println("Connection problem: " +
                e.toString());
            if (queueConnection != null) {
                try {
                    queueConnection.close();
                } catch (JMSException ee) {}
            }
            throw e;
        }

        try {
            System.out.println(prefix +
                "Receiving synchronize messages from " +
                controlQueueName + "; count = " + count);
            queueReceiver =
                queueSession.createReceiver(controlQueue);
            while (count > 0) {
                queueReceiver.receive();
                count--;
                System.out.println(prefix +
                    "Received synchronize message; " +
                    " expect " + count + " more");
            }
        } catch (JMSException e) {
            System.err.println("Exception occurred: " +
                e.toString());
            throw e;
        } finally {
            if (queueConnection != null) {
                try {
                    queueConnection.close();
                } catch (JMSException e) {}
            }
        }
    }

    /**
     * Sends a message to controlQueue.  Called by a subscriber
     * to notify a publisher that it is ready to receive
```

```
   * messages.
   * <p>
   * If controlQueue doesn't exist, the method throws an
   * exception.
   *
   * @param prefix     prefix (publisher or subscriber) to be
   *                   displayed
   * @param controlQueueName  name of control queue
   */
public static void sendSynchronizeMessage(String prefix,
        String controlQueueName)
        throws Exception {
    QueueConnectionFactory  queueConnectionFactory = null;
    QueueConnection         queueConnection = null;
    QueueSession            queueSession = null;
    Queue                   controlQueue = null;
    QueueSender             queueSender = null;
    TextMessage             message = null;

    try {
        queueConnectionFactory =
            SampleUtilities.getQueueConnectionFactory();
        queueConnection =
            queueConnectionFactory.createQueueConnection();
        queueSession =
            queueConnection.createQueueSession(false,
                Session.AUTO_ACKNOWLEDGE);
        controlQueue = getQueue(controlQueueName,
            queueSession);
    } catch (Exception e) {
        System.err.println("Connection problem: " +
            e.toString());
        if (queueConnection != null) {
            try {
                queueConnection.close();
            } catch (JMSException ee) {}
        }
        throw e;
    }
```

```
        try {
            queueSender =
                queueSession.createSender(controlQueue);
            message = queueSession.createTextMessage();
            message.setText("synchronize");
            System.out.println(prefix +
                "Sending synchronize message to " +
                controlQueueName);
            queueSender.send(message);
        } catch (JMSException e) {
            System.err.println("Exception occurred: " +
                e.toString());
            throw e;
        } finally {
            if (queueConnection != null) {
                try {
                    queueConnection.close();
                } catch (JMSException e) {}
            }
        }
    }

    /**
     * Monitor class for asynchronous examples.  Producer signals
     * end of message stream; listener calls allDone() to notify
     * consumer that the signal has arrived, while consumer calls
     * waitTillDone() to wait for this notification.
     */
    static public class DoneLatch {
        boolean  done = false;
        /**
         * Waits until done is set to true.
         */
        public void waitTillDone() {
            synchronized (this) {
                while (! done) {
                    try {
                        this.wait();
                    } catch (InterruptedException ie) {}
```

```
                }
            }
        }

        /**
         * Sets done to true.
         */
        public void allDone() {
            synchronized (this) {
                done = true;
                this.notify();
            }
        }
    }
}
```

Code Example A.4 `SampleUtilities.java`

Glossary

This glossary contains terms related to the JMS API and to the J2EE platform and used in this book. *Italics* indicate terms defined elsewhere in the glossary.

administered object A preconfigured JMS object. The *Java Message Service (JMS) API* has two kinds of administered objects: *JMS connection factories* and *destinations*. These objects are created by an administrator for the use of *JMS clients* and are placed in a *Java Naming and Directory Interface (JNDI) API* namespace.

API Application Programming Interface. In the Java programming language, a set of classes and interfaces that specify a particular functionality, for example, the *Java Message Service (JMS) API*.

application client A first-tier client *component* that executes in its own Java virtual machine. Application clients have access to some J2EE platform APIs, including the *Java Naming and Directory Interface (JNDI)* and the *Java Message Service (JMS)* APIs.

bean-managed transaction A *transaction* whose boundaries are defined by an *enterprise bean*.

business method An *enterprise bean* method that implements the business logic or rules of an application.

commit The point in a *transaction* when all updates to any resources involved in the transaction are made permanent.

component An application-level software unit supported by a *container*. Components are configurable at deployment time. The J2EE platform defines four types of components: *enterprise beans*, *Web components*, applets, and *application clients*.

connection See *JMS connection*.

connection factory See *JMS connection factory*.

Connector architecture An architecture for integration of J2EE products with enterprise information systems. This architecture has two parts: a resource adapter provided by an enterprise information system vendor and the J2EE product that allows this resource adapter to plug in. This architecture defines a set of contracts that a resource adapter has to support to plug in to a J2EE product, for example, transactions, security, and resource management.

container An entity that provides life cycle management, security, deployment, and runtime services to *components*. Each type of container (EJB, Web, JSP, servlet, applet, and application client) also provides component-specific services.

container-managed persistence Data transfer between an *entity bean*'s variables and a resource manager managed by the entity bean's *container*.

container-managed transaction A *transaction* whose boundaries are defined by an *EJB container*. An *entity bean* must use container-managed transactions.

deployment The process whereby software is installed into an operational environment.

deployment descriptor An XML file, provided with each module and application, that describes how each should be deployed. The deployment descriptor directs a deployment tool to deploy a module or an application with specific container options and describes specific configuration requirements that a Deployer must resolve.

destination An *administered object* that encapsulates the identity of a JMS queue or a topic. See *point-to-point messaging domain* and *publish/subscribe messaging domain*.

durable subscription In the *publish/subscribe messaging domain*, a subscription that continues to exist as long as it has subscribers. Subscribers may become inactive; the *JMS provider* retains the subscribers' messages until the subscriber becomes active again or until the messages expire. Durable subscriptions give the reliability of queues to the publish/subscribe messaging domain.

EAR file A JAR archive that contains a *J2EE application*.

EJB See *Enterprise JavaBeans*.

EJB container A *container* that implements the EJB component contract of the J2EE architecture. This contract specifies a runtime environment for *enterprise beans*, including security, concurrency, life cycle management, *transaction*, *deployment*, naming, and other services. An EJB container is provided by an EJB or a *J2EE server*.

enterprise bean A *component* that implements a business task or a business entity and resides in an *EJB container*; an *entity bean*, a *session bean*, or a *message-driven bean*.

Enterprise JavaBeans (EJB) A component architecture for the development and deployment of object-oriented, distributed, enterprise-level applications. Applications written using the Enterprise JavaBeans architecture are scalable, transactional, and secure.

entity bean An *enterprise bean* that represents persistent data maintained in a database. An entity bean can manage its own persistence, or it can delegate this function to its *container*. An entity bean is identified by a primary key. If the container in which an entity bean is hosted crashes, the entity bean, its primary key, and any remote references survive the crash.

J2EE See *Java 2 Platform, Enterprise Edition*.

J2EE application Any deployable unit of J2EE functionality. This can be a single module or a group of modules packaged into an *EAR file* with a J2EE application *deployment descriptor*. J2EE applications are typically engineered to be distributed across multiple computing tiers.

J2EE server The runtime portion of a J2EE product. A J2EE server provides EJB and/or Web *containers*.

Java 2 Platform, Enterprise Edition (J2EE) An environment for developing and deploying enterprise applications. The J2EE platform consists of a set of services, application programming interfaces (*APIs*), and protocols that provide the functionality for developing multitiered, Web-based applications.

Java Message Service (JMS) API An *API* that allows applications and *components* to create, send, receive, and read *messages*. It enables communication that is loosely coupled, asynchronous, and reliable and allows applications and components written in the Java programming language to communicate with applications that use other messaging implementations.

Java Naming and Directory Interface (JNDI) API   An *API* that provides naming and directory functionality. A *JMS application* uses the JNDI API to look up *destinations* and *connection factories*.

JavaServer Pages (JSP)   An extensible Web technology that uses template data, custom elements, scripting languages, and server-side Java objects to return dynamic content to a client. Typically, the template data is HTML or XML elements, and in many cases, the client is a Web browser.

JMS   See *Java Message Service (JMS) API*.

JMS application One or more *JMS clients* that exchange *messages*.

JMS client A Java language program or *component* that produces and/or consumes JMS *messages*.

JMS connection An object that encapsulates a virtual connection with a *JMS provider*. For example, it could represent an open TCP/IP socket between a *JMS client* and a provider service daemon. A JMS client uses a connection to create one or more *JMS sessions*.

JMS connection factory The object a *JMS client* uses to create a *JMS connection* with a *JMS provider*. A connection factory encapsulates a set of connection configuration parameters defined by an administrator.

JMS provider A messaging system that implements the *Java Message Service API*, as well as other administrative and control features.

JMS session A single-threaded context for sending and receiving JMS *messages*. A JMS session may be part of a *transaction*. If it is, the transaction may be local or distributed.

JNDI   See *Java Naming and Directory Interface (JNDI) API*.

JSP   See *JavaServer Pages (JSP)*.

MDB   See *message-driven bean*.

message In the *Java Message Service (JMS) API*, an asynchronous request, report, or event that is created, sent, and consumed by an enterprise application, not by a human. A message contains vital information needed to coordinate enterprise applications, in the form of precisely formatted data that describes specific business actions. The JMS API defines five types of message objects: `BytesMessage`, `StreamMessage`, `MapMessage`, `ObjectMessage`, and `TextMessage`.

message consumer An object, created by a *JMS session*, that is used for receiving *messages* sent to a *destination*. This object can consume messages synchronously or asynchronously. A *message-driven bean* is an asynchronous message consumer created by the *EJB container*. In the *JMS point-to-point messaging domain*, a message consumer is called a receiver; in the *JMS publish/subscribe messaging domain*, it is called a subscriber.

message-driven bean An *enterprise bean* that is an asynchronous *message consumer*. It is created by the *container* to handle the processing of the *messages* for which it is a consumer. A client accesses a message-driven bean by sending messages to the *destination* for which the message-driven bean is a *message listener*. A message-driven bean has no state for a specific client, but its instance variables may contain state across the handling of client messages, including an open database connection and an object reference to an EJB object.

message listener An object similar to an event listener. A *JMS client* registers a message listener with a *message consumer*. Whenever a *message* arrives at the *destination*, the *JMS provider* delivers the message by calling the listener's `onMessage` method, which acts on the contents of the message.

message producer An object, created by a *JMS session*, that is used for sending *messages* to a *destination*. In the *JMS point-to-point messaging domain*, a message producer is called a sender; in the *JMS publish/subscribe messaging domain*, it is called a publisher.

native client A messaging client program that uses a messaging system's native client API instead of the *Java Message Service (JMS) API*.

nonpersistent messages *Messages* not guaranteed to be preserved in the event of a *JMS provider* failure. Nonpersistent messages may offer a performance advantage over *persistent messages*.

persistent messages *Messages* guaranteed not to be lost in the event of a *JMS provider* failure.

point-to-point (PTP) messaging domain A messaging model built around the concept of message queues. Each JMS *message* is sent to a specific queue, and each message has only one consumer. The queue retains all messages sent to it until a *JMS message consumer* consumes the message or the message expires, in which case the message does not have a consumer.

publish/subscribe messaging domain A messaging model built around the concept of broadcasting to subscribers. Each JMS *message* is published to a topic, and the system distributes the messages to all the topic's subscribers. Each message may have zero, one, or many *JMS message consumers,* depending on how many subscribers are registered with the topic when the message is published. See also *durable subscription.*

queue See *point-to-point messaging domain.*

rollback The point in a *transaction* when all updates to any resources involved in the transaction are reversed.

servlet A Java program that extends the functionality of a Web server, generating dynamic content and interacting with Web clients, using a request-response paradigm.

session bean An *enterprise bean* that is created by a client and that usually exists only for the duration of a single client-server session. A session bean performs operations, such as calculations or accessing a database, for the client. Although a session bean may be transactional, it is not recoverable should a system crash occur. Session bean objects either can be stateless, or they can maintain conversational state across methods and transactions. If a session bean maintains state, the *EJB container* manages this state if the object must be removed from memory. However, the session bean object itself must manage its own persistent data.

SQL Structured Query Language. The standardized relational database language for defining database objects and manipulating data.

SQL92 The version of SQL standardized by ANSI in 1992.

stateful session bean A *session bean* with a conversational state.

stateless session bean A *session bean* with no conversational state. All instances of a stateless session bean are identical.

topic See *publish/subscribe messaging domain.*

transaction An atomic unit of work that modifies data. A transaction encloses one or more program statements, all of which either complete or roll back. Transactions enable multiple users to access the same data concurrently. See also *commit* and *rollback*.

transaction attribute A value, specified in the *deployment descriptor* of an *enterprise bean*, that is used by the *EJB container* to control the transaction scope when the enterprise bean's methods are invoked. A transaction attribute can have the following values: `Required`, `RequiresNew`, `Supports`, `NotSupported`, `Mandatory`, `Never`. For *message-driven beans*, only the `Required` and the `NotSupported` attributes are valid.

Web component A *component* that provides services in response to requests; either a *servlet* or a *JavaServer Pages (JSP)* page.

Index

The Java™ Series

 The Java™ Programming Language Third Edition — *Ken Arnold · James Gosling · David Holmes*
ISBN 0-201-70433-1

 Effective Java™ Programming Language Guide — *Joshua Bloch*
ISBN 0-201-31005-8

 The J2EE™ Tutorial
ISBN 0-201-79168-4

 The Real-Time Specification for Java™
ISBN 0-201-70323-8

 The Java™ Tutorial, Third Edition — A Short Course on the Basics
ISBN 0-201-70393-9

 The Java™ Tutorial Continued — The Rest of the JDK™
ISBN 0-201-48558-3

 J2EE™ Technology in Practice — Building Business Applications with the Java™ 2 Platform, Enterprise Edition
ISBN 0-201-74622-0

 The Java™ Developers ALMANAC 2000 — *Patrick Chan*
ISBN 0-201-43299-4

 The Java™ Class Libraries Second Edition, Volume 1 — java.io · java.lang · java.math · java.net · java.text · java.util
ISBN 0-201-31002-3

 The Java™ Class Libraries Second Edition, Volume 2 — java.applet · java.awt · java.beans
ISBN 0-201-31003-1

 The Java™ Class Libraries Second Edition, Volume 1 — Supplement for the Java™ 2 Platform Standard Edition, v1.2
ISBN 0-201-48552-4

 Programming Open Service Gateways with Java Embedded Server™ Technology — *Kirk Chen · Li Gong*
ISBN 0-201-71102-8

 Java Card™ Technology for Smart Cards — Architecture and Programmer's Guide — *Zhiqun Chen*
ISBN 0-201-70329-7

 JavaSpaces™ Principles, Patterns, and Practice
ISBN 0-201-30955-6

 Inside Java™ 2 Platform Security — Architecture, API Design, and Implementation — *Li Gong*
ISBN 0-201-31000-7

 The Java™ Language Specification, Second Edition
ISBN 0-201-31008-2

 Java™ Message Service API Tutorial and Reference — Messaging for the J2EE Platform
ISBN 0-201-63456-2

 The Java™ FAQ — *Jonni Kanerva*
ISBN 0-201-63456-2

 Designing Enterprise Applications with the Java™ 2 Platform, Enterprise Edition — *Nicholas Kassem · Enterprise Team*
ISBN 0-201-70277-0

 Concurrent Programming in Java™ Second Edition — Design Principles and Patterns — *Doug Lea*
ISBN 0-201-31009-0

 JNDI API Tutorial and Reference — Building Directory-Enabled Java™ Applications — *Rosanna Lee · Scott Seligman*
ISBN 0-201-70502-8

 The Java™ Native Interface — Programmer's Guide and Specification — *Sheng Liang*
ISBN 0-201-32577-2

 The Java™ Virtual Machine Specification Second Edition — *Tim Lindholm · Frank Yellin*
ISBN 0-201-43294-3

 Applying Enterprise JavaBeans™ — Component-Based Development for the J2EE Platform — *Vlada Matena · Beth Stearns*
ISBN 0-201-70267-3

 Programming Wireless Devices with the Java™ 2 Platform, Micro Edition — *Roger Riggs · Antero Taivalsaari · Mark VandenBrink*
ISBN 0-201-74627-1

 Java™ 2 Platform, Enterprise Edition — Platform and Component Specifications
ISBN 0-201-70456-0

 J2EE™ Connector Architecture and Enterprise Application Integration — *Rahul Sharma · Beth Stearns · Tony Ng*
ISBN 0-201-77580-8

 The Java 3D™ API Specification, Second Edition
ISBN 0-201-71041-2

 Java™ Look and Feel Design Guidelines: Advanced Topics
ISBN 0-201-77582-4

 The JFC Swing Tutorial — A Guide to Constructing GUIs — *Kathy Walrath · Mary Campione*
ISBN 0-201-43321-4

 JDBC™ API Tutorial and Reference, Second Edition — Universal Data Access for the Java™ 2 Platform
ISBN 0-201-43328-1

 Java™ Platform Performance — Strategies and Tactics — *Steve Wilson · Jeff Kesselman*
ISBN 0-201-70969-4

 The Jini™ Specifications Second Edition
ISBN 0-201-72617-3

Please see our web site (http://www.awl.com/cseng/javaseries)
for more information on these titles.

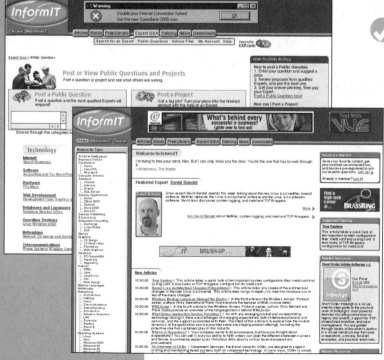

Register
Your Book
at www.aw.com/cseng/register

You may be eligible to receive:
- Advance notice of forthcoming editions of the book
- Related book recommendations
- Chapter excerpts and supplements of forthcoming titles
- Information about special contests and promotions throughout the year
- Notices and reminders about author appearances, tradeshows, and online chats with special guests

Contact us

If you are interested in writing a book or reviewing manuscripts prior to publication, please write to us at:

Editorial Department
Addison-Wesley Professional
75 Arlington Street, Suite 300
Boston, MA 02116 USA
Email: AWPro@aw.com

Addison-Wesley

Visit us on the Web: http://www.aw.com/cseng